D1595804

Shakespeare's Miracle Plays

Shakespeare's Miracle Plays

Pericles, Cymbeline, and *The Winter's Tale*

H. W. Fawkner

Rutherford • Madison • Teaneck
Fairleigh Dickinson University Press
London and Toronto: Associated University Presses

Associated University Presses
440 Forsgate Drive
Cranbury, NJ 08512

Associated University Presses
25 Sicilian Avenue
London WC1A 2QH, England

Associated University Presses
P.O. Box 39, Clarkson Pstl. Stn.
Mississauga, Ontario,
L5J 3X9 Canada

The paper used in this publication meets the requirements of the American National Standard for Permanence of Paper for Printed Library Materials Z39.48-1984.

Library of Congress Cataloging-in-Publication Data

Fawkner, Harald William, 1946–
Shakespeare's miracle plays : Pericles, Cymbeline, and the Winter's tale / H.W. Fawkner.
p. cm.
Includes bibliographical references and index.
ISBN 0-8386-3442-7 (alk. paper)
1. Shakespeare, William, 1564–1616—Tragicomedies. 2. Mysteries and miracle-plays, English—History and criticism. 3. Shakespeare, William, 1564–1616. Winter's tale. 4. Shakespeare, William, 1564–1616. Cymbeline. 5. Shakespeare, William, 1564–1616. Pericles. 6. Miracles in literature. 7. Tragicomedy. I. Title.
PR2981.5.F39 1992
822.3′3—dc20 90-56175
CIP

PRINTED IN THE UNITED STATES OF AMERICA

Contents

Preface

The first and second parts of this book were written in central Sweden in the late months of 1989; the third part was written in Saas Fee, Switzerland, in January 1990. The three parts correspond in a rough way to the three plays that are discussed: *Pericles, The Winter's Tale,* and *Cymbeline.* Since the study attempts a holistic approach to the miracle plays in general, however, each part contains analyses of all three plays.

The general idea behind this book was conceived during a university course focusing on the last plays of Shakespeare. Then, over a period of several years, that idea became little more than a visionary possibility at the farthest horizon of critical thought. Finally, the last plays once more materialized as specific entities haunting the immediate centers of critical attention, and analysis of individual plays became a possible reality.

The introductory section on *Pericles* is illuminated by this sense of the mysterious, almost hermetic, quality of the last plays: their willingness to hide beneath appearances that are nothing but their own theatrical obviousness. In that section, I try to convey the sense of a "spectral" quality in the Shakespearean miracle play. Much excitement is generated today by the "parallel *King Lear*"; but what this book might have called the "parallel *Pericles*" is an equally elusive entity—not, this time, because the text is double, but, more complexly, because it in the final analysis is not.

This doubleness that is not a doubleness was something I sighted in *Pericles* (and parts of the other miracle plays) during my first serious encounter with these dramas. It then became an analytical intuition—part vision, part notion—that came and went . . . like Stevens's "first idea." When it came, I was sure of it; when it went, I was sure of nothing. Eventually I accustomed myself to this coming and going, gradually realizing, perhaps, that it was a fluctuation that was not external to Shakespeare or to his final dramatic purposes.

The reader looking for simple readings of Shakespeare should take warning from this account of the analytical genesis of this book: I have always taken it for granted that the creative conditions operating in Shakespeare's final phase are the most complex conditions thinkable in the history of the literary imagination. Anybody unwilling to grant Shakespeare that amount of imaginative sophistication will not only find this book unsatisfying—but utterly unreadable. It is a war on unsophisticated readings of Shakespeare's last plays and is from that viewpoint not only a demanding project, but implicitly also a spacious one.

The analytical procedures of this work follow the rationale I have already forwarded in *Deconstructing "Macbeth"* and *Shakespeare's Hyperontology:* the hyperontological outlook. Such criticism implies a massive release of the transcendental capacities—an emancipation of those transcendental energies of the intellect that in various crude and sophisticated ways have been systematically repressed since the Enlightenment era. Today there is no need to start a civil war or a nuclear holocaust in order to do away with the iron curtain or apartheid; on the contrary, a hyperontological world is a world where ideas themselves spontaneously take power over matter. The arms race between the superpowers is *thought* away; the iron curtain itself is *thought* away. Transcendentality, in this radical situation, is not merely idealism but a heightening of idealism. In mind, man discovers not only his prisons but also the imaginative implications of his farthest dreamings. Hyperontology, whether externally political or internally analytical, is thus an encounter with an excess of freedom and an excess of space. It is, above all, a sensation of the vanishing of intellectual repression. The hypertranscendental dimensions of William Shakespeare's work cannot be *forbidden*. And partly that is so because those free dimensions simply are there.

The freedom that this enterprise in this way enters results in two main theoretical claims. The first of these concerns the nature of the relationship between discourse and recognition in Shakespeare's last plays. The second claim amounts to a theory of the miraculous. These innovations on the level of theory are at once the conclusions and the conditions of the practical criticism forwarded in these pages. A hyperontology, in this way, is neither method nor final vision, but both.

Acknowledgments

In the stages of revision, editing, and production I have been kindly assisted by Thomas Yoseloff, Julien Yoseloff, Claes Schaar, Maurice Charney, Caterina Mercone, Michael Koy, and Julie Korman. Acknowledgment is also made to the presses that have granted me permission to reprint material from certain works of criticism: to Routledge Ltd. for G. Wilson Knight, *The Crown of Life,* Ruth Nevo, *Shakespeare's Other Language,* and the Arden editions of *Pericles, The Winter's Tale,* and *Cymbeline;* to Macmillan Ltd. for Frank W. Brownlow, *Two Shakespearean Sequences;* to Faber and Faber Ltd. for John F. Danby, *Poets on Fortune's Hill;* to Harvester Wheatsheaf and Twayne/G.K. Hall for Wilbur Sanders, *The Winter's Tale;* to Cambridge University Press for Anne Barton, "Leontes and the Spider" and Inga-Stina Ewbank, "My Name Is Marina"; to the University Press of Kentucky and Harvester Wheatsheaf for Stevie Davies, *The Idea of Woman in Renaissance Literature.* Excerpts from *The Art and Life of William Shakespeare* by Hazelton Spencer, copyright 1939 by Harcourt Brace Jovanovich, Inc. and renewed 1967 by Louise S. Spencer, are reprinted by permission of the publisher.

1
Miracle

Shakespearean Recovery

As William Shakespeare moves into his final phase of creative discovery, his plays frequently discuss the opposition between art and nature. This is partly so because the difference between the aesthetic and its negation itself becomes of interest to the dramatist, partly so because the aesthetic moves toward a state of crisis in the last plays. On a mere empirical level of analysis, we might simply say that certain Shakespearean dramas begin to run the risk of failure: failure in relation to new tastes or failure in relation to the restless expectations of the artist. In a sense, therefore, the transition between the tragedies and the miracle plays is a transition from tragic danger to aesthetic danger. The main risk in the tragedies is a risk that primarily affects the hero: the dangers of jealousy, of ambition, of paranoia, of self-pity, and so forth. But in the last plays, risk has no such easy human contour but is the fragility of the whole aesthetic frame. The play is no longer just about a danger, but is itself danger. Tragic crisis begins to merge with aesthetic crisis. Danger, if you like, gets aestheticized.

I will be discussing this phenomenon in considerable detail as we move along. And, above all, I will be discussing how the concept of recovery operates on a number of levels in order to cope with aesthetic risk, aesthetic gambling, and aesthetic failure.

If "recovery" and "failure" are about to figure as the conceptual protagonists of our inquiry, we need to consider these notions against the intellectual background of modern Shakespeare criticism—a criticism that some generations ago thought of the last plays as failures and that more recently has attempted to recover them from such aesthetic disgrace. The strictures of Johnson, Dryden, Shaw, and Lytton Strachey are well known: the last plays were often directly dismissed as substandard material.

Today we are more enlightened. Yet the notion of "failure" does not drop completely out of view. I shall indeed try to show that the successfulness of the last plays in a curious way is structurally interwoven with the *notion* of failure. As Norman Sanders observes, there is nowadays some sense of critical consensus about the need to recognize "that all Shakespeare is good even in its badness."[1] That does not mean that we generously translate what is bad in Shakespeare into goodness; it means that what is "bad" in a writer as complex and remarkable as Shakespeare fails to be bad in any simple way. Badness itself is rich in Shakespeare.

Engaging in that type of discussion is not to separate the last plays from everything else in Shakespeare; for there are bad spots in Shakespeare's best tragedies, just as there are moments of ecstatic beauty in the miracle plays. What is involved here, rather, is the critic's willingness to understand the peculiar strain on badness in the last plays—a strain that from the outset might have been a fortuitous and external misfortune (the ineptitude of a collaborator, the shallowness of taste and fashion), but that Shakespeare exploited in order to create (and perhaps discover) an unprecedented type of theatrical gamble. What needs to be recovered in the last plays, in other words, is recovery itself. Thus I will not simply be recovering these plays from some situation of intellectual or aesthetic neglect imposed by a complacent critical community; on the contrary, I will be discussing recovery as something that is always in operation in the plays themselves. This internal recovery is not a finite feature or event with certain clearly distinguishable empirical limits; instead it is a possibility. Inside the last plays, the possibility of recovery is a fluctuating sheet of imaginative thought—in a sense the veil of miracle as such.

The investigation I have in mind presupposes some hostility toward interpretations of a symbolic kind. I think such reviews of the last plays are of limited usefulness; and to explain just why this is so, I first refer to the parallel scepticism of Ruth Nevo, as she rejects "the main methods of recuperation" traditionally used by criticism to meet the "challenge" of the last plays.[2]

> One such method has been to identify folklore or fairy-tale motifs, appropriate to the mode of romance, to account for the weirdness of the invented events. These are then, in effect, set aside while attention is given to the wit and wisdom of a great humanist culture and the incomparable high mimetic art which are inscribed everywhere

> in the text. Another has been to interpret allegorically, and a variety of ingenious anagogical themes, mythological, philosophical, theological, have been energetically advanced to sweeten the irrational pill and ease the strain the plays' implausibilities make upon our powers to suspend disbelief. Perhaps we should not allow ourselves to be thus diverted by extrapolated conceptual schemes, however inventive and ingenious. Perhaps what we should take seriously is precisely the raw, the odd, the counterrational in them. . . . I believe that if they are to speak to us . . . their familiarities must become strange and their strangenesses familiar in a new way. It is an investigation into the uncanny that we must undertake.[3]

I could not agree more. As Nevo remarks, the last plays should not be neutralized and get appropriated by a preexisting humanist paradigm or by intellectual complacency. But if "familiarities must become strange," why must the strangenesses become "familiar"? Here I find myself in radical disagreement with Nevo—for my own view is that strangenesses are to be evaluated as strangenesses, and not as items belonging to a reassuring and familiar scheme thought of as "the strange" (what Nevo calls "the uncanny"). In fact, Nevo makes exactly the kind of mistake that she accuses her humanist opponents of: she makes the strange familiar by comfortably inserting it within a preexisting ideology or scientific system: theirs was "humanism"; hers is "the uncanny." But the uncanny in Nevo's criticism is not itself uncanny at all; on the contrary, it is the reassuring edifice of "post-psychoanalytic semiotics."[4] Nevo's entire analysis of Shakespeare's last plays is haunted by what it seeks to exclude: the canny, the predictable, the familiar. We are back in the familiar workshop of "unconscious signification."[5] Attention is turned from humanist wisdom to psychoanalytic wisdom: we are dragged through the recognized schemes of weak psychoanalytic theory, re-creating the kind of "extrapolated conceptual schemes" we should have abandoned.[6]

The assumptions of the present enterprise are quite different: *all* symbolic readings are weak. It is of course legitimate to interpret individual clusters of words in terms of specific symbolism, but there can be no conclusive "symbolic reading" of an entire miracle play. All such readings will be reductive for the simple reason that complex drama is not reducible to any system of thought outside it. A system, a dogma, defines some things as possible, some things as impossible; but in Shakespeare, and particularly in the miracle plays, there is constantly a jerky defiance of what is supposed to be possible. The possible varies from moment to moment; indeed, that is the ultimate type of suspense in the miracle plays. Each line and each linguistic impression has to be examined from scratch: not in the sense that we could imagine some sort of interpretative innocence for ourselves, a state where we might be unblinded by the prejudices of our egos and cultural outlooks; but in the sense that we need to be ready for an act of appreciative revision at the shortest possible notice.

If we are to achieve an open reading of the miracle plays, we must make ourselves ready—in fact open—for the task of letting the openness of the plays hit us suddenly from an unexpected direction. One such source of absolute openness, I shall be suggesting, is muteness, a muteness that we cannot quickly align with any comfortable notion safely discoverable inside contemporary theory. The theory for understanding a miracle play thus arises from the miracle play itself. Such theory is not a system; it is not external to the works it illuminates and cannot be exported indiscriminately into each and every corner of the literary universe.

The criticism generated by such a theory of the miraculous will need to focus precisely the things that Nevo focuses: the overlooked detail, the marginal. As in strong psychoanalysis, one will be looking for certain telling types of overemphasis, certain quaint silences, certain fascinating absences and ellipses; but unlike the weak psychoanalyst, we are not going to organize these fascinating odds and ends into neat, rationalistic constellations of fixed symbolic meaning. We are not going to translate the oddities into program and proper thinking. On the contrary, we are going to stare oddity itself in the face. Hopefully, it will do the same to us. I want to understand the otherness of the miracle plays without having to translate their sense of otherness into a convenient theory of otherness preexisting the critical venture.

To a certain extent, this type of problematic is related to the question of seriousness. "We are," writes Charles Frey, "rediscovering for ourselves both the seriousness and craft of romance."[7] But that kind of general seriousness is not what I am aiming for in this study. Taking all of Shakespeare's last plays "seriously" seems to me to be the surest way of missing what is seriously other in them—for they simply do not contain any ordinary seriousness. Ordinary seriousness only leads to the kind of weak symbolic translation I have already referred to. To *seriously* believe that the miracle plays really are about some hidden order of symbolic truth seems to me to be patently naive. It is to grossly overvalue their symbolic power and to grossly undervalue their nonsymbolic power: their otherness. What is interesting about the last plays is in the final analysis not how they signify, but how they do not signify. Not-signifying, here, is not the same as failing to signify. On the contrary, negative signification is itself moving toward success in the last plays—moving, in fact, toward the upper limits of success, toward the miraculous. We need to understand exactly how the miracle plays do not signify and exactly what the miracle plays do not signify. For the absence of (ordinary) signification (the presence of otherness) is not simply a formal aspect of the plays, but on the contrary a theme and inner concern that they dramatize as an inward inspection of their own hard substance.

What I am perhaps aiming at, for the explication of these plays, is a notion of indeterminacy that is more scientifically rigorous than the casual one implemented by symbolic criticism. In the case of the symbolic critic of the last plays, indeterminacy is mainly a direct function of the arbitrariness of the symbolic order used to "explain" the plays. Norman Sanders discusses this sloppiness in his keen and informative survey of some twentieth-century criticism: "there seem to be no limits to the critical imagination when its focus is the final plays. . . . If their symbolism is so complex that it can embrace so many apparent contradictions, are they not, in thus symbolizing everything, drawing perilously close to symbolizing nothing?"[8] I think they are. In fact, from a hyperontological view, this is a very good and thought-provoking manner of defining the "essence" and challenge of the miracle plays: they come "perilously close to signifying nothing." Not close to signifying nothing. But perilously close.

The systems of symbolic belief are various: the urgently Christian critic believes that Shakespeare's canon is too good not to everywhere exemplify the Christian vision; the myth-oriented critic sees each unit of action as a reanimation of the age-old human vocabulary of symbolic dismemberment, fertility ritual, and cyclic resurrection; the weak psychoanalyst, I have argued, has a quite different symbolic faith—but it is still a faith, still a symbolic attitude, still an eager concern to translate verbal otherness into symbolic signification. The diligent source-hunter and the generic critic are in a sense performing similar acts of symbolic translation: the literary source or the literary genre is used as a symbolic frame, and as the critical process unfolds, Shakespeare's words are related to the frame rather than to themselves—so that the primacy of the frame "guides" our understanding of Shakespeare's language. As Sanders correctly points out, however, Shakespeare's originality always tends to break the genres he seems to be serving, and there are powerful patterns of a general nature that cut right across the notion of genre in Shakespeare.[9] Indeed, as Nevo claims, we need to be provisionally free from "generic intelligibility" to at all appreciate Shakespearean otherness in a radical manner.[10]

What I am suggesting, at this point, is that it is necessary to abandon "safe ground"; we should avoid anxiously identifying an external ground for the critical enterprise: Freudian ground, Lacanian ground, Derridean ground, Christian ground, mythic ground, generic ground . . . symbolic ground. We must bring ourselves to a state where we have no ground to refer to, refer ourselves to. This sense of groundlessness is in a way what the miracle plays, and particularly *Pericles*, propose as ontological climate and spectatorial condition: that we must, like Pericles himself, experience that permanent offshore sensation of being grounded in the loss of ground:

> *Lysimachus.* Upon what ground is his distemperature?
> *Helicanus.* 'Twould be too tedious to repeat;
> But the main grief springs from . . . loss
>
> (5.1.27–29)

The sea in *Pericles* functions as this ground without ground, and not merely for the sake of creating atmosphere. Marina's answer to Pericles' inquiry as to whether she is "of these shores" is poignant: "No, nor of any shores" (5.1.103). Being without a shore, being out of sight of the visible limit of any ground, is not being in the void. On the contrary, it is being in the *place* where the absence of the ground is what always itself moves visibly into view. "Where do you live?" asks Pericles: "Where I am but a stranger; from the deck / You may discern the place" (5.1.113–15).

But art, surely, is itself a ground? Yes, and no. It is true, as Northrop Frye insisted, that Shakespearean drama in a sense takes us to a transcendental level of understanding where symbolic meaning only is operative as aesthetic meaning; yet the really interesting question is whether Shakespeare in the last plays actually bothers to take us to that artistic transcendentality (ground us there), or whether he in fact only uses such a transcendental artistic ground as a starter and first condition. I would like to suggest, in point of fact, that the miracle plays mainly sport the sense of artistic transcendentality in negative fashion. (The emphasis here is on "mainly.") That is precisely why the notion or sensation of failure is so crucial for Shakespeare's final performances. Without the usage of an inverted sense of artistic transcendentality (aesthetic ground), the crucial failure/success hesitancy in the miracle plays could not be worked into a hyper-ontological device that is at once enframing and enframed. Yet this negative magnetization of the aesthetic ground is not, as is commonly thought nowadays, a function of irony, absurdity, or any other form of dialectical distance. As I shall explain in the next section, "failure"—like its hypersuccessful opposite, the miraculous—is not a dialectical construct. Irony is. If the miracle plays question their own aesthetic ground, they do not do so from the objective viewpoint of an exterior distance (as irony does), but on the contrary from the vantage of an internal (and therefore "absent") site of negative vision—one without dialectical, spatio-logical existence. All quests are questions in these plays (things in need of an answer, things moving consciously or unconsciously toward response); but the questions often fail to be properly present to those who might have formulated them. Also, they seem to fail to be truly present (dialectically visible) to the discourse that makes them possible. They are thus, as I shall argue, easily drawn into the nondialectical ground of muteness. They are questions without questioning ground.

Crisis and Fading

One way of recovering Shakespeare's miracle plays in traditional fashion, of recuperating them in the name of dialectical seriousness, is to discuss their otherness in terms of irony. Irony is a very reassuring and philosophically proper notion, since it cuts a firm line between itself and its object. But Shakespeare does not use irony to make his miracle plays displacements of romance; he uses failure. Irony creates distance, and failure creates negativity without distance. Irony creates withdrawal, but Shakespeare creates negativity without withdrawal. Irony can only recover from irony by means of double irony (ironization of irony, a further dialectical reversal); but Shakespeare creates recovery in the miracle plays without dialectic or reversal. Such recovery is not, as many traditional critics think, simply a new version of the old theme of "regeneration"; on the contrary, recovery is now the miraculous. The miraculous is not dialectical (a suspended irony) and requires a different (more potently negative) platform. I suggest that this platform is failure, and I suggest that muteness is what negotiates the extremes of failure and miracle by being their ideally shareable suspension of proper articulation.

For reasons such as these (to be clarified later on), I will have to reject Howard Felperin's dialectical conception of Shakespearean romance as a to-and-fro between demystification and remystification, irony and the ironizing of irony. Felperin informs us that the "complex interaction" (dialectic) between "demystification and remystification" is something to be found not only in modernist works like *Heart of Darkness,* but also in early types of romance.[11] This insight is correct in a limited sense: it is true that there is no simple one-way development of the demystifying dimension in literary history; demystification is always there from the outset—in romances, in mystification, in the earliest texts. What is wrong with Felperin's analysis, however, is its dialectical bias. He claims that Shakespearean romances "reveal a *dialectic* between the demystification and remystification of their own romance mode."[12]

This error is in its turn based on an archetypal fallacy typically promoted by the average twentieth-century intellectual: the ironic fallacy (or dialectical illusion) that leads one to conclude that the entire cultural past of the West (including medieval and Renaissance miracle plays) is comprehensible in terms of some cheap epistemological theory about the split between subject and object. Ironic man, characteristically, tells us that Romanticism was (or is) a "crisis,"[13] that this crisis is produced by a subject/object split, and that "ironic sophistication"[14] involves the recognition of the fact that the subject (man) has "broken irreparably" with the objective world.[15] Paradise, the "mythic source," is eternally lost[16] and can only be recuperated artificially—for instance through art. We cannot regain paradise, but we can pretend that we can. This reductive way of conceiving our whole cultural past is highly prejudiced, severely tainted by the anachronistic, epistemologizing pessimism of the modernist intellectual.

What involves romance and the experience of the miraculous cannot be conceived in merely negative and ironic terms, so that the romance moment is something that appears as a latecomer. One cannot merely define the miraculousness of the romance moment negatively and passively, in terms of what happened *despite* originary ironization. A miracle is not reducible, even in secular times and secular forms of cultural experience, to something as trivial as a recovery from irony and modern disenchantment. The necessary conditions for the experience of the miraculous—as Shakespeare's best romance moments show—is neither what Felperin calls a "mystified state of mind" nor an ironic condition of being "ruthlessly demystified."[17] In fact, we might dispense altogether with this mystified type of critical terminology: discussions based on the shallowly epistemological distinction between "mystification" and "demystification" are themselves mystifications, and very dangerously so. What Shakespeare ideally requires of his audience is neither of these states, but simply a readiness to suddenly experience the radically other—and to accept that other, unconditionally, for what it is. That kind of process signals its orbit of possibility in a space altogether different from the one prepared by the modernist universalization of ironic secularity. There is some irony in a play like *Pericles,* but nobody is going to make me believe that I first need to be in an ironically secular mood to achieve the sense of the miraculous whenever it happens to be offered in that play.

What I am prepared to grant, however, is that there is something negative enframing the possibility of the miraculous. But this negative frame, or groundless ground, which in *Pericles* very much is felt to be the dark encircling pavilions of the ocean, is not primarily ironic. I am therefore anxious to distinguish between recovery from irony and recovery from failure. "Pericles" (the play as well as the man) is constantly threatened by failure, by a premature and constantly possible "drowning." Out of that drowning or submergence (aesthetic as well as personal) emerges the miraculous as such (personal as well as aesthetic). Thus, there is a background, an encircling "wet" negativity; but the darkness and contrastive threat of this watery (aesthetic) abyss is not dialectical or ironic. Irony has never survived any real tempest. The contrastive is not the dialectical here, nor is the negative ironic. This is precisely why the impact or general sensation of a Shakespearean romance is so different from the overall impression created by an ironic play *(Troilus and Cressida, Timon of Athens).*

It is at this point that we can brace ourselves for our first strong encounter with the notion of failure and its operative importance. Frye's discussion of Greek drama in relation to Shakespearean romance is a helpful pedagogical model in this context, for it facilitates the completion of the rejection of the facile notion of the preeminence of irony discussed a moment ago. (My sceptical attitude to strong generic thinking persists in the ensuing commentary; I am using Frye's genre-thinking in "negative" terms: I am not trying to define the generic situatedness of the romances, but instead trying to eliminate erroneous criticism of them by identifying the ways in which they do *not* function, the dramatic genealogy they do *not* belong to.) As Frye contrasts Greek New Comedy (related to Shakespeare's comedies of love) with Greek Old Comedy, he discusses the difference between the teleological character of the former and the nonteleological character of the latter.[18] The lovers in New Comedy overcome various obstacles in order to achieve sexual fulfillment. (The situation is radically ironic and dialectical, I may add, since the audience must have a clear a priori intuition of the distance between the subjectiveness of love and the objectivity of social fact.) In Old Greek Comedy, however, the constructional principles are much wider and looser. There is a dislocation of the sense of hierarchical order—in society and universe (the chain of being), but also in the play.[19] Movement takes place for its own sake, is processional rather than developmental,[20] facilitating the experience of the sense of the absurd, as in Aristophanes.[21] Such freedom of dramatic imagination also breaks up rational hierarchies and reflexes, including our need to constantly generate the comforting feeling that there is a cause for every event. In the less-than-causal world of Greek Old Comedy, even the appearances and disappearances of characters are faintly inexplicable. The same goes of course for much that happens in Shakespeare's last plays: people, as Frye puts it, "appear without introduction and disappear without explanation."[22] To use our analytical tool "failure" for hyperontological definition: entries and exits too malfunction, too fail—and successfully.

It is this antiteleological drive of Old Comedy, incidentally, that increases the explanatory irrelevance of symbol criticism: for symbol criticism is always teleologically overdetermined, always wants to achieve the preexisting aim of demonstrating that literary material is logically dependent on an exterior order of established symbolic meaning. *Pericles* is dramatically less-than-causal, yet Ruth Nevo is determined to supply the missing causal connections: "the progress of the play is the haunting of Pericles by the Antiochus in himself, the incest fear which he must repress and from which he must flee."[23] The missing of the cause is safely translated into the missing cause: "Why so much punishment? What crime has been committed [by Pericles] that his thoughts should be so full of punishment?"[24] If Pericles' gloom can be traced back to unhappy childhood by causal criticism,[25] so can Leontes' irrational behavior in *The Winter's Tale*.[26] But strong romance is not manageable in terms of that type of petty causal reasoning. Instead, as Frye remarks, there is in nonteleological drama a contest between forces.[27] And these forces, I might add, are in Shakespeare's miracle plays primarily the forces of failure and averted failure, catastrophe and recovery, despair and miracle.

The *power* of failure is to a certain extent explicable in relation to the fact that, unlike irony, it is never totally within the controlling sphere of authorial mastery. The "breadth" of failure is a function of its natural capacity to be semipassive and, as a consequence, to look "larger" than dialectic, irony, or intentionality. "General failure" is outside dialectic (irony, intention, all systems of internal tension), and therefore failure is also outside the difference between romance and its other. That is why irony (a merely finite reflex) gets marginalized in the last plays. And that is why—according to the fascinating inner law of Shakespeare's conclusive phase of creativity—the miracle play cannot fail as other plays can. This means, in practical terms, that the a priori introjection of a dimension of aesthetic catastrophe in the miracle plays from the outset inoculates them against ultimate failure. For failure here is, as it were, necessary for the production of its opposite: and particularly so for the production of the miraculous. A naively "successful" romance can *depict* a miracle; but only a romance that from the outset flirts with general aesthetic failure can *become* a miracle. An aesthetic one.

Aesthetic miracles of the pure kind need to make some dramatic recovery: and the only patient who makes a genuinely miraculous recovery is one for whom hope is gone. Saying that much is not saying that Shakespeare's other plays fail to contain "miracles"; it is to say that those miracles do not attempt the type of instantaneously wholesale recovery visualized in the miracle plays. Nor does saying that much mean that Shakespeare deliberately worked drama in the direction of catastrophe. Yet to a dramatist of such outstanding intellectual force, the aesthetic reality of that abyss must have been permanently within view as the negative shadow of ongoing glory. It is possible that Shakespeare finally realized that he could situate glory *in* that shadow: that he could make the shadow of his art into a new theater.

The idea of recovery surfaces consciously on numerous occasions inside the plays: "nothing we'll omit / That bears recovery's name" (*P* 5.1.52–53). When Shakespeare makes Leontes imagine a Hermione restored to life, the words chosen suggest a theatrical and artistic recuperation ("on this stage") and not merely an empirical one. What is being recovered is not merely the character as a revivable human being but the character as an artistically potent construct—the "characterness" of the character. Leontes thinks that a rival wife to dead Hermione "would make her sainted spirit / Again possess her corpse, and *on this stage* . . . *appear*" (*W* 5.1.57–59). In *Pericles* dramatic action is really "beyond recovery." Only the most extravagant recovery in the play can turn the whole performance into something that *is* a thing properly recovered. No ordinary type of Shakespearean revision can save the play from its state of dumbness. Whatever theory we develop to account for the un-Shakespearean dimension of *Pericles,* we are still left with the recuperative sensation: that discourse, as it unfolds, is being rescued from a state of chaotic inertia that parallels the one affecting the characters on the existential level of struggle for survival. This sensation is real whether the printed version of the play is a corrupted text inadequately memorized from the original[28] or a Shakespearean improvement of a weak first effort compiled by a collaborator. The basic feeling remains: that the text fights for its life, that the play struggles against the sucking waters of its own mute oblivion. The desperation is external as well as internal. There is everywhere an ongoing life-and-death struggle between a mute *Pericles* and an audible *Pericles,* a play that is able to speak for itself and a play that voices its unspeaking.

"Muteness" here is not simply a minus, deficit, and drawback, but a resource. In a sense—and precisely for the extension of the possibility of the miraculous—it is the most important reserve that the play has access to. In fact, the active potential of the deadness/muteness/numbness of *Pericles* strengthens the case for the view that the surviving text is a play revised, patched up, and *recovered* by Shakespeare.[29] Generally speaking, all such questions need to be asked against the background of the cumulative evidence focused in the present study: Shakespeare's extraordinary concentration on the idea of miraculous recovery. It is surely unlikely that this almost obsessive notion could lack significant relation to the dramatist's own actual predicament as a professional writer caught in a particular phase of work—reconstructive work.

These considerations, together with others, influence the way one epochalizes Shakespeare's plays. *The Tempest* is traditionally looked upon as the crowning romance in the Shakespearean corpus, but from the viewpoint I have recently been forwarding as the hyperontological one, *The Tempest* is not a miracle play. There is no magus in *Pericles, Cymbeline,* or *The Winter's Tale:* no father figure who centrally authorizes the possibilities and exact limits of miraculous manipulation—therefore in the final analysis no "author" who in transcendental manner overdetermines the magic of recuperation itself. Precisely because *The Tempest* is too strongly dominated by the central presence of an author-izing and patriarchal male, the sense of the miraculous is never dramatically free. (All yearning for the freedom of the miraculous is compressed in the servitude of Ariel.) This means that we recognize in Prospero the type of authorial egocentricity already encountered in Lear, Coriolanus, and Timon. Thus, we need to think of *The Tempest* as mainly belonging to an altogether different cluster of plays, and also to quickly recall how different the father/daughter relationship appears in the alternative dramatic worlds of *Pericles, The Winter's Tale,* and *Cymbeline.* In these plays, fathers have very few scenes with their daughters, the father appropriating neither the daughter nor the loss of her. This, I think, is not primarily a question of involvement and counterinvolvement in the depths of Shakespeare's psyche (suppression, sublimation, release) but a question of the totally different roles played by central authorial mastery in the two types of plays.

This discrepancy obviously leads to a quick understanding of how futile and meaningless it is to ask questions like: Did William Shakespeare intend the miracle plays to float undecidedly on the ungrounded ground of immanent failure? This type of question cannot be asked, because in these plays there is no central field of authorial consciousness where a mind capable of giving an intelligent answer to that question could—in the manner of Lear or Prospero—be truly present. We cannot ask if Shakespeare yearned for failure; but we might in an oblique fashion ask if failure yearned for Shakespeare. This latter yearning could well be experienced in terms of absolute intensity—perhaps one that Shakespeare, like most great artists, could sense as the mystique of a permanent lateral beckoning.

One different way of looking at this tricky question is perhaps at hand if we return to Aristophanes and the possibilities of Old Greek Comedy. There, direct address, or parabasis, was an important ingredient; and in Shakespeare's miracle plays recovery itself speaks to us in terms of such direct address. Something intervenes: and this something is really neither the voice of the author, nor anything objectively generated by the causal givens of the action. Failure, here, by being the contrastive substratum necessary for the emergence of such direct address, too travels along the pathways of address. Failure directs *its* success into those parts of our dramatic attention that need to be directly activated if we are to understand miracle as miracle and not primarily as the depiction of human action and self-present speaking.

The discrepancy I am discussing between *The Tempest* and the miracle plays may be felt by considering the role of Leontes in *The Winter's Tale*. He initially threatens to set himself up in the centrally authorial position of a Lear or a Prospero; but this power is taken away from him, so that he has to submit to the inorganic world of romance and magical causation. This causation that is not a causation is not engineered by the central self-presence of a self-congratulatory magus, but is on the contrary engineered by a weird type of constructional recklessness suggesting a slight surrender of centered authority. It is naive to read this type of loss of power (in Leontes) as the function of a shift in power balance from the male to the females opposing him. That shift is important, it is there; and we shall be discussing it in some detail. But it is not a causal shift. What happens is that human self-presence itself gets shattered, so that the play abandons the causal and psychological intricacies that it for a moment feigns to want to portray—and instead gives in to the altogether different romance formula that energizes the creative core. That is why the play can "get away" with a feminine counterplot that is ridiculously improbable and hilariously artificial. Nothing connects these two arbitrary imitations of plot: Leontes' jealousy strikes from out of the blue, and so do the miracles of feminine recovery. No Jacobean spectator, however masculine, could have been seriously troubled by the feminist U-turns, for they are immediately perceived to be playfully organized according to the most mechanical and arbitrary of principles. That does not mean that there is no feminist dimension in *The Winter's Tale;* it means that that dimension is as autonomous, inorganic, and free as any other motif.

In the miracle play, no central and self-present mind, *no strongly self-assertive creative ego,* "successfully" organizes disparate dimensions into powerful theme or proper meaning. What is at stake, suddenly, is no longer the performative potency of a capable magus at the center of his work—capable or incapable of making things cohere. As shattering, that mind ("William Shakespeare") is not aspiring to a success that is immediate. The pen, more slanting and less erect than ever, now defers and stalls its maguslike powers to the limit. This pure relinquishing of power is what makes miracle possible. Miracle gives back all that in this way is relinquished: but its giving (which is not a return of interest or investment) is no longer internal to the poetic ego. In miracle there is a poetry that the ego cannot itself write. As terminal event in a Shakespearean drama, miracle is from this hyperontological viewpoint the most extreme instance of the possibility of deferred writing and deferred power. Authorial self-presence and self-centering are from the outset canceled in the name of creative shattering. Genius removes itself from center to periphery, from creation to observation, from meaning to spectacle, from spell to sportive unconcern; yet a terminal miracle *immediately* collects the energies of such shattering into its own objective and hyperobjective solidity. It is almost, in *The Winter's Tale,* as if the magician had changed his craft: become sculptor instead of dramatist; as if his betrayal of the pressures of centered authorial performance has actually led to an abandonment of the proper medium—as if the poet would have preferred to bring his heroine to life as stone rather than words. Perhaps, as I shall suggest, he has.

Muteness speaks in all this too. It is hard to avoid the thought that the final phase of Shakespeare's career involves some sort of protest; and it is hard to avoid experiencing that elusive protest as mute protest. Muteness here is of course not literal, empirical muteness (although Shakespeare will be happy to utilize that possibility as often as he can). For as a craftsman working in an audible medium, Shakespeare could only forward the mute in terms of its opposite. To make muteness speak—that is one of the defiances of the miracle plays. It includes not only the muting of personal commitment to the profession (the muting of William Shakespeare) but also the muting of genius (of "Shakespeare").

There is a difference here between muting and toning down. Or there is *perhaps* a difference between muting and toning down. Shakespeare knew that he was fading: fading out of his career, his youthful vitality, his cultural status, his life. Shakespeare knew what an end was. Thus a "toning down" is operative whether Shakespeare likes it or not, whether his plays (written and to be written) like it or not. In this kind of situation the strong craftsman (to rework a Bloomian notion) can cooperate with the toning down of existence: gradually muffle his voice, slacken his pace, weaken his presence, blur his profile, marginalize his authority, dilute his discourse, whisper his wrath. But it seems to me that there is a trace of an alternative procedure in the miracle plays—and a trace that is all the more cunning in that it is virtually indistinguishable from mere toning down. This trace is what I am here calling the mute. Its difference/mark/identity is itself mute, does not give way to announcement, the vulgar adieus of a Prospero. It is as if, in some delicate phase of Shakespearean fading, the dramatist had provisionally intuited some way of fading out fading itself, of turning all the powers of his art completely around, in a 180 degree swerve: so that his powerfulness would become the instrument of its opposite, and so that the decline of powerfulness therefore would signal its reanimation. It is as if, ending writing, Shakespeare could write less and less while still feeling the accumulative processes of pure creative growth.

This is the secret of the mute person, of a protest whose passivity is completely pure: that power grows spontaneously out of impotency. Had you been Shakespeare, you might eventually have wanted to silence Shakespeare; but that silencing, you would have realized, would never become genuinely efficacious without there also being the supplementary feeling of a cessation of genius and writing—of drama as a noetic ideal (a perfectly successful performance, a perfectly successful play, a perfectly successful playwright). The point, then, would be that of achieving a strange position—the very one I believe Shakespeare situated himself in—where it is possible to go on writing when writing already has been abandoned and emptied as a means of proper speaking and significant saying. It is to go on writing without writing, to go on creating without creating. On the one hand, this sensation will shape altogether new demands and exhilarating challenges; on the other hand, all those new obstacles and creative peaks will be fundamentally empty. In my terminology, they are going to be radically mute. Both of these sensations, I think, are conspicuous in the miracle plays. Even muteness is slightly feigned. Even muteness is mute.

The Muteness of Pericles

Is not Shakespeare in love with Pericles? And is not this love based on the recognition of the muteness of Pericles rather than on any appreciation of him as a pliable character ready to speak proper lines? Is not the proper action of Pericles alien, belonging to some other writer? But an other writer who is not other than Shakespeare. Is not Shakespeare's real collaborator here Shakespeare himself? Could he not have collaborated with a fellow writer *and* with himself? And could he not have collapsed those two collaborations into one another: not only technically, but metaphysically?

Shakespeare was of course used to welcoming literary figures from other texts, used to introducing alien, precreated personalities into his own imaginative world. But does he not greet the alterity of Pericles in a rather different way? Frankly, I perceive the distance of Pericles as a mute distance, his alterity as a mute alterity. In Shakespeare's theater, and perhaps even in Shakespeare himself, this seems to give him the position of a deafmute. That circumstance is special, no doubt something that helps *Pericles* to be a special play among Shakespeare's plays. For what is mute collapses the difference between proximity and distance, identity and foreignness, presence and estrangement. The mute does something to difference itself. Pericles thus seems to me to be excessively close to Shakespeare through his radical estrangement from Shakespeare. In this manner, the muteness of the autistic schoolboy simultaneously makes him the most inconspicuous and conspicuous member of his class. Silence is your special drama. The inability to speak your lines is your preeminent status as leading actor. Such semiotic activity refuses to belong either to the metaphysics of presence or to the metaphysics of difference.[30] The charm of Pericles, in this way, is that he does not speak lines given to him by Shakespeare, but that Shakespeare, as it were, first listens carefully in order to determine if Pericles has anything to say, if the moment is ready for proper speaking as such. The relationship between writer and character becomes therapeutic. The character is cherished because of his inadequacies. And instead of just wanting to remedy these inadequacies (improve the speech-deficient Pericles delivered by an inferior cowriter), Shakespeare decides to give voice to the inadequacies themselves. This is the source of the ability of dumbness and inadequacy and failure to grow in *Pericles*. The insufficiencies of Pericles themselves speak in *Pericles;* and in an important sense the play (as something written by Shakespeare rather than by anyone else) is organized around this general insufficiency. Without its central muteness, failure, and unspeaking, *Pericles* is not *Pericles*.

Pericles is at once dumb and rescued from the dumb. If Shakespeare falls in love with him, this is one of the main reasons. Shakespeare is moved by the therapeutic possibility, the idea of giving speech to Pericles, of saving him from silence; yet at the same time, and as love deepens, Shakespeare realizes that he is more in love with the silences of Pericles than with his speeches. Or rather: that recovering Pericles for speech is curiously dependent on recovering his inability to speak. Recovery, here, can only totalize its recuperative thrust by not totalizing itself. To have an integrity, therapy must preserve some part of the originary malaise it is wiping out. While first thinking that he wants to make Pericles speak and come alive everywhere, Shakespeare may progressively realize that he does not care for Pericles' speeches as much as for the speechlessnesses that frame them.

Yes, Pericles is rescued from the dumb. Perhaps this is one of the sadnesses of Pericles: one of several reasons for that peculiarly beautiful melancholy that swims around him from the outset. Not as if he were a stranger in his own play (as Macbeth is) or alien to his own greatness (as Coriolanus is), but as if he is always originally appearing in the play for the second time—as if he had played the mute Pericles so well and so often that he is more familiar with the silent lacunae of the play than with its verbosity; as if he is more at home in moments of awkward dumb show and primitive oceanographic disarrangement than in full linguistic performance; as if he knows that dumb speaking is more befitting and natural in this play than the ostentations of meaning, power, proper place, and true expression.

Because *Pericles* is centered on the sensation of dumb speaking (a feature we shall return to with frequent concern), the play is from the hyperontological perspective neither talkative nor silent, neither expressive nor retentive. That (to Shakespeare's relief?) is why nothing is really said in *Pericles*. But the fact that nothing is spoken (in the profound, metaphysically grounded sense) is exactly what prevents the play from speaking (about) nothing. *Pericles* cannot thematize, essentialize, or philosophize nothingness. *King Lear* and *Macbeth* can portray nothing and nothingness by encapsulating "blank" zones of negative discourse, where an individual or discursive voice enters the possibility of the void. But *Pericles*, by "belonging" in its whole bulk to the silent void from which it emerges, by being framed by the originary muteness that crosses it, can never take a decision to move in the direction of unspeaking, unmeaning, and decelerated signification. No muteness in it could ever surprise us.

This means, in practical terms, that there is no real exit from the primitive and archaic in *Pericles*.[31] (Let us incidentally recall that this archaic level of romance purity is not of a primarily symbolic kind, not the symbolically archaic.) We, with the characters, can leave the hovel in *Lear* and get back to the ironies and dialectical conflicts of fully human speech; we can make some kind of recovery (similar to Lear's) from the *un*speaking speech monitored by the Fool and by archaic madness. But in *Pericles* that kind of return to speaking as plenary speech is never possible (except in a crudely theatrical fashion), or even desirable. Since speech as self-presence (plenary speech, what, ideally, we see Lear portion out in the opening of his play) is dialectical speaking, and since all dialectical speaking involves the basic human competitiveness that shapes society as a sphere of mundane prestige, this total inability of *Pericles* to reenter the world of abolished muteness is also the inability of the play to engage in any significant way with human competition and its meannesses. That is one of the refreshing dimensions of the play: that we are not, as in *The Winter's Tale* and *Cymbeline,* constantly thrown back and forth between the archaic purities of romance imagination and the petty rivalries of human affairs. There is human egoism behind the pride of men like Leontes and Posthumus Leonatus, but in *Pericles* selfishness is stylishly marginalized even when the plot seems to call for its activation.

A consequence of this general hyperontological sensation is that negativity in *Pericles* never seems to truly originate in humans, never seems to inhere in what, despite the odds, gets spoken. As the negativity of the language of Lear's fool seems to be incompletely connected to the inner personality of that likable fellow, so the negativity that *Pericles* speaks (tempests, destructions, losses, griefs, natural catastrophes, elegies) does not come across as the speaking *of* a negative voice that could be thought of as transcendentally coextensive with the play itself. Shakespeare and Prospero organize a tempest together; negativity—centered, masculine, and self-assertive—appropriates negation and makes it serve language, meaning, and action. But *Pericles* withdraws from that kind of centered, self-presencing negativity. *Pericles* does not write negativity; negativity writes it.

This shattering of negativity from center into space means that the tempest blows harder in *Pericles* than in *The Tempest,* but that this very intensity of the storm is harmless in terms of calculated viciousness, calculated revenge, calculated violence, and calculated power. The tempest in *Pericles,* by belonging to a free economy without telic, authorial truthfulness, is open. It is, like all genuine tempests, the experience of openness itself.

This sense of the external, inorganic nature of negativity in *Pericles*—its nomadic, free-roaming arbitrariness—is related to the special quality of otherness in the play. I have already pointed out that a theory of the role of the other in the miracle plays cannot be made reducible to finite, materialist dogma—whether narrowly Freudian or not. Finite otherness of the symbolic kind always involves our intuition of how humans can hurt one another through the dialectical to-and-fro of statement and counterstatement; all symbolic orders with a decipherable "meaning" negotiate cultural truth in relation to hierarchical positioning, social equilibrium, and anthropocentric violence of a quasi-political kind. But in *Pericles* the other is harmless even while doing harm. Elemental and archaic—in fact mute—the other escapes dialectic, and in a sense even difference. As blank, numbness, or primordial negation, the alien is utter reducibility. This also means that all reductions in *Pericles* go without the quality or sensation of diminution or shrinkage. The zero-level—mute, pure, hard, absurd, or simply beautiful—is nothing less than the rock-bottom elementality of direct ontic possibility: what is naked without being unconcealed, what is "there" without being evident. *Pericles* shows the freshness of the more simple than the simple (the mute) by casting it in terms of otherness projected toward the limit of structural indifference. The lack of (dialectical) structure here itself becomes the other: what remains mute in discourse by being an embedding with a structural complexity that is always a bit lower than that of "language." The mute, as (hyperontological) in-difference, or structural naiveté, speaks in language by setting itself off from language in terms of the refusal of difference and relatedness (human relatedness as a function of a conventionalized code of differential relations). If language is a semiotic network of differences without positive terms (which it is, in a limited sense), the mute is *positive* here by refusing to participate in the differential system.

Since Pericles on numerous occasions (as we shall see) identifies his dramatic reality in terms of some state of muteness, and since this muteness of his is paradigmatic of muteness in general as manifested by the primary agents of Shakespearean romance, I wish to clarify this hyperontological status of the mute a bit further before moving on to more concrete matters. We can understand the particulars of muteness (the mute particulars of romance discourse, including dumb shows) only through some general insight into the constructional role of muteness as a creative condition of theatrical possibility.

The mute is the most other of differences; the refusal of difference itself. True, the mute is "different" (it can be distinguished from voice and inscription); in fact, a dictionary merely defines it negatively, in terms of a negative difference: "lacking the power of speech"; "unable to speak," "not expressed in uttered words"; "lacking some usual attribute or accompaniment"; "lacking in intelligence." Yet the difference of the mute is not just negative, not just of a "differential" kind. On the contrary, the difference of the mute is itself mute. That is its secret. The mute does not say: "I am the mute." The mute does not enter speech in order to proclaim: "We are unspeakability." Instead the mute *is* the difference/protest, already, that it intends to claim for itself. If the mute has a purpose (to be silent), this purpose is already attained before the mute actually enters its effective program. From this viewpoint, the mute is continuation as such: not a continuity, not a system of connections between various points of differential reference. When what is mute *continues* (sets up its epochal regime) it extends an otherness that has never needed to cross into any notion, awareness, or territory of difference. Power extends without there being implemented any cut or dis-continuing violence. The cut/break/disconnection of the mute, its feigned difference, is already "contained" within the a priori natural situatedness of the mute one.

This sublimity of the very question and vastness of the mute has much to do with what I have already discussed as the open—the ability of pure romance to open up all horizons recklessly, the sense in *Pericles* that its hero has access to a freedom or openness of possible itineraries that is more than a geographical openness. The mute partakes of this free openness by being what stands mutely on its threshold.

Stones and trees are open. They stand primordially and mutely in an openness. This archaic standing in what is open is mute, and its primordial force, captured by the elemental sensations of romance, "precedes" difference and relatedness, just as it "precedes" presence as the voiced "I am here" of centered belonging. One does not have to be different to be archaically visible; nor does one have to belong. But one has to endure, and one has to endure in silence. Pericles attaches himself to Shakespeare's fond care in this way: by refusing to manifest any radical concern for identity, difference, or belonging. He is (dare I speak the word?) natural.

The mute, in the final analysis, does without inscription. The power that the mute person has over all those who speak (over the world) is that she or he does not have to enter the quasi-regulated system of differences (language proper, proper language) that the others (the linguistic ones) subscribe to in terms of convention and law. The mute one is different without being a function of difference. The mute one is other without being a part of otherness-as-difference. The *others* may wish to take part (as nonpositive terms) in a system of (semiotic) difference; but the mute one establishes silence as the positive and hyperoriginary term that breaks this system by always preceding it.

For reasons such as these, even murder and incest lack negative emotional content in *Pericles*. They are, quite simply, mute. But this muteness of murder, of incest—this muteness of sin itself—is not a function of the muffling of these things, a function of some phony "suppression" that at some hypothetical point in the past made a mess of the tribal innocence of a community or family. Far from being suppressed, sin here is absolutely open (witness the brothel scenes). At the beginning of *Pericles*—and in a sense also at the beginnings of *The Winter's Tale* and *Cymbeline*—we do not see "signs" and tokens of sin, but the surface of sin, sin as surface. This surface, precisely by being a surface without a past or a depth to conceal, is the locus of what is openly sinful. Sin here is astonishing even to those who are producing it as an emotive phenomenon in their own incredulous beings. In *Pericles,* which in this context always tends to be paradigmatic for the Shakespearean miracle play, incest and murder seem to be inorganic, cosmological facts of a narrative.

The Rusting of the Ground

I have already stated that the noncompetitive atmosphere in *Pericles* is related to the sense of muteness. We can identify this sensation, and consider its wider implications for the romances in general, by looking at Pericles' behavior in the first parts of the play. When he makes his first entry in act 2, he is as wet and miserable as Lear was in the storm; but unlike Lear, Pericles has no background of deeply knowable error to support the sustained sense of unhappiness. Perhaps he is not unhappy, but melancholy ("Yon knight doth sit too melancholy" [2.3.54]). This melancholy stirs those who behold him, including the spectator: "Now, by the gods, I pity his misfortune, / And will awake him from his melancholy" (2.3.90–91). The supposed reason for his sadness is shipwreck (2.3.83–85); yet in the rather acausal world of romance it is hard to separate cause and effect—causation is circular. Thus the violence of the sea is simultaneously the reason for melancholy and the cause of its removal: "The king is not at the palace; he is gone aboard a new ship to purge melancholy and air himself" (*W* 4.4.763–64).

The wrong that has been done to Pericles, whatever it really could have been, is not felt to be the kind of wrong done to Lear, for there is no sufficient background of dialectical prestige and human competition to ever correspond to the gloom of the protagonist's comportment. Ruth Nevo, we have seen, argues for a causal, explanatory, and dialectical review: "The parent-child configuration gives a particular tinge to the melancholy he expresses."[32] But is "configuration" important? What is important, surely, is not the specific causal constellation (which in any case remains obscure and conjectural) but the general atmosphere. This general atmosphere is melancholic; but it is also noncompetitive and feminine.

Femininity here is not mainly thinkable in terms of the countercompetitive power of individual women, but is instead the opening of a world largely free from masculine types of prestige (the narrowly dialectical). It is true, as Cyrus Hoy observes, that this type of femininity can be reviewed as idealization and escape: Shakespeare avoids the tragic turbulence of strong father-daughter encounters by distancing daughter from father in the miracle plays.[33] As tenderness without strong suggestion of sexual desire, femininity can now become a pure imaginative ideal.[34] But I do not think femininity in the romances is reducible to some mere sublimation of the guilty love of father and daughter. The strength of the miracle plays is precisely their ability to affirm femininity without surrendering to the banal temptation of letting it lose itself in a puerile power contest with the dominant male.

Because we in such states lack an immediate involvement in the directly causal issues of masculine tension and masculine competitiveness, it is futile to ask narrowly causal questions about the "origin" of melancholy and other primordial emotions. There is pity, there is guilt; but in a strange way it is important that there are no obvious reasons for these things: either for us or for the hero. Pity and guilt are now *without foundation*. It is necessary that we love Pericles without knowing why, just as it is necessary that we love his world without knowing why. It is necessary that we pity this world, and pity its nomadic protagonist; and it is important that we base this pity on nothing—on pity and sympathy themselves. It is essential that we become moved (not rent) by a grief we cannot trace back to some source of negativity that would be more sad than it. In this way, as pity becomes pitiful in the radical loss of its own cause, and as love becomes miraculous in the radical institution of its own unreasonableness, romance plays man and woman in an acausal oscillation. Now femininity is not merely subject to distancing but to magnification and dilation. The feminine is not restricted to the sphere of interpersonal dialectic with the dominant male (Lear, Coriolanus, Prospero).

The feminine dislocation of dialectical competitiveness is felt immediately. When Pericles emerges victoriously from the offstage tilting tournament against the other knights, we do not experience this victory as a dialectical winning, as power (2.3.9–11). Winning, here, as in the case of Marina being able to "win some words" of her father (5.1.43), is basically a question of being at all able to articulate some sort of rudimentary imitation of full presence. (As rusty armor, Pericles' performance in the tilting tournament is not the optical brilliance of a lustrous presence.)

Pericles is radically unable to fill or fulfill his role as ideally chivalrous knight. His chivalrousness does not come from knighthood but from its muffling, not from his performances but from their muteness. His situation is not ironic, however; he is not an antihero. He is, heroically, what silently antecedes the heroic. He is dumb (5.1.24–40), deaf (5.1.83), unscissored (3.3.29; 5.3.75), and—in spite of constant proximity to water—unwashed (4.4.28). But these things, including his rustiness, do not suggest secondariness; on the contrary, they suggest primordiality. And the primordiality is gentle, not savage or dialectically brutal.

A rusty armor is by chance retrieved from the sea by some fishermen, and Pericles quickly identifies it as belonging by right to him: "part of mine heritage, / Which my dead father did bequeath to me" (2.1.122–23); but the spectator, far from associating this rust with wear and tear, will associate it with the primordiality and freshness of the element from which it originates. Rust is, as it were, always wet here: so that whenever

Pericles sports his rusty garments, these remind us of water rather than deterioration. Rust too, like pity, love, and guilt, is "without cause." It speaks as phenomenon rather than as explanation. This is another way of saying that it does not speak at all, that it is mute. Rusty armor is mute armor, and a rusty knight is a mute knight. By wearing rusty garments at the tilting tournament, Pericles marks victory itself with rust: not with the tarnish of what *has* rusted, but with the muting of what otherwise would have been glossy, polished, reflexive, and dialectical. Rust abolishes the mirror effect.

But the absence of the mirror effect (of dialectical reflexivity, whether temporal, causal, or sexual) also affects the father image. The father image is itself rusty here, itself goes without reflexive power to project a strong patriarchal profile into the dramatic present. The "rough seas" that in some past have taken the fatherly armor "in rage" (2.1.130–31) have swallowed the human equipment *so much* that it is no longer a human signifier: the rusty armor does not signify the father, but the rust; and the rust signifies the ocean, femininity, the preprimordial. Superbly rusted, in this way, the masculine attire par excellence suffers from a radical corrugation that removes fatherliness and human origin altogether. Pericles does not appear as a *son* in any fundamental way; he appears as rust. The father lacks foundation (generally) and so does the son (generally); and this means that family relations in general are unfoundational in *Pericles*. It follows, let it be understood, that they are feminine. The relations of Pericles to women (to Thaisa and Marina, wife and daughter) spring out of this possibility—the largest possibility that the play makes possible (perhaps its most moving miracle). Precisely because Pericles cannot have dominant fatherly relations to Marina or marital relations to Thaisa, he can in an unprecedented manner have relations to *a* daughter, *a* wife. The daughter only becomes possible across the nihilating void where the father-to-daughter dialectic is swamped into its abyss; the wife only becomes possible as the personification of the loss of the marital ekstasis. This does not simply mean that daughters are lost and then found; that wives perish and get resurrected. It means that the ungrounding (the rusting) of dialectical reflexivity in *Pericles* makes possible a world where there is no place or relevance for the dominant manipulations of a dialectical Prospero or a dialectical Lear. The rusting of the male (which in a sense has its equivalent in *The Winter's Tale*) permits the emergence of ungrounded and different attitudes to woman. The rusting of the male permits a vision of the female as something other than a modification of the male—permits relations of a family nature to be more than family relations.

When Pericles presents himself in rusty armor to Thaisa prior to the tilting tournament, he enters without a shield, giving his "device" directly to Thaisa. His present to her is "A wither'd branch, that's only green at top; / The motto, *In hac spe vivo*" (2.2.42–43). This, again, is the suggestion of growth without cause or foundation: how what is new and fresh, if it is radically miraculous, starts its growing from the very point where the *dead* foundation has totalized its numbness. How hope, if it is faith, is without base, precedent, reason, origin, trunk, or root.

Because Pericles, like a Flying Dutchman, seems to be eternally at sea, he seems to belong to nonbelonging, seems to originate in a flawed origin. He emerges from the sea as one emerging from the absence of ground. This gives us the feeling that he is *thrown up* on land: thrown up from unground to ground. His appearances, therefore, are odd, inexplicable—perhaps also impossible. This sense of the otherness of Pericles—his manifestation of himself as the manifestation of the unprecedented—is given to us in the description of his impact on the fishermen. On the beach, he catches sight of the three men just before they notice him:

> *Pericles. (Aside.)* How from the finny subject of the sea
> These fishers tell the infirmities of men;
> And from their wat'ry empire *recollect*
> All that may men approve or men detect!—
> Peace be at your labour, honest fishermen.
> *2.Fisherman.* Honest! good fellow, what's that? If it be a day fits you, search out of the calendar, and nobody look after it.
> *Pericles.* May see the sea hath cast upon your coast—
> *2.Fisherman.* What a drunken knave was the sea to cast thee in our way!
> *Pericles.* A man whom both the waters and the wind,
> In that vast tennis-court, hath made the ball
> For them to play upon, entreats you pity him;
>
> (2.1.48–61)

What is shown here is the unacceptability of Pericles; he is ontologically grotesque. He does not fit. The fisherman tells him that *if* there had been a day in the year (in time as the ground of its own foundation in itself as "calendar") that could have fitted

Pericles ("fits"), then this day would have been so other that it would not have fitted its own possibility ("nobody look after it"). Such a day cannot be grounded in the calendar; the calendar, as temporal ground, cannot accommodate such a man/day. If that day is proper to Pericles, it is not a proper day. Recollection (memory), with its binary opposite, "forgetting," forms an important motif in *Pericles* as well as in the other miracle plays. Here the fishermen are supposed to be men who can "recollect" human understandability from the ocean (2.1.50–51); but this recollection is framed by our larger sense of Pericles as always melting into the oceanic as one melts into forgetting: we wait only a few lines to receive this impression: "What I have been I have forgot to know, / But what I am, want teaches me to think on" (2.1.71–72).

But this forgetting is not only an erasure of memory, not only something negative; it is a resource. Precisely because Pericles always can emerge from a nonground (ocean/shipwreck), and precisely because each new ground in this way becomes absolutely new, the ground as such can be presented as the purest possible instantiation of freshness. This freshness taken to the extreme limit of the thinkable is internal as well as external: Pericles' inner being is like that "wither'd branch, that's only green at top" (2.2.42). His memory, and therefore his life, always has this marvelous ability to start from scratch. At any moment, because of the constant totalization of the loss of the past, existence can start a new shoot: not in spite of the deadness of the branch/trunk/root, but because of it. The miraculous is related to this intuition of unthinkable freshness. That is why Marina is a miracle; and that is why Thaisa becomes a miracle too. A miracle is the experience of an incomprehensible freshness. The sensation is known to those who can recollect a vivid experience of childbirth (Pericles meets Thaisa on her birthday [2.1.107]). Although we know that there are causal explanations for the appearing of a new child, and although we therefore can situate it reasonably in a present that is connected to the past (to what is *not* fresh), we do not in the actual moment of birthgiving perceive the miraculous present as a function of the past. The child, we understand for a few hours or minutes, has been given and created out of nothingness. The baby has not emerged from possibility or ground but from impossibility without ground. Indeed, those causally "responsible" for the child (the parents) are the ones most struck and impressed by this strange new cosmic situatedness of the newborn. Marina, the freshest possible image of miraculous birth and miraculous birthgiving, is in this way shown hesitating (like all babies) on the plank of the tiniest possible ground: what she rests on (that crumbling ship) is what birth itself rests on, a foundation so tiny and fragile that its very materiality needs to be questioned and doubted.

What generally speaking keeps happening to Pericles, then, is that he finds himself stranded in fresh territories where, much like Gulliver, he understands the uselessness and redundancy of past experience. He is always starting from scratch. Indeed, he understands that *surviving* is very much this knack of beginning afresh. A melancholia is retained in the process of restarting, yet the melancholia is not caused by past events, but on the contrary by their absence, irrelevance, and sad marginalization into unmemorized vanishing.

In each fresh ground, then, Pericles is awkwardly out of place: not simply because he is a stranger *there*, but because he brings with himself a sensation of encircling ungroundedness that itself is strange: strange for him and strange for others; strange for the world and strange for us. It follows that he could be mistaken for one suffering from amnesia or aphasia. He does not, as we just saw, make an appearance that in any way "fits" (2.1.54) temporal grounding (time as "calendar"); nor does he make an appearance that convincingly suits spatial grounding: "*Marshal.* Sir, yonder is your place. / *Pericles.* Some other is more fit" (2.3.23). Macbeth had no place at his banquet, and he had a reason for perceiving his place as a nonplace. But in *Pericles* this constant transformation of place into nonplace has no proper foundation. The lack of ground for the protagonist does not itself have a ground; the lack of ground itself lacks ground. Such a man cannot be brought to his senses, like a distracted Macbeth; he must simply be made to assume a knowable position: "Sit, sir, sit" (2.3.27).

We have seen that the sensation of the constant removal of Pericles from his proper ground/memory/past/foundation/being is not unrelated to the question of muteness. Muteness is *the* token of the absencing of proper ground in the play—for the play as a verbal construct could discover no more immediately negative ground than that of inarticulation. Muteness is primarily negotiated through the prevalence of dumb shows. An intelligent production of the play does not underemphasize the role of such moments of pure muteness. Hyperontologically speaking, a dumb show in *Pericles* is not simply a show that happens to be dumb, but on the contrary the *showing* of the dumb. The space between these two notions—in a sense the space of the play *Pericles*—is oceanic.

Delivery

The feeling that Shakespeare in the miracle plays moves into the area of the visionary where "words fail" and where conventional verbal representation is impotent (however skilled) is conveyed to us massively by the general sensation that discourse everywhere needs to be assisted and supplemented: by dumb shows, prologues spoken by Gower, music, and so forth. The notion of delivery is crucial in this context. We speak of verbal delivery in terms of the felicity of what is spoken: in speaking, what gets spoken is delivered clearly or unclearly; a speech is eloquently delivered or inelegantly delivered. Thus words, as they move from the dumb to the voiced, are delivered from muteness. But in *Pericles,* this wrenching of speech from the mute is overemphasized, so that—perhaps on account of the recalcitrancy of the protoscript—we feel that what gets delivered has rescued itself from the abyss of inarticulation. As the first two acts suggest, an awkward silence is imposed on the play by some unknowable obstacle impeding the course of a more direct eloquence. Delivery, then, is on an obvious level delivery from dumbness. But the point, of course, is that dumbness also can deliver itself, that dumbness can deliver dumbness. Or that it could want to. Dumbness can deliver. From this viewpoint, dumbness is not simply the epiphenomenon of the miraculous, but its condition of possibility. It is not simply that a miracle strikes us dumb, that wonder silences us; it is also that a kind of silencing of the world is a prerequisite for the emergence of the miraculous. Something has to be hushed for the miracle to be born; and if this thing that needs to get hushed is language itself (for protagonist as well as spectator, for writer as well as "dumb" actor), then we are in some trouble if our profession is a linguistic profession.

Shakespeare's miracle plays are in a sense based on this single conflict. This means that Shakespeare is provisionally in a situation where he wants to be delivered from language. In such a situation the delivery of words is a peculiarly delicate delivery. Hyperontologically speaking, it becomes a risk. What is risked is not only the words, language—but delivery itself. That is why child-delivery is so poignant in *Pericles*. When Thaisa delivers

Marina, the dangers of delivery are totalized. In that shipwreck, we feel that there is infinite risk for *what* is delivered (Marina, the baby, the delivered entity, the product of delivery), but what we really learn is how delivery/delivering itself (Thaisa, motherliness) is thrown into the abyss. In that tempest, there is no ground for what is delivered, but there is no ground for delivery either. The groundlessness of what is delivered never gets delivered from the groundlessness of delivery. Marina may survive (she does), but her survival is marked by the trace (or rather the muteness) of the supposed nonsurvival of her mother. Marina is delivered from death, canceled birth; but she is not delivered from the abyss of birthgiving. Nor are we.

Now the nonsurvival of the mother (the abyss of delivering) itself can be transformed into survival—according to the reduplication of miraculous possibility that Shakespeare eventually implements; but that more unthinkable salvation is not merely made possible by the whims of authorial omnipotence, but on the contrary made possible by the fact that Shakespeare from the outset has imagined the project of delivering the abyss of delivery. When Pericles begins the process of dissolving the estrangement between himself and Marina, he tells the sad story of his lost wife in terms of delivery: "I am great with woe / And shall deliver weeping" (5.1.105–6). The Arden editor explains: "he will deliver his tears as a mother frees herself from her burden in the process of birth."[35]

The entire passage deserves our special attention, and the best place to begin is perhaps the moment when Marina promises the lords of Mytilene to do what she can to recover Pericles from dumbness. He is not known to her (or to himself) as her father but is simply "A man who for this three months hath not spoken / To any one" (5.1.24–25). The final act has just opened, like the previous ones, with a prologue spoken by Gower; but, significantly, there is no inaugural dumb show here. Why? Because Pericles' own presence is about to take upon itself the sensation of a dumb show. *Recovery,* here, is making Pericles speak, making Pericles deliver ("he will not speak" [5.1.33]; "he will not speak" [5.1.40]). We have already encountered some of the significant units. To "win some words of him" (5.1.43) is to take part in what "bears recovery's name" (5.1.53). But Pericles' speechlessness is so radical, as we are about to see in a few seconds, that we get the impression that he is malfunctioning not only as a human being but also as a character; that his refusal to speak is not merely a refusal to become a normal speaking man in the "real" world of

Mytilene but also a refusal to become audible in the play—to have a proper role there, a proper voice. He seems to want to cling to an optional role, one with a voiceless voice, a speechless speaking, a dumb presence. The entire recuperative action—as initiated and implemented by Marina/Shakespeare—seems to involve the impression of a much larger process of recovery: as if the miracle we are waiting for is not only one that the (non)father of Marina requires, but also one that the play itself badly needs. From this viewpoint, the protagonist's stuttering hesitancy between voiced and unvoiced presence is more than a hesitancy between his human ability to speak and his human ability to abstain from speaking: his entire status as a "full" character in the play appears to waver. This wavering takes place between his failure to be present to the play and his ability to overcome that failure; but it also takes place between a force wanting him to be present there as presence and a force wanting him to be present there as something else. That other wavering is a contest over Pericles between the mute and the delivered. This contest does not unfold "in" Pericles, as some sort of "inner conflict" engineered by split disposition or conflictual predicament.

As we attend to the language of the crucial passage with the closest possible vigilance, we perceive the traits outlined above: the hyperconstructional role of muteness, the tendency of "recovery" to spill out into the aesthetic enframing of the character as a viable theatrical being (his cue is to miss his cue, to seek to recover it, reinterpret it in terms of muteness), and the sliding of delivery into deliverance.

Muteness, now, will need to convey itself at some length:

Marina. Sir, I will use
My utmost skill in his recovery, provided
That none but I and my companion maid
Be suffer'd to come near him.
Lysimachus. Come, let us leave her;
And the gods make her prosperous!

(Marina sings.)

Mark'd he your music?
Marina. No, nor look'd on us.
Lysimachus. See, she will speak to him.
Marina. Hail, sir! my lord, lend ear.
Pericles. Hum, ha!
Marina. I am a maid,

My lord, that ne'er before invited eyes,
But have been gaz'd on like a comet; she speaks,
My lord, that, may be, hath endur'd a grief
Might equal yours, if both were justly weigh'd.
Though wayward fortune did malign my state,
My derivation was from ancestors
Who stood equivalent with mighty kings;
But time hath rooted out my parentage,
And to the world and awkward casualties
Bound me in servitude. I will desist;
But there is something glows upon my cheek,
And whispers in mine ear "Go not till he speak".

Pericles. My fortunes—parentage—good parentage—
To equal mine—was it not thus? what say you?

Marina. I said, my lord, if you did know my parentage,
You would not do me violence.

Pericles. I do think so. Pray you, turn your eyes upon me.
You're like something that—What countrywoman?
Here of these shores?

Marina. No, nor of any shores;
Yet I was mortally brought forth, and am
No other than I appear.

Pericles. I am great with woe
And shall deliver weeping. My dearest wife
Was like this maid, and such a one
My daughter might have been: my queen's square brows;
Her stature to an inch; as wand-like straight;
As silver-voic'd; her eyes as jewel-like
And cas'd as richly; in pace another Juno;
Who starves the ears she feeds, and makes them hungry
The more she gives them speech. Where do you live?

Marina. Where I am but a stranger; from the deck
You may discern the place.

Pericles. Where were you bred?
And how achiev'd you these endowments which
You make more rich to owe?

Marina. If I should tell my history, 'twould seem
Like lies, disdain'd in the reporting.

Pericles. Prithee, speak;

. . . .

Report thy parentage. I think thou said'st
Thou hadst been toss'd from wrong to injury,
And that thou thought'st thy griefs might equal mine,
If both were open'd.

Marina. Some such thing I said

(5.1.75–132)

The uncertainty of delivery, here, is related to the uncertainty of deliverance. Also, the re-creation of speech appears to inadvertently promote the risk of the decreation of speech. We almost feel that Marina risks getting drawn into the abyss of nonspeaking from which her father is to be rescued. This sensation is of course related to the literal meaning of the unit "starves the ears she feeds" (5.1.112). The "real" meaning is no doubt that she intensifies attention in those who listen to her; the more they hear, the higher grows their yearning for more of her speaking; yet on the literal level the unit actually discusses a starving of the ears, precisely what muteness creates. These spots of countersignification should not be overemphasized; but we need to recognize how delicate traces of the notion of muteness pervade the drama on all possible levels of linguistic action. Speech tends to be the positive thing promoting the interidentifications of character; yet the negative sensation of simulation or dissimulation is there to disturb and quiver at the very moments when recognition ought to be pure instantaneity. This feeling is brought out when Thaisa, before she recognizes Pericles, is *about* to recognize him: "*Like* him you spake, / *Like* him you are" (5.3.32–33).

It is perhaps possible to understand this persistence of the suggestion of the *trace of muteness* by thinking of this trace as a minute quantum of nonspeaking perpetually wedged inside the imagined completedness of plenary speech. This minute depletion of full voice does not necessarily mark a deviation from speaking, but can, as in the case of the refusal to sing in *Cymbeline*, sometimes even mark a deviation *toward* speaking. When Imogen is thought to be dead, Cymbeline's son Guiderius informs his brother Arviragus that he cannot take part in the musical lamentations ("I cannot sing" [4.2.240]); and they then agree to perform the tune unmelodiously: "We'll speak it then" (4.2.242). The displacement is quite odd, almost uncanny. Why on earth should they speak instead of sing? Here speaking is a sort of muteness, a form of articulatory reticence; and the withdrawing of the plenary voice rests on no visibly rational foundation whatsoever; nor does it seem to rest on an irrational foundation. The withholding of the fullness of the voice is *other*, a sign of the mischief of active otherness. Speech here is mute music, or muffled music. What gets spoken speaks dumbness, voices a certain vocal restraint or vocal timidity.

Music is not usually betrayed in this way in the miracle plays, but instead supplies the visionary moment with the mystique of transcendental ecstasy and reverbatory euphoria. Yet music still comes to indirectly associate itself with dumbness and reduced articulatory plenitude, since music tends to want to make the sound of what ordinary language and ordinary speaking cannot convey. At precisely the moment when the ordinariness of speaking gives way to the extraordinariness of revelation and the extraordinariness of suspended speech (wondrous silence), music floods in to fill the semiotic void. But this filling is affected by what it fills—affected by the void. If wondrous silence is the voiding of ordinary linguistic performance, and if music comes to "express" that wondrous silence, then music incorporates traces of the very silence it removes. Music supplements silence by (1) transforming silence into reverberation and by (2) furthering the cause of the silencing of voice.

For reasons such as these, music in the miracle plays, which is often combined with the sense and traces of lingering dumbness, negotiates our impressions of a delicate threshold of awareness as it is caught between articulation and silence. Music is the fading of speech, or is the fading of silence (the recovery of speech). But the recovery of speech is never entirely free from an other recovery, a negative recovery. It is as if the moment when recuperated speech is ready to speak is also somehow the moment when silence itself is about to be ready to speak: so that when the mute one is on the threshold to revelation/recovery, he or she is infinitely ready to tell us something about the joy of recovery, but also infinitely willing to transmit signals from the area of sleep in which he or she has been lost. On the threshold of recovery, floating on music, the recovering person hovers magically in a special zone where he or she recognizes the miracle of speech/recovery but also the miracle of muteness and incomplete recovery. Only by being slightly incomplete can recovery come across as miracle; for in that transient musical moment of dumb, semi-articulatory bafflement, the subject still gloriously has the negative world of lost speech in full view.

In *Pericles*, Gower tells us that his task is that of harmonizing the dumb and the spoken: "Your ears unto your eyes I'll reconcile" (4.4.22); but in a strange way the interplay of speaking, music, and silence (including dumb shows) never becomes a quite transcendental trinity. Music is the catalyst facilitating the resurrection of Thaisa (3.2.93); and Marina, "train'd in music's letters" (4.1. Chorus. 7–8), sings her father back to speaking life (5.1.79), releases the "heavenly music" of the spheres (5.1.231). Yet from the outset Pericles has decided that he is the "worst" of all the scholars of music (2.5.31) and that he is "unworthy" of being the musical schoolmaster of the king's daughter (2.5.40). The recovery of Pericles' speaking is in addition never really a matter of simply taking him back to normality, for there is no past in which we intuit him as entirely free from originary muteness. The music of the spheres first actually sends Pericles to sleep—returns him provisionally to the very zone of dumbness from which he is to be rescued. In each of these cases one can of course work out a rational account for the deviation; in the case of his alleged musical insufficiency, for instance, one would state that he is merely being excessively humble and polite. Yet taken together these cumulative instances of the irreducibility of dumbness affect the spectator and shape a general sensation of the wavering complexity of the mute/nonmute interface. Music does not always stabilize or harmonize the interface, because its powers of enthrallment are undecided.

As Stevie Davies correctly observes, we do not know if the music of the spheres heard by Pericles is a normal event in the mind of a man regaining his health or if it is a mad ecstasy only acknowledged as real by others for therapeutic reasons.[36] Whatever the case, the passage quickly manifests the precariousness of the interfaces we have been discussing: those of speech, dumbness, and music.

> *Pericles.* Now, blessing on thee! rise; thou art my child.
> . . . .
> Give me my robes; I am wild in my beholding.
> O heavens bless my girl! But hark, what music?
> Tell Helicanus, my Marina, tell him
> O'er point by point, for yet he seems to doubt,
> How sure you are my daughter. But what music?
> *Helicanus.* My lord, I hear none.
> *Pericles.* None?
> The music of the spheres! List, my Marina.
> *Lysimachus.* It is not good to cross him; give him way.
> *Pericles.* Rarest sounds! Do ye not hear?
> *Lysimachus.* Music, my Lord? I hear.
> *Pericles.* Most heavenly music!
> It nips me unto list'ning, and thick slumber
> Hangs upon mine eyes; let me rest.
>
> (5.1.212–33)

The text is no doubt somewhat corrupt at the moment when Lysimachus is supposed to say "Music, my Lord? I hear" (5.1.

231). This is a strange line, as we have it, and parts of it are probably either a stage direction or words to be spoken by Pericles. But this editorial problem is not purely editorial; and that is so because Shakespearean writing itself is here an "editorial" problem—not for editors, but for meaning; not for the corrupted text but for an uncorrupted one. The interfaces created by music/muteness/ecstasy/speech themselves suggest mislineation. The interrelatedness of music and speech, speech and muteness, muteness and music: these folds are themselves weird. Do *we* hear the music of the spheres? Somehow we too are doomed to deafness. Should we hear the music of the spheres or should we indeed hear the absence of that music—hear silence? Should we hear what Pericles hears or should we hear an unhearing—*hear* precisely what the other staged figures hear, nothing at all? It is our own fate to become the victims of a curious deafness here, whether we hear or fail to hear. For we cannot simultaneously hear what all the characters hear: we cannot hear hearing as well as nonhearing, the music of the spheres as well as the absence of that music. We do not know if our deafness is caused by what we hear or by what we fail to hear; we do not even know, in view of the preeminence of dumb-showing, whether the ability to hear what is being said is an asset or a radical failure of attention. Pericles' "hearing" of the music of the spheres is probably in itself a form of dumb show. And if that is so, it is one of the finest shown things in the play.

The "editorial" aspect (as discussed above) is again conspicuous as something larger than anything any editor could manage when we consider the speech acts in *The Winter's Tale* that necessarily remain mute for the spectator because the speakers "talk aside" (4.4.507, 595). Such mute talking is of course a dramatic commonplace and no extraordinary thing in Shakespeare; but it remains tantalizingly suggestive in *The Winter's Tale* in view of the fact that characters almost seem aware of the inaudibility of the words they are supposed to speak. "O Perdita," cries Florizel, "what have we twain forgot?" (4.4.660). The play here *forgets* what the characters have forgotten; yet at the same time, given the general hyperontological bias toward muteness/dumbness/forgetting in the miracle plays, it is almost as if they can speak about this forgetting in advance, almost as if the characters are vainly trying to recall what the play *will* soon have forgotten. All an external and empirical editor ends up with, however, is what J. H. P. Pafford ends up with in the Arden edition: certain factual assertions about a textual muteness that is merely seen in terms of deficient information, the objective unavailability of certain lacking units of discourse:

> 660.*forgot?]* We never learn what Florizel and Perdita have forgotten or what he said to her. In *F* [Folio] the question mark is often used where modern practice would use an exclamation mark and the line may mean: "What, Perdita! Have you and I forgotten our vows, our resolution to stand by each other—that nuptial which we two have sworn shall come!" . . . But the passage may merely be, in common stage convention, just another of many similar passages introduced to allow an aside. We never learn what Perdita had to listen to at 507 or Florizel at 595.[37]

Pericles and Femininity

For the facilitation of an analytical deepening of what has been discussed so far in terms of dumbness, I would like to situate the mute more precisely in relation to the masculine/feminine continuum. Let us provisionally consider the miracle plays in holistic fashion as basically feminine. Why feminine? Because, we have seen, Shakespeare's miracle plays project a dramatic world whose theater is primarily unfoundational or defoundational—and the foundation itself can only be thought inside Renaissance patriarchy in terms of masculinity (in terms of dominance and originary power). This fact is of course not limited to an individual writer called Shakespeare or to an individual epoch called Shakespearean, but applies to the cultural cognizance of the West in general.

In her excellent discussion of the feminine forestructure of the late plays, Stevie Davies calls attention to this Shakespearean emptying of masculine power and masculine dialectic (competing for prestige). "Pericles' political power is seen from the first as already maimed."[38] Without being effeminate, passive, or cowardly, the protagonist moves away from traditional masculine self-assertiveness:

> *Pericles* is a sustained evasion of action, insofar as action is to be equated with battle-antagonism. This makes the actions he does undertake all the more significant: the bringing in of the corn, his marriage, his response to the birth of his daughter and his reunion with Marina and Thaisa. Each of these acts either impersonates a feminine role (the nurture of the city) or ties the hero to the feminine.[39]

Davies argues that the visionary experiences of the hero thus in the final analysis amount to a complete surrender of masculinity: "Pericles abdicates his gender."[40] This is no doubt an exaggerated phrasing, but it is certainly true that Pericles has (and is meant to have) "an experience that is visionary";[41] and it is certainly obvious that the removal of masculine attitudes is a prerequisite for such visionariness. This feminine forestructure of ecstatic vision is something we have already discussed: the connection between delivery and deliverance. In the vision, in fact, Pericles "conceives of himself as a woman in labour."[42] The vision itself, Davies stresses, is one where the sense of the miraculous intensifies pleasure to the extreme limit where it actually begins to become indistinguishable from pain. Thus suffering is not simply transcended or overcome in the visionary moment, but stays with us there as the shadow of its own totalization:

> With full recognition comes a state of mind which is close to the accounts by Cicero, Sophocles and Plato of the ecstasy experienced at the Mysteries as producing clarity of insight, accompanied by wild and enduring joy which ensures for the initiate the cleansing of fear from the whole future. Shakespeare communicates a sense of the nearly unbearable character of such joy, joy as pain.[43]

From this visionary potential (which, as potential, is there from the first in *Pericles*) there springs a softening. The male is affected by this softening. But he does not become "soft," does not become a soft male. What is forwarded, instead, is the general sense of our capacity to endure adversity in terms of extreme patience, suffering, and tolerance. Man emerges as something significantly more sensitive and compassionate than the world he must inhabit. The attitude is close to Greek and Christian resignation; but the afflicted subject skirts the metaphysical center of such tragic suffering by demonstrating his constant readiness to avoid self-pity and to confront the tempests of his predicament.

The softening in *Pericles* also involves its telling. Gower keeps asking us for our imaginative cooperation: "In your imagination hold / This stage the ship, upon whose deck / The sea-tost Pericles appears to speak" (3.1. Chorus. 58–60). "Imagine Pericles arriv'd at Tyre . . ." (4.1. Chorus. 1). This imagining always either supersedes the muteness of dumb show or prepares to fall back into that world of muteness and unspeaking: "Now our sands are almost run; / More a little, and then dumb" (5.2.1–2). The absence of story is dumb story, or dumbness; and this dumbness makes itself felt as something entirely enveloping story-telling as its condition of tellability: anteceding telling, superseding telling. But muteness has also "leaked" in from the circular outside, invading the very "gaps" (4.4.8) where Gower stands to rectify things. His presence is strikingly apologetic, as if he too is suffering: at once tolerating the show and asking us to share his tolerance. As he stands next to the mute monument of Marina, he seems to negotiate *mute proximity* itself: to be what stands closest to dumb show, silence, and unspeaking. He softens the transitions (the difference?) between the mute and the audible:

> Scene 4. *Before the monument of Marina at Tharsus. Enter Gower.*
> Thus time we waste, and long leagues make short;
> Sail seas in cockles, have and wish but for't;
> Making, to take our imagination
> From bourn to bourn, region to region.
> By you being pardon'd, we commit no crime
> To use one language in each several clime
> Where our scene seems to live. I do beseech you
> To learn of me, who stand i'th'gaps to teach you
> The stages of our story.
>
> (4.4.1–9)

In the real world we would *hear* the difference between one language and another: what was spoken in one place would not speak to those arriving from another. In addition, all such southern languages would be "mute" and significantly dumb for any contemporary spectator familiar only with the sounds of his native tongue. In this general situation, the "gaps" that Gower says he is standing in are not felt to be simply the gaps between one leg of the narrative and the next, between one act and another; instead he seems also to stand in the (mute) gaps between those various languages. The "stages of our story" (4.4.9) are thus not felt to be simply temporal entities, but to be structural and narratological ones—all kept apart *and* unified by a polyglot sense of ontological variety. But in this polyphony and polyglotism, *one* of the languages is muteness itself. In fact, Gower's strategically typical position in the play is (as I have emphasized) that of immediately superseding a dumb show. He thus comes over to the spectator as a grafting of the mute and the audible; and if he apologizes, as graft, for this awkward hinge, his apology might be felt to have the purpose of sometimes consoling the dumb ones: the dumb ones, while the play unfolds in the theater, being of course not only those working in silence in the dumb shows, but also us, the spectators. We, as we watch without ever uttering a syllable, are unconsciously the ideal sensory equipment for the general apperception of the ontological limitlessness of mute signification. Indeed, even at the opening of act 5, where the inaugural dumb show has been omitted, Gower appeals to our vision rather than to our hearing. To "suppose" ("suppose him now at anchor" [5.Chorus.16]) is to imagine; and to imagine, already, is to move not simply into greater hearing but into greater seeing, into the visionary (what soon is to be the dramatic climax)—perhaps into mute vision, visuality *without* hearing: "In your supposing once more put your *sight*" (5.Chorus.21). As I shall soon be suggesting, this emphasis on the visual side of experience is exceedingly important in *The Winter's Tale* too.

The miracle play requires a type of dramatic cooperation that is special, that is other. It is not simply demanded of us that we believe the story but that, inside the story, we generate the kind of belief that the participants generate when they approach the possibility of the miraculous. R. S. White discusses such dramatic cooperation when considering the "miracle" that concludes *The Winter's Tale*. "The play . . . comes alive not only by what it gives us but also by what we give to it. Paulina carefully prepares her spectators for a cooperative enterprise which involves both the work of art and the feelings of the perceivers, as she brings a 'statue' to life."[44] But whereas such miraculousness is dangerously deferred in *The Winter's Tale* (seeming, and perhaps being, a constructional addition), it is in *Pericles* felt from the first to be a natural dimension of the poetic sensation. Miraculousness is simply the heightening of the poetic spell that language is gradually falling into. That does not mean that the miraculous is not abrupt, but that its abruptness is not itself aesthetically or linguistically jarring. The miraculous is in harmony with itself in *Pericles* in a way that it is not in *The Winter's Tale*. We may perceive this difference by comparing the (linguistic) presentation of the birth of the two daughters, Perdita and Marina. Let us begin with Perdita:

> *Emilia*. She is, something before her time, deliver'd.
> *Paulina*. A boy?
> *Emilia*. A daughter; and a goodly babe,
> Lusty, and like to live: the queen receives
> Much comfort in't; says, "My poor prisoner,

I am innocent as you."
Paulina. I dare be sworn:
These dangerous, unsafe lunes i'th'king, beshrew them!
He must be told on't, and he shall: the office
Becomes a woman best. I'll take't upon me:
If I prove honey-mouth'd, let my tongue blister,
And never to my red-look'd anger be
The trumpet any more. Pray you, Emilia,
Commend my best obedience to the queen:
If she dares trust me with her little babe,
I'll show't the king, and undertake to be
Her advocate to th'loud'st. We do not know
How he may soften at the sight o'th'child:
The silence often of pure innocence
Persuades, when speaking fails.

(*W* 2.2.25–42)

There is muteness, here, as the last lines indicate: just seeing the child might possibly reverse the entire situation for Leontes. That moment of mute purity could be the therapeutic masterstroke. But the poetry and emotion of the situation are of course soiled by the fact that the newborn child is already being used here as a pawn in a human and sexual dialectic. The femininity of Perdita is at this moment reduced to the (dialectical) fact that she may or may not prove visually strong enough to bring the erroneous male over to the side of the nonerroneous females. Nothing is "wrong" with that possibility as such; the problem instead is that femininity here is finitized and dialecticized in a manner that severely limits the aesthetic and imaginative power of femininity as a cosmic drive. Like Pericles, Leontes may "soften" (2.2.40) at the sight of his newborn daughter (in fact he does not); but that hypothetical softening is simply the finite relinquishing of a finite prejudice caused by finite, determinable factors (incorrect information about Hermione). Perdita is just as *exposed* as Marina; but the exposure is simply the tempestuousness of marital bickering and human quarreling: Marina is chafed by the winds of a furious gale, Perdita almost by the "trumpet" (2.2.35) of Paulina's sharp tongue. To understand femininity as delivery in *Pericles*, then, is to see it in possible contrast to feminine delivery in *The Winter's Tale*. It is not difficult to perceive, in fact, that the entire staging of the sensation of cosmic femininity in *Pericles* is propelled by the infinitely poetic and moving account of Marina's first moments of existence and pain.

Enter Lychorida, with an infant.

Lychorida. Here is a thing too young for such a place,
Who, if it had conceit, would die, as I
Am like to do. Take in your arms this piece
Of your dead queen.
Pericles. How? how, Lychorida?
Lychorida. Patience, good sir; do not assist the storm.
Here's all that is left living of your queen,
A little daughter: for the sake of it,
Be manly, and take comfort.
Pericles. O you gods!
Why do you make us love your goodly gifts,
And snatch them straight away? We here below
Recall not what we give, and therein may
Use honour with you.
Lychorida. Patience, good sir,
Even for this charge.
Pericles. Now, mild may be thy life!
For a more blusterous birth had never babe;
Quiet and gentle thy conditions! for
Thou art the rudeliest welcome to this world
That e'er was prince's child. Happy what follows!
Thou hast as chiding a nativity
As fire, air, water, earth, and heaven can make,
To herald thee from the womb.
Even at the first thy loss is more than can
Thy portage quit, with all thou canst find here.
Now the good gods throw their best eyes upon't!

(Enter two Sailors.)

1. *Sailor.* What courage, sir? God save you!
Pericles. Courage enough: I do not fear the flaw;
It hath done to me the worst. Yet for the love
Of this poor infant, this fresh-new seafarer,
I would it would be quiet.
1. *Sailor.* Slack the bolins there! Thou wilt not, wilt thou?
Blow, and split thyself.
2. *Sailor.* But sea-room, and the brine and cloudy billow kiss the moon, I care not.
1. *Sailor.* Sir, your queen must overboard; the sea works high, the wind is loud, and will not lie till the ship be clear'd of the dead.
Pericles. That's your superstition.
1. *Sailor:* Pardon us, sir; with us at sea it hath been still observ'd; and we are strong in custom. Therefore briefly yield'er, for she must overboard straight.

Pericles. As you think meet. Most wretched queen!
Lychorida. Here she lies, sir.
Pericles. A terrible childbed hast thou had, my dear;
No light, no fire: th'unfriendly elements
Forgot thee utterly; nor have I time
To give thee hallow'd to thy grave, but straight
Must cast thee, scarcely coffin'd, in the ooze;
Where, for a monument upon thy bones,
And e'er-remaining lamps, the belching whale
And humming water must o'erwhelm thy corpse,
Lying with simple shells.

(3.1.15–64)

Once poetry in this way has simplified strong emotion to the point of absolute aesthetic purity, it is utterly impossible ever to turn back to the finite world of dialectical contest and sexual prestige. Therefore, we feel no self-pity whatsoever in Marina, when she later on describes her cosmic situatedness in terms of personal sorrow: "Ay me! poor maid, / Born in a tempest, when my mother died, / This world to me is as a lasting storm" (4.1.17–19). Yet self-pity is precisely what one (rightly or wrongly) can imagine in Hermione, when she is reported to have described the condition of her newborn child in terms of her own condition: "My poor prisoner, / I am innocent as you" (2.2.28–29). Here in *The Winter's Tale* innocence is not itself innocent—for it is tainted by the sexual rhetoric of human power. In this discursive field, the word *innocence* is itself charged with assertiveness. This assertiveness may in itself be innocent, may in itself be counterassertive, something thrown *at* assertiveness; but since the word is spoken dialectically, it is contaminated by the competitive context it helps to intensify and sharpen. But the violence that surrounds Marina in *Pericles* is not of this dialectical quality, and therefore she is never *linguistically* corrupted by the negativity that she inherits. Perdita inherits a competitive negativity that she can overcome; Marina inherits a noncompetitive negativity that she can absorb, sometimes even love.

Human negativity is for such reasons marginalized in *Pericles*, dwarfed to the dimension of the comical. Marina is empirically speaking constantly threatened by rape, by the severest possible type of masculine aggression. But Shakespeare has maneuvered his play so dexterously that even rape itself—*particularly* rape itself—looks strangely feeble, harmless, innocent. It is fun watching the pirates carry Marina off to instant sexual rending ("Half-part, mates, half-part! Come, let's have her aboard suddenly"

[4.1.94–95]); and it is fun watching her being badgered in Mytilene by the lords of the brothel. We do not distance ourselves from her delicate sexual predicaments simply because art idealizes her innocence or simply because many romance events have a fairyland quality; the sense of relativity, rather, is a function of our inaugural experience of Marina's cosmic status as emblematic of originary loss (3.1.35).

By situating Marina from the start in the middle of a cosmic vortex large enough to swallow all ground or sense of realistic hope, Shakespeare provides her with *narratological* foundations that immediately come to relativize all ensuing mishaps of a finite and worldly nature. Absolute loss always precedes loss itself for Marina ("at the first thy loss is more" [3.1.35]), and therefore the negativity that time has in store for her can never "catch up" with the negative foundation that primordially neutralizes it. What we also very much feel in (and after) that long storm passage cited a moment ago is that Pericles has a significant capacity for sympathy and empathy. And his pity for others does not diminish the capacity of others to pity him—these "others" of course being inclusive of the spectators. Indeed, the types of emotional receptivity that Pericles permits himself to express are inadvertently feminine (or nonmasculine) from this viewpoint, since they are identifiable as the very response mechanisms that males characteristically suppress in order to enter dialectical contests with the optimal sense of professional purpose. In dialectic, pity is "useless."

If death, then (in battle), is the locus where the dialectical male collects the transcendental awards of the sacrifice of emotion and sensitivity, the miracle is (at least aesthetically speaking) the site where the mute, "genderless" person meets the visionary realizations of an other commitment. In the foundational arena of death, masculinity collects meaning—its meaning. In the unfoundational abyss of the miracle, cosmic femininity does not collect, but simply *beholds* what has been delivered. Therefore, as in the quasi-feminine world of Spenser's *Faerie Queene*, what seems to be a lineal quest for a dominant and conclusive truth is really a process rather than a drive. The questing (something self-sensitizing) is more important than the quest (something true). In *Pericles* we are *en voyage*. And that is all we really need to be.

2
Negative Miracle

Negative Shakespeare

With *The Winter's Tale* we are already in a world where the cosmic principles of miraculousness are on the wane: where these principles, although staged more conspicuously and theatrically, risk degenerating into a state of spiritual emptiness. That emptiness, as I shall argue, is not necessarily a negative thing on the aesthetic level, but simply implies that Shakespeare gradually "returns" miracle to the patriarchal secularism that is the basic cultural condition of his profession.

It is always tempting to imagine for great writers some logically pure pattern of "development," according to which all that happens to their creativity is viewed as growth toward ever-increasing "maturity." Each step that the writer takes is a step making him a more mature artist and his art a more mature art. According to this fallacy, all the late plays of Shakespeare can be called "romances," and that entire group of dramas can be conceived as the *most* mature part of the Shakespearean corpus. From this viewpoint *Pericles* is only a fragile and incomplete beginning, the least "mature" and "Shakespearean" of the romances, as it were, while *The Tempest* is the final fullness of what *Pericles* merely promises and faintly foreshadows. There is some truth in this type of psychobiographical generalization; but I think such thinking blinds us to other developments in Shakespeare that are more important and that have little to do with that larger, sweeping sense of a general Shakespearean step-by-step progression toward *The Tempest*. As I have already emphasized, the three plays that concern us in this study need to be respected and considered quite individually; and that kind of scholarly and critical respect entails some disrespect for the facile assumption that Shakespeare everywhere "progresses." I do not think Shakespearean progression is an exclusively (or even primarily) lineal event, and I think that various innovations and artistic switchovers in Shakespeare are triggered by the fact that there is a certain loss of vitality within some of his play sequences. This decline may not be general; it may be affecting only a certain dimension of the particular play sequence. But such partial weakening is enough, in the long run, to empty that particular play sequence of the energy it needs to survive in the restless space of Shakespeare's creative workshop.

From this viewpoint, I am prepared to say that Shakespeare's miracle plays do develop in step-by-step fashion, if we think of them in terms of an artistic complexity of a technical and (perhaps) theatrical kind. But I am also prepared to say that in terms of *miraculousness* the miracle plays do not "develop" in any conventional sense. On the contrary, they empty out. As I shall presently argue, this emptying-out of the Shakespearean miracle play is governed by a process of secularization and humanization that takes the edge off miracle itself. Thus I will be asking myself whether *The Winter's Tale* is not a decline from *Pericles:* a decline in seriousness, in miraculousness, in vision, in purity . . . in femininity. And I will be asking myself if *Cymbeline* does not complete this decline. Also, however, I will be asking what accrues from this decline: for in decline itself various possibilities make themselves available for Shakespeare; and as Shakespeare progressively learns to exploit these unprecedented possibilities, he lifts his creative resources to the level of an artistic sense of challenge previously undreamed of. (I refer the reader interested in the *Pericles/Winter's Tale* interface back to the sections in chapter 1 where I discussed some of the differences and contrasts between the two plays.)

In one of the best works ever written on the miracle plays, *The Crown of Life,* G. Wilson Knight emphasizes the peculiarly important role of *Pericles* in the Shakespearean corpus and also the way in which *The Winter's Tale* is unable to quite follow suit. Knight primarily understands *Pericles* in terms of vision:

> The blindness of past Shakespearian criticism is at no point more completely in evidence than in the comments on this play. To the discerning mind it will be evident that we are here confronted with the furthest reach of Shakespeare's poetic and visionary power: if we except *The Tempest,* the latter half of *Pericles* has no equivalent in transcendental apprehension in all Shakespeare but the latter half of *Antony and Cleopatra* . . . Now if, as is probable, the greater part of *Pericles* is the work of Shakespeare grafted on to an earlier play of different authorship, of which signs are apparent in some of the early

> scenes, it is not surprising that, after his composition of these supreme latter acts, he found another plot of the same kind for his next play; nor is it surprising that the next play, *The Winter's Tale,* though more perfect as a whole, lacks something of the paradisal radiance of *Pericles.* The great artist does not well to repeat himself: in *Pericles,* as the writer handles an old theme, some mystic apprehension of a life that conquers death has sprung to vivid form, as it were, spontaneously: a shaft of light penetrating into the very heart of death. The studied repetition that follows is less vital.[1]

My own inclination is very much to share this view, including the assumption that Shakespeare's major contribution to *Pericles* has shaped itself in terms of grafting. But what Wilson Knight really fails to explain is why the artist could not "repeat himself." Shakespeare repeated himself on numerous occasions, if by repetition we mean the reactivation of a generic possibility: comic repetition, tragic repetition, and so forth. A great artist can always vary his art so that repetition does not make itself felt as repetition. Why, then, could not Shakespeare safely go on repeating the "miracle" formula of *Pericles?*

I have a very definite answer to this question—and an answer that is so crucial that this entire critical enterprise hinges on the possible power of its relevance. A miracle play, as something organized around a sense of the miraculous, involves the feeling that something is *rescued;* and I suggest that this sense of actually *rescuing everything* was available to Shakespeare (as a total creative sensation) only in a professional situation where what had to be rescued was the play as such (and not merely something that was part of the action inside the play). No one will ever know exactly what it was in the operative blueprint for *Pericles* that actually moved Shakespeare to this unprecedented sense of salvational necessity. Perhaps the radical wretchedness of the operative stock (to be supplemented by his graft) was such a cause (as the hopelessness and aesthetic disarrangement of the first two acts would suggest to a critic not chiefly attributing such inadequacy to the mischief of poor reporting by theater pirates); or perhaps some private sense of hopelessness at that specific moment joined up with the provisional sense of insurmountable technical difficulties. Whatever the case, I suggest that the very hostility of the creative conditions framing the genesis of *Pericles* may have contributed to its peculiarly sincere and fresh engagement with the miraculous; and I suggest that the *lack* of the urgent need to achieve a creative graft may well explain the rather more "studied" miraculousness of the other miracle plays.

I am basing this line of thinking not simply on conjecture, but on the evidence (to be progressively elucidated in what follows) scattered throughout the miracle plays of the traces of a Shakespearean obsession with the idea of recuperation, recovery, and restoration. Unlike many a positivist critic, I do not mainly see these salvational motifs in terms of theme ("regeneration") or as a function of some personal Shakespearean yearning for recuperative bliss or existential convalescence. As I shall try to demonstrate, nearly all of the salvational moments in the miracle plays (moments touching the idea of miraculous recovery) are directly or indirectly related to the sense of technical and aesthetic recovery on the level of artistic self-questioning (am I creating/improving a failure or a success?). For me, therefore, the entire play sequence of the three miracle plays is the most uncertain and uncertainizing period of Shakespeare. A miracle is actually needed at times, and it is the reality (sincere urgency) of that need that in the final analysis determines the operative potency of the miracle play *as* miracle play.

It is important to observe, here, that the sense of the uncertainty of the aesthetic project (the final successfulness of the play) is not necessarily a personal or private matter. If Shakespeare for the first time is really uncertain about the future fate of a play he is writing with serious commitment, and if this play already is the fully available text of something written by a collaborator, Shakespeare can face the sense of aesthetic abyss without actually sensing any directly personal involvement in that abyss—without sensing the abyssing of Shakespeare in the abyssing of his writing.

This, I suggest, is an immensely possible, immensely important, and immensely novel situation: that Shakespeare could be facing an abyss (total failure) without feeling that that abyss had any significant relation to his own psyche, own inner darkness, own perversions, own foibles, own neuroses, own weaknesses, own hungers, own drives, own frustrations, own prestige, own power. Such premises, technical and professional rather than private and existential, might supply us with an alternative way of speculating about the reasons for the important sea-change in the creative period of the late plays. Personally, I find it hard to imagine that the special atmosphere of *Pericles*—a Shakespearean world free from Shakespearean fever—could have been generated by conditions other than those outlined above. Nor can I explain the oddness of the treatment of the notion of "recovery" without considering a Shakespearean exposure to the lateral influence of other dramatists. Shakespeare was of course always conscious of the parallel contributions of rival playwrights, and his plays consciously absorb the discourse and structures of predecessors. But what I am calling lateral influence is neither a self-confident awareness of the parallel achievement of peers nor a shameless exploitation of predecessors. It is the sense of being uncertainized by the immediate activity of copresent dramatists—whether these are upstart crows (Beaumont and Fletcher) or drastically incompetent journeymen (traceable in *Pericles* and elsewhere).

Much of what has recently been said is speculative; but the difficulty with Shakespeare's late plays is that they need some frame of speculative thought to at all become real objects of criticism. This indispensability of the speculative is triggered by our sense that the late plays are engineered by a sudden change of attitude in Shakespeare to his own writing. Essential things in the late plays seem to be understandable only in relation to such a change. Since the shift involves a writer whose innermost attitudes are destined to remain unknowable and mysterious, speculation of some sort has to be undertaken. As John Danby points out, the late plays all point to a single crucial question about Shakespeare's new position: "What is his attitude to himself in the act of writing?"[2]

If, as I have suggested, Shakespeare in a striking way benefits from the challenge of the "lateral," from the copresence of a collaborator or rival who at first inspires negatively, then the play sequence constituted by the miracle plays becomes strangely reversed from the viewpoint of aesthetic evaluation. It no longer becomes a drawback to have half one's play written by an alien hand. Interference seems to me to be structurally positive in the miracle plays, because only the miracle is going to be able to put an end to interfering. Or, rather, only radical interfering is going to make a miracle the *necessary* terminal climax of the creative and dramatic process. This means that, as Shakespeare gradually adjusts himself to the task of writing miracle plays where the miracle is not *aesthetically* necessary (because he is himself doing the planning from the outset), he has to create his "own" interference. He has, in a sense, to mix up his material so badly (imitating the work of a poor journeyman) that he finds himself driven to a final point of hopelessness where he may attack, decreate, and salvage his own play. I will be suggesting that the miracle plays are full of references to this type of process. Such deliberately "negative" writing and such last-minute recuperation may be operative on the macrolevel of the entire drama as well as on the microlevel of individual scenes, lines, or motifs.

The creation of "negative writing" (the decreation of writing) involves the decentration of writing. The collaborator, if he exists, removes the writer from the center of the creative process by already stamping the artifact with the inaugural determinations of his own shaping willpower, just as the dominant rival playwright (by swinging the taste of the entire public) removes the writer from the center of his imaginative freedom. Now this "decentering" of the creative ego, as I have remarked, is not necessarily a negative thing—and certainly not so for a Shakespeare who by now has accumulated so much reputation and artistic self-confidence that "loss" of the creative ego only becomes sport: provisional and experimental. A loss of the center is in the late plays not something serious, because some important part of Shakespeare is beginning to stand aloof from loss in general as well as from the artistic ego.

What we thus witness in *Pericles* is the formation of *a hero whose psyche is not a centered consciousness*. In creative and personal terms, this means that Shakespeare's attitude to the hero is one of total engagement without total identification. The hero is not only someone else's hero (the collaborator's, the text's), he is also a hero in whom Shakespeare *feels* that his (self-) identification dissolves. What is miraculous in the miracle plays is from this creative viewpoint the absolute indifference between total engagement and total disengagement, the complete vanishing of the difference between a private, caring Shakespeare and an aesthetic, distanced Shakespeare. In the best moments of the miracle plays (and there are more of them in *Pericles* than anywhere else) there is a complete personal involvement of an emotive kind that is as pure and free as that of the impersonality of aesthetic commitment itself. Because of the peculiar conditions of the dramatic genesis, there has been no need to create such a blissful state by utilizing the semidistanced world of comedy; on the contrary, Pericles, while remaining pure, can carry the existential darkness that tragedy carries. Yet no part of this dark burden is contaminated by the murky idiosyncracies of Shakespeare's passionate ego.

In discussing the difference between the poor opening acts of *Pericles* and the three more Shakespearean acts that follow, John Danby tries to identify the two types of writing by maintaining that the first acts lack "a consciousness centred in the writer."[3] Discussing Sidney's different treatment of romance, he argues that there is "no one, in fact, who seems as securely centred as are any of the four lovers in the *Arcadia*."[4] I would like to suggest that this disappearance of "a consciousness centred in the writer" in a sense is permanent in *Pericles*, and in the miracle plays in general. Furthermore, this absence of the writerly control center is by no means exclusively a drawback—although, as Danby justly points out, those first two acts are simply *too* centerless. This is another way of saying what I asserted some moments ago: that in the miracle plays Shakespeare profits from things that in a "normal" play would be aesthetically and theatrically negative.

To give these types of preliminary remarks is to at once indicate the difficulties posed by a play like *The Winter's Tale*. There, precisely, miracle is reduced to *coup de théâtre;* and if we want to understand that *reductive* (and therefore negative) move in terms of some aesthetic purpose that is affirmative (and therefore positive), we must grasp the general importance of what I have recently been discussing in terms of Shakespeare's "negative writing." Shakespeare flirts with difficulty in the miracle plays; and while he may at first to a certain extent be flirting with failure in order to enhance the drama of miracle, he is also, by progressively making miracle itself a difficulty, extending the entire lure of "failure"—pushing it toward those limits (catastrophe) where, in the adventurous moment of writing, the artist cannot know anything certain about last resources.

Jealousy and Miracle

Important structural connections between *Pericles* and *The Winter's Tale* are negotiated through the leading principles we have already begun to review: the lack of ground, the lack of motive, and the lack of center (of pronounced aesthetic cogito). We shall be discussing all of these principles.

I intend to focus jealousy in *The Winter's Tale* in relation to the lack of motive, but I wish first to anchor this notion of absent motive in the fashioning of such motivelessness in *Pericles*. This is quickly done by simply pointing to the fragmentation of all viable causal structure in that play. In fact, as soon as we enter the miracle plays, we are no longer in the mainly causal world of other Shakespearean drama—and the failure of critics to appreciate the scope and significance of this change is, as I shall argue, one of the main sources of confusion about the miracle plays. Donald Stauffer is pleasingly free from such blindness:

> In *Pericles* there are none of those masterful persuasion scenes, no more dialogues of the mind with itself as it reaches toward a painful choice. The reversals in situation come like bolts of lightning. Men are struck without reference to their own wills; their faults and virtues do not lie in themselves, except for a predisposition to evil or good; free will in the piece exists beyond men, in the stars.[5]

Unfortunately, certain critics stubbornly refuse to recognize this general Shakespearean promotion of a world not mainly understandable in terms of ordinary causation. A recent example is Wilbur Sanders, who not only defends the psychologistic approach,[6] but who also goes on to construct one of the most absurdly complicated "causal" accounts ever printed in the history of Shakespeare criticism. Having mocked Leavis's criticism,[7] he establishes "a profusion of explanations" to clarify Leontes' behavior through logical causation.[8] Such exaggerated and unbalanced causal criticism implements a false and narrowly reductive logic, bringing the investigator close to the risk of becoming the very "fool-critic" derided by Leavis.[9] Most important Shakespeare critics have already successfully established the reasons for marginalizing the causal mode of interpretation. For Wilson Knight, in this way, Leontes does not belong to a world of external causation: "His evil is self-born and unmotivated."[10] E. M. W. Tillyard's commentary is even more to the point:

> Leontes's obsession of jealousy is terrifying in its intensity. It reminds us not of other Shakespearean tragic errors, but rather of the god-sent lunacies of Greek drama, the lunacies of Ajax and Heracles. It is as scantily motivated as these, and we should refrain from demanding any motive. Indeed, it is as much a surprise to the characters in the play as it is to the reader.[11]

The final sentence here is peculiarly important: that the jealousy is alien not only to Leontes but also to the supposedly organic nature of the play. Jealousy is *inorganic* in *The Winter's Tale*, and this ability of any unit in the miracle plays to appear atomically—isolated from any kind of causal or logical context—is structurally decisive in epochalizing the miracle plays of Shakespeare and in determining the rationale we require in order to identify them. The "inorganic" quality of events in a miracle play is what makes the miracle itself possible; because in an "organic" and logically developmental process, a miracle cannot plausibly take place—it is superfluous. A miracle is not simply the logical outcome of a sequence of logically connected events; nor is it simply a reversal or rupture of such a classical sequence. The atomistic and inorganic ordering of dramatic structure is, as F. W. Brownlow emphasizes, the very world that *Pericles* has already made available:

> The arrangement of its incidents is chronological, and there is no necessary connection between one incident and another. Although Pericles leaves Tyre a second time for fear of Antiochus, there is no reason why he should call at Tarsus. In this example there is a general motivation, but not a specific one; sometimes there is no motive of any kind, as when Pericles gives no reason for leaving Marina at Tarsus, or when Thaisa gives no reason for entering the temple at Ephesus. The plot's resolution begins when Pericles arrives by accident at Mytilene; and although he proceeds to Ephesus in response to a vision, he has no idea what he will find there. In a tale so lacking in motivation the characters represent ways of being that we take for granted, not persons who become what they are through choice.[12]

It is precisely this atomic, inorganic, and acausal nature of events that creates the special need for the cooperative efforts of the audience in the miracle play. Events are not "supported" by other events so much as by our own faith in their sheer isolated self-manifestations. Strangely, this somehow applies to many inner events too. Characters have difficulties interpreting events taking place in their own heads—almost as if they were strangers to the causal realities voiced by those heads. (The beheading of Cloten/Posthumus in *Cymbeline* is not unrelated to this problematic of displaced identity, as I shall argue later on.) In general this means that Shakespeare is moving toward the creation of a dramatic possibility, or unthinkable situation, where the crowning event of one of his plays is going to lack all real supportive and logically causal context. As a theatrical event, this is precisely what the miracle amounts to in *The Winter's Tale* (the resurrection of Hermione after sixteen years of certain death). We have all along been preparing ourselves for the "reality" of such an isolationist event, because all along, right from the first presencing of Leontes' ludicrous jealousy, inner and outer events have supported themselves on little but their own emergent reality. Time itself, in *The Winter's Tale,* promotes this "inorganic" and disjunctive sensation; for although Time bridges a gap of fifteen or sixteen years (the gap between these two figures itself has to be bridged),[13] Time also creates the violence of the rupture of that gap: for the spectator, the news delivered by Time that it has jumped sixteen years does not simply harmonize two dramatic and empirical epochs; the news also startles us with the negativity of its disjunctive leap.

Thus, in a play heading toward a final improbability, the shocks of jealousy and temporality are suitable events in a world where the isolationist constantly triumphs over the developmental. As I have emphasized, the harmonizing of the atomically isolated items of dramatic narrative in this way becomes a significantly spectatorial duty—so that we during the finale are prepared to do just about anything, to cooperate in just about any way, to achieve final sense-making. This is of course exactly what Shakespeare demands of us. He has not only created the miracle (the revival of the statuesque Hermione) but also the specific spectatorial attitude that is its condition of theatrical possibility. Shakespeare creates a miracle, but he also creates "eyes" capable of seeing it. These eyes cannot primarily be looking for logical causes during actual revelation; they must supply the miraculous vision with the supportive and isolationist faith of miraculous participation. Here participation itself is a form of vision, for such vision requires the total exclusion of all context (of everything not belonging to the sighting of miraculous possibility). This new and radical stress on the hyperactivity of the spectator is already evident in *Pericles*, as Brownlow observes in his lucid review. There, the role corresponding to that of Time is played by Gower.

> The chief effect of Gower's presence is that narrative is restored to its ancient pre-eminence over character. A character like Hamlet embodies the notion, which is a very modern one, that the self is autonomous: "Before me," he seems to say, "nothing is." Pericles, however, is obviously the creation of another mind. Indeed, as Gower insists, Pericles is as much the creature of our imaginations, almost, as he is of Gower's. His reality depends upon an agreement between the storyteller and his audience.[14]

But agreement here, the "contract" between dramatic telling and dramatic attention, is more than suspension of disbelief; for suspension of disbelief is vaguely and generally applied to the story in general, while the spectatorial hyperactivity sought by the miracle play implies a disjunctive on-and-off attention that at any moment is prepared to make a fresh start and point the mind in context-defying fashion at an individually ultrailluminated object of immanent fascination. Close as it appears to be (and come) to vulgar sensationalism (not an altogether remote theatrical option in Jacobean times), such a type of dramatic attending is in the final analysis an attitude reaching down richly to the complex subterranean roots of medieval consciousness.

Because he at any time is quite free from the story in which he is being told, Pericles requires our cooperative support *to at all exist.* The story cannot by itself, as it were, hold him in any organic state of viable dramatic belonging. Or, if the story can do so, it is through our unusual narratological sympathy (an unusualness Gower is specifically designed to promote). But such exceedingly cooperative efforts are required of us in *The Winter's Tale* too. We spontaneously become involved in the jealousy of Othello and in the innocent sufferings of Desdemona; but the innocence of Hermione is at first almost interchangeable with her supposed adultery, because the isolationist and uncontextual nature of the presencing of her moral reality does not *immediately* call for any type of normal dialectical participation. Her ambiguity is a matter of indifference, and Leontes shouts his recriminations straight across the space of this indifference.

In time, of course, the issue of her fidelity will ideally come to touch us; but that touching is only possible once the play has strained itself to the limit in a form of reconstructive work where the urgency of the sense of causal meaning is imposed retrospectively.

For some time now, I have been discussing motivation. And my central thesis in this subsection is that action in Shakespeare's miracle plays is governed by principles overriding those of logical causation and consistent "development" of a classical kind. This notion of the marginalization of dramatic motivation, we have seen, is one shared among a host of Shakespeare critics. There is also support for such a notion in the knowledge we have about the theatrical climate in which Shakespeare was working. Here the question of the lateral influence of Beaumont and Fletcher is not one I wish to overstate on the grounds of direct influence; but it can certainly be said that Shakespeare's ongoing awareness of the efforts of his professional rivals also was an awareness of the diminishing role of motivation in English drama. Beaumont and Fletcher were strikingly shameless and innovative in creating situation for the sake of situation, thus violating habitual forms of dramatic expectation. What might have impressed (and perhaps shocked) Shakespeare in this context may not have been the use of this technique but its successfulness and popularity. Having spent so much time and energy on causal probability, he might have asked himself a whole set of new questions not only about the technical procedures of dramatic persuasion but also about human beings. The easy aesthetic conscience of Shakespeare's rivals shifted the dramatic focus. Writes Ellis-Fermor: "it is the situation or emotional crisis that is preserved, while the motivation shows unmistakable signs of patching."[15]

It may be asked at this point why Shakespeare chose to center two of his miracle plays on the idea of jealousy. The answer I shall give is very simple: from the hyperontological view, *jealousy is a negative miracle*. Why? Because a miracle is essentially something without foundation, cause, or necessary motivation, and this is what potentially characterizes all radical jealousy. Where a miracle is ultrapositive, giving the sense of the paradisal, jealousy is ultranegative, giving the sense of the diabolic. In miracle we are in Heaven; in jealousy we are in Hell. *The Winter's Tale* essentially traces the journey from the former extreme to the latter, from a negative miracle to a positive miracle. This strange symmetry is destroyed if either of the extremes is humanistically rationalized in terms of classical causation. As functional opposites in the isolationist fabric of miracle play, jealousy and revelation need to hover "above" strict causal foundation. A foundation, ground, and causal platform may be suggested; the characters perceive the ground they should be standing on (the logic that could have accounted for everything they are experiencing); but the "space" between that solid foundation and the horror/wonder of their disengagement from it is what counts.

I am saying, then, that jealousy, like miracle, is unfoundational and defoundational. It can have a ground, and often does have a ground; but it belongs to its nature not to necessarily have a ground. *Othello* briefly identifies this crucial dimension of jealousy:

> *Desdemona*. Alas the day, I never gave him cause.
> *Emilia*. But jealous souls will not be answered so.
> They are not ever jealous for the cause,
> But jealous for they're jealous. 'Tis a monster
> Begot upon itself, born on itself.
>
> (3.4.152–56)

This definition of jealousy, a self-begotten monster lacking cause, fits Leontes perfectly—and is indeed a clue to the entire dramatic commencement of *The Winter's Tale*. Curiously, it is not the same kind of clue to the world of *Othello;* for while *The Winter's Tale* presences jealousy as such, *Othello* presences a dramatization of jealousy.

This difference, as I have argued, is based on the fact that while jealousy in no way actually is dependent on the existence of a motivation (it can be something entirely self-begotten in the imagination), it *can* be supplemented by causal or pseudo-causal triggers. Thus Othello has no factual cause for his jealousy, but Iago has manipulated affairs to the point where the world looks exactly like a world where there would have been real reasons for jealous behavior. We are back in the dialectical world of false appearances and logical causation—for the spectator can in step-by-step fashion follow the rational plan according to which Iago will lead Othello further and further into *concluding* that Desdemona is unfaithful. The conclusion is false, but it is nevertheless a conclusion; the evidence is fallacious, but it is nevertheless indistinguishable from evidence that in a similar situation would have been empirically conclusive. But in *The Winter's Tale* all such "realistic" evidence is lacking. The "signs" of infidelity in Hermione are precisely the kind of signs that are empty of strong empirical content and that typically get overinterpreted in the hyperimaginative hothouse of the jealous mind. No Iago is required for the fabrication of jealousy's totalization, and no elaborate plot is required, no staging of a complex rationalist scenario where a multitude of individuals with various motives intercreate a theater of tragic causation. Here in *The Winter's Tale* there is no genuine tragic causation; yet jealousy still roars at full throttle, and pain is still there to torment love and selfhood.

To fail to understand this ontological difference between jealousy in *Othello* and jealousy in *The Winter's Tale* is to fail to understand the radical discrepancy between the basically causal world of the tragedies and the basically acausal world of the miracle plays. I touched this difference a moment ago when I spoke of the distinction between jealousy and a dramatization of jealousy. What is new in the miracle plays is that Shakespeare, a dramatist, does not *dramatize* everything he stages. Critics have great difficulty understanding, accepting, and digesting this innovation; they think that a dramatist is to be measured by his powers of dramatization, and that a dramatization of something always is superior to the absence (refusal) of its dramatization. But in the miracle plays, the purpose is no longer to humanize the world according to the limitations of humanist drama, but on the contrary to focus individual situations and to understand them in splendid isolation. Jealousy, in this way, is questioned as such. So are happiness, suffering, ecstasy, and endurance. What we want to do in a miracle play is to remove the normal causal supports for an experience, its logical world-context, and analyze it on its own terms. *Pericles* shows us what suffering *is* without relating it to anything beyond itself. The same goes for love, joy, patience, and cosmic bewilderment. *The Winter's Tale* shows us what jealousy *is* without fabricating some fantastically clever plot that is going to make it look tragically pure—without, therefore, giving us the elaborate comforts of catharsis. The visionary enlightenment of Leontes comes long after the time of the purgation of his negative emotions, and thus there is no direct causal bridge between tension and release from tension, between jealousy and its sublimation in a final sense of spiritual renewal. The huge gap (sixteen years) instituted by Time is here again structurally significant, for it disconnects the negative and positive poles of emotion from one another. When Leontes eventually is seen bursting with tension in the revelation scene (will Hermione come to life again? is that possible?), that tension is not dramatic tension at all in any ordinary sense, not tension that has been "preserved" from the negativity of his jealous frenzy; on the contrary, that frenzy lies subdued and annihilated in the annals of a chronicled past safely buried more than a decade away from the theatrical present. The tension he feels is mainly generated by the "now" of the isolationist event and possibility of miracle itself.

In this way, jealousy and miracle form an absolute tension in *The Winter's Tale,* being one another's pure opposites; but the tension between them is not communicated dialectically as any tension that moves between the two extremes in terms of dramatized conflict. The contrast between negative miracle (jealousy) and positive miracle (resurrection) is not a dramatic conflict. The absence of such a dramatization (Shakespeare's deliberate discontinuation of psychological tension in spectator and hero) absences the theatrical possibility of catharsis and ordinary spiritual renewal. But this absencing of ordinary renewal is what makes possible the presencing of unusual renewal: spiritual ecstasy that, like jealousy itself, is "begot upon itself, born on itself." Miracle too is a "monster" (to cite *Othello* once more), at least aesthetically; for it is drastically oversized in relation to any normal ground that could account for it. But Shakespeare, at this point, is not concerned with the task of harmonizing miraculous experience (whether positive or negative) with any "order," least of all a preexisting one. What he is interested in is the "reality" of miracle qua miracle; and that reality is unthinkable in a relativistic world of plenary contexts.

The intensity of focus granted by the "miracle technique," with its isolationist capacity to bring direct atomic focus on an individually illuminated phenomenon (like jealousy or revelation), has caused certain able critics to fall into the trap of believing that the material yielded in the miracle plays is *better* than the material produced by earlier plays. Wilson Knight himself walks into this trap with characteristic enthusiasm, telling us that "Leontes is more complex than Othello as a study of jealousy and more realistically convincing than Macbeth as a study of evil possession."[16] The "full authenticity of these crowning works"[17] is such that there is "an advance in human delineation" permitting Iachimo in *Cymbeline* to outshine Iago as "convincing" stage figure.[18] This, of course, is an exaggerated view, full of wishful thinking. Wilbur Sanders walks into exactly the same trap when he speaks of Leontes in terms of "the three-dimensional depth of Shakespeare's characterisation."[19] In point of fact, the world of Shakespeare's miracle plays is hardly ever a world of either "depth" (in this sense) or "characterisation" (in the normal sense); and Shakespeare's miracle plays work toward situations of structural crisis as soon as they too closely approximate that former type of human delineation.

This fallacious notion that the *parts* of Shakespeare's drama grow more complex as his art grows more complex tends to be accompanied by the ancillary fallacy (intelligently skirted by Wilson Knight) that ecstasy in Shakespeare cannot be of a religious type. We thus learn from Sanders that it is naughty to commit the "offence" of "giving *grace* a capital 'G' " in comments on *The Winter's Tale*.[20] Grace "is far too rich and human a quality to be abandoned to the theologians."[21] But this choice between humanity and theology is of course strained, false, and absurd. It may well be that we should refrain from *translating* the Shakespearean miracle into the language and thinking of religious doctrine; but that in no way gives us the right to "humanize" the Shakespearean miracle according to the psychologizing rationale of twentieth-century humanism. It is not simply that such a rationale, determined to have its way everywhere in Shakespeare, superimposes a questionable and totalistic set of preexisting intellectual values; it is that such a subjective determination to "humanize" the Shakespearean text in universalist fashion actually leads to logically preposterous conclusions. The obstinately "human" reading of *The Winter's Tale* creates bias and evaluative narrowing in the understanding of plot, character, meaning, transcendence, and aesthetic purpose. I shall return to this issue in order to clarify just what that type of distortion destroys on the level of the function of character.

It is perhaps important at this point, already, to recognize that the motif of infidelity (pivotal for the delineation of the effects of jealousy) also has a bearing on the aesthetic frame of the miracle plays (and not merely on their "content"). Let me relate the particular and internal sense of infidelity (the one operating on the level of plot and character) to a larger and more enframing sense of infidelity—what we may call *aesthetic infidelity.* I have already pointed to the outline of this general phenomenon, or epiphenomenon, when discussing the "negative writing" discernible in Shakespeare's late plays. By that term I was referring to what Danby and Kermode view as a slightly self-destructive feature in the writerly attitudes of the late-play Shakespeare: our "sense that the dramatist is somehow *playing* with the play."[22] In his late plays, Shakespeare can actually manifest a tendency that is thinkable as a sort of infidelity toward his own art. In that statement the word *art* includes a variety of possibilities, ranging from "genius" to "technical competence" and "representational capability." Such a "self-destructive" impulse (which is incidentally precisely what the naive "all-humanizing" critic of the miracle plays never dreams of) can amount not only to a personal stand of the artist against his own artistry (or some aspects of it) but also to a hostility against art as such. As Kenneth Muir remarks in his survey of the late plays of various great writers, "Tolstoy, like Racine, turned against art in his last period."[23] Shakespeare did not do that; but it seems crude not to recognize that there are traces in the miracle plays of a similar de-struction of full artistic excellence. This process is not simply negative or "destructive," as I keep emphasizing, but on the contrary the clearing of a space for new creative experiments. It is possible, as Danby puts it, that this loosening of artistic structure expresses the "relaxed" attitudes of a man who now "makes a toy of thought";[24] but on the other hand there may be more seriousness (and less relaxing) in the miracle plays than the feeble concentration needed to fabricate what Danby calls "entertainment."[25]

What I am calling "aesthetic infidelity" is thus not simply a relaxing from the true strains of artistic commitment, or from the precisions of professional craftsmanship; it is instead a readiness to allow certain familiar devices of the craft to run counterclockwise. We have already touched this sensation, when we heard Tillyard claim that Leontes' jealousy, "scantily motivated" as it is, "is as much a surprise to the characters in the play as it is to the reader."[26] If the characters are in a state of surprise, and if the characters are Shakespeare's, then inevitably Shakespeare himself ought to have been in a state of surprise. Indeed, I suggest he was. For in drama of an atomistic and isolationist kind (a string of sensations free from the cement of "organic development"), the artist has the unique privilege of somehow being able to "listen" to what the characters themselves want to do. The dramatist may have a rough idea of what is going to happen, but more freely than in developmental drama, he can follow through to the limit whatever the whim of the moment seems to suggest.

If the whim of the moment in this sense *rules* (which is not at all to say that the artist is "relaxed" or "careless"), the loss of centered consciousness (already conspicuous in the amnesias of Pericles) is heightened to the extent that we may begin to sense what Danby identifies as the displacement of voice. Discourse does not properly belong to character, for the "voice" of the character is a belated construct that is superimposed on him:

> Recent commentators have argued that Shakespeare's technique in the Last Plays can best be regarded as a development towards symbolism. It is more accurate, I think, to regard the development as a move not towards the symbolic but towards the schematic—the schematic with one addition: Shakespeare imposes on the characters schematically conceived what we have called a *voice*.[27]

This, to me, is a precious form of insight; and as I shall argue in the concluding hours of this enterprise, it is fairly futile to try to understand a play like *Cymbeline* without some sense of the importance of such vocal superimposition. This kind of appreciative outlook pulls out the carpet from the feet of "all-humanizing" criticism—for such criticism is often centrally dependent on the fixed idea that an important speech act always belongs to an important Shakespearean character in the way that a bank account belongs to a conscientious businessman. If Leontes' voice in some way is sensed as being superimposed on him, then his jealousy too will come across as something oddly superimposed on him. I suggest that the average intelligent spectator generates that kind of impression, and I suggest that Shakespeare was fairly conscious of wanting the spectator to sense such a "gap" between Leontes and his voice of jealousy. This peculiarly immediate and vociferous jealousy is in fact one of the queerest structural things ever to emerge from the hand of Shakespeare; and it may be wise to acknowledge the impact of that vocal rupturing before one prematurely starts to psychologize and moralize the play. In what follows, I shall now open the play itself in order to discover how a notion of vocal rupture can interact with what we have been reviewing as the absencing of foundational ground in the shadow of jealousy.

"O!"

We are now at a point where we have come to recognize the "active" part played by "nothingness" in *The Winter's Tale:* jealousy is based on "nothing" and so is the supposedly causal chain of dramatic events. As Brownlow remarks, the significant scenes of *The Winter's Tale* are in the final analysis contextualized by nothing:

> Technically they are like Posthumus' repentance and dream, Pericles' finding of Marina and his hearing the heavenly music. In all these cases reality, the moment of discovery and truth, is shown *coming to men from sources outside the sequence of cause and effect* that is usually, and has been in Shakespeare's own work, the stuff of drama.[28]

I now want to examine what it is that the "nothing" founding (hence not founding) Leontes' jealousy actually amounts to as Shakespearean discourse: as the specific language of the play. If jealousy of the extreme and "mad" kind, as I have argued, is a "negative miracle," and if, like miracle in general, its foundation or cause is a logical "nothing," then we can agree with Wilson Knight that *The Winter's Tale* commences by opening the chasm of the (im)possibility of nothingness:

> The impossible has happened: worse, it is even now happening; the known creation has had dallyings with the "unreal," the "nothing," and thence given birth (as in *Macbeth*) to an only-too-real action of hideous obscenity in the visible order. We are close to Macbeth's

> "horrible imaginings" of his own as yet "fantastical" crime, with "function smother'd in surmise" until "nothing is but what is not" (*Macbeth* I.iii.137–42). In both plays we have evil impinging as essential "nothing," unreality, a delirium, which yet most violently acts on the real.[29]

Thus, as Wilson Knight also observes, the "nothing" that is the (non)foundation of jealousy does not only open the horror of accepting a world where the negativity of infidelity is possible, it also opens the vision of a cosmic sense of all-invading nothingness that *replaces* the positivity of the existing world. Since infidelity is inconceivable, and since it at the same time is real fact, the factual reality of the world itself becomes void of foundational substance:

> In *The Winter's Tale,* the plot turns on Leontes' distrust of Hermione's conjugal loyalty. Now too much stress cannot be laid on the importance attached to infidelity in Shakespeare. The horror at the passing of love's faith is twin to the horror of death: the difficulty is quite as much a metaphysical as a moral one—Troilus cannot understand the patent fact of its existence.[30]

I shall in a moment discuss the relationship between Leontes and "nothing" as it materializes from this type of sensation and predicament; but I would first like to situate such a discussion in the general context of an awareness of the implications for language of such trauma. We have already reviewed the language of *Pericles* in relation to the mute, so that the dominant potential of miracle in that play could be thought of as radiating "muteness" into parts of discourse not really under the direct influence of miraculous experience. The "nothing" of miracle—its impossibility and lack of "real" foundation—translates itself into the nothing-state of language, into "dumbness," "muteness," and visionary silence. But if jealousy is a "negative miracle," it too will have to affect discourse, speaking, and hearing. I have already indicated the nature of such a possible linguistic dislocation by pointing to Danby's analysis of "voice" in *The Winter's Tale* as a function of superimposition. If you like to think of such rupture in commonsensical terms, simply say that Leontes speaks "out of character." But the connection between the absencing of voice and the experience of "nothing" is typically suggestive in all the miracle plays. Consider the role played by the unit "O" in the following speech by Posthumus in *Cymbeline,* at the time of his most unrestrained jealousy:

Is there no way for men to be, but women
Must be half-workers? We are all bastards,
And that most venerable man, which I
Did call my father, was I know not where
When I was stamp'd. Some coiner with his tools
Made me a counterfeit: yet my mother seem'd
The Dian of that time: so doth my wife
The nonpareil of this. O vengeance, vengeance!
Me of my lawful pleasure she restrain'd,
And prayed me oft forbearance: did it with
A pudency so rosy, the sweet view on't
Might well have warm'd old Saturn; that I thought her
As chaste as unsunn'd snow. O, all the devils!
This yellow Iachimo, in an hour, was't not?
Or less; at first? *Perchance he spoke not, but*
Like a full-acorn'd boar, a German one,
Cried "O!" and mounted; found no opposition
But what he look'd for should oppose and she
Should from encounter guard. Could I find out
The woman's part in me—for there's no motion
That tends to vice in man, but I affirm
It is the woman's part: be it lying, note it,
The woman's: flattering, hers; deceiving, hers:
Lust, and rank thoughts, hers, hers: revenges, hers:
Ambitions, covetings, change of prides, disdain,
Nice longing, slanders, mutability;
All faults that name, nay, that hell knows, why, hers
In part, or all: but rather all. For even to vice
They are not constant, but are changing still;
One vice, but of a minute old, for one
Not half so old as that. I'll write against them

(2.4.153–83)

We notice here that the "O!" that finally marks sexual assault is operative in earlier parts of the speech ("O vengeance," "O, all the devils!"). Thus the sense of the abyssal silencing of discourse in the preverbal site of erotic catastrophe/rape/bliss/rapture makes itself felt as a general aspect of Posthumus' language: he too is in an "O!"-state, a madness "before," "beyond," or "below" language. His language is from this viewpoint, like the equivalent languages of Lear, Troilus, and Othello, a blinding of language—a discursive blizzard where language approximates what normally is exclusive of language. Hence the average spectator brackets the language of passion in the "O!"-state of passion, brackets the primarily *linguistic* (semiotic) powers of Posthumus' speech, seeing it (indeed hearing it) as the "O!"-equivalent of Iachimo's supposed sexual penetration of his mistress and of the courtly norms of erotic decorum. We sense that Posthumus' *entire* speech is the hyperontological equivalent of a long, protracted "O!". In fact we sense that this long "O!"-speech of Posthumus', as the counterbalancing equivalent of the "German" O!, "opposes" that O! exactly as the female animal of sexual madness opposes the male animal of sexual madness: one instinctual blindness faces another, one energetic loss of linguistic coherence faces another, one abyssing of language faces another.

The "bracketing" performed by the spectator, here, is ontological rather than simply cognitive or hermeneutic. It is not simply a question of the spectator recognizing that Posthumus is too mad to be taken seriously in all his pronouncements; it is not simply a matter of us understanding the exaggerated nature of his discourse. Instead it is a sense that such discourse somehow is breaking the referential and semiotic boundaries of linguistic reality itself. There is as it were no point in speaking once the imagination has penetrated to a vision of a possible violation of love where the intelligible world as such fades away into worthlessness and insubstantial mockery. In a world where one's most precious possession is mounted, *without a word,* by a German boar, the word itself, with the exception of the not-word "O!", loses the precisions of its signifying force. Even as he speaks, Posthumus senses this. He enjoys the increasing ruination of referential relevance.

It is of course correct that many a true word is spoken in jest; and it is of course true that the mad things Posthumus says about womankind echo deep-lying Renaissance prejudices of a sexist kind. Yet it is also true that Shakespeare wanted to keep himself and his audience at some distance from such views. The speaking of Posthumus is maneuvered into a position of self-deception where his pronouncements are qualified by the deceits that have made them possible.

It is clear that Posthumus wants to tear out the "woman's part" in himself (2.4.172, 174). And this view can be generalized: Shakespeare—Renaissance man, if you like—wants to tear out the "woman's part." Go even further, go all the way: say that *man* wants to rip off the "woman's part." But the point is that this feeling, while being totalistic at the moment of its impingement, is only operative intermittently. We all know that Posthumus (and Shakespeare) can feel this way about woman in a quite "genuine" way; but we also know that there are hosts of moments when the general feeling about woman is altogether different.

It is clear, then, that man here is vulnerable in a general fashion, but mainly at the moment of specific revelation (negative miracle) when his relation vis-à-vis woman becomes one of defenselessness. This defenselessness, no doubt, is a function of the possibility of what I have all along been referring to as the disappearance of the foundation. Woman can make the *ground* vanish (and not just psychologically, personally, or erotically), for she happens to hold the key to an aspect of foundational reality that is indispensable to foundational masculinity and at the same time totally outside its sphere of control. This defoundational and foundational key is the notion of origin.

A foundation or ground is an origin; it is where we "come" from. In our culture, this origin is masculine insofar as it is "God," but it is feminine insofar as it is mother (and by implication wife). The origin/ground is masculine insofar as it is an idealized philosophical and quasi-theological construct in the ideological mode of cosmic self-identification institutionalized by patriarchy and the masculine West; but the origin/ground is feminine insofar as it is the biological and sexual reality of human dialectic and human procreation. The *idealization* of woman, which nowhere is out of sight in Shakespeare's late plays (with the possible exception of *Timon of Athens*) becomes an exceedingly equivocal and explosive nexus in this general Western tension between patriarchal culture and feminine eroticism. Posthumus can launch himself into a universalist discourse on the fall of man, and sense the *complete* abyssing of the ground, because the possible ruination of the ideality of the origin (birth, woman) is also the possible ruination of the universe itself (ideality, value, foundational belonging). By idealizing woman and *connecting* her to the preexisting idealization of the ground/origin/foundation, the male of late Western culture has put all his idealist eggs in one basket. In an important sense, modern Western man risks everything by instituting the contemporary (and almost universally operative) notion of love for an ideal mistress. And in contrast with early Western man (the heroic individual of classical times), the late male of the West in this way situates all the burden of risk in a site outside his own person: the infidelity and dishonor of *another* individual can in a second ruin all my own sense of cosmic foundation and existential ground. The feverishness and metaphysical pathos with which Shakespeare always enters such a problematic cannot be grasped without a recognition of this general ontological predicament of Western masculinity. Shakespeare's "hot" attitude to infidelity and woman is not reducible either to private sufferings (however real these may have been) or to something as banal as the "prejudices" of contemporary males. Worse conflicts are going on in Shakespeare than battles of the sexes and ideological dialectic.

These remarks, I hope, will in some way facilitate an analytical engagement with the question of jealousy in *The Winter's Tale*. In that play, precisely, it is the ideality and idealization of woman that hang in the balance. And the reason why the drama becomes exquisitely interesting from the hyperontological perspective is that criticism here faces a Shakespearean attempt to negotiate the difference between miracle and ideality. This negotiation, moreover, is conducted through woman: for woman here is at once what is idealized and what is miraclized. The basic hyperontological question must therefore be: Is it at all possible, especially in the theater, to harmonize the femininity of ideality with the femininity of miracle? Is idealized woman compatible with woman as miracle? The ancillary (and more complex) question would be something like this: Does Shakespeare actually want these two notions to harmonize? And finally: Do we, the spectators, accept a harmonization of conflicting renditions of transcendental femininity? Can we digest idealization and miracle at once?

What looms dangerously for the male, we have seen, is the ability of woman to be "destructive" through passivity. This sensation is frightening, because it suggests that woman *as such* can remove the foundation. By woman "as such" I mean woman devoid of any violent supplement. A man can become hostile and destructive toward another man by supplementing his being with some amount of violence that will add itself to his personality as a free "extra." I can distinguish between a man and the blow he gives me. I can intuit the logical connection between the two things, but they do not come across as a single identical unit whose sides cannot be separated in the mind. With woman as an object of jealous thought, however, things are different. Since her passivity can increase rather than decrease her "destructive" power (her capacity to be seduced and taken by a rival male), and since her absolutely passive state of erotic surrender is ontologically indistinguishable for the jealous mind from her being as such (her mere passive state of being a being), man can experience a cruel vertigo (the hypernegative miracle of jealousy itself) in which woman *is* infidelity and the totalized abyssing of cosmic security. Shakespeare drives home this point in the O!-discourse of Posthumus recently cited:

> Perchance he spoke not, but
> Like a full-acorn'd boar, a German one,
> Cried "O!" and mounted; found no opposition
> But what he look'd for should oppose and she
> Should from encounter guard.
>
> (2.4.167–71)

What here "opposes" the "German" physique of the mounting male is itself "no opposition." There is "no opposition" in the organ-to-organ opposition formed by the sexual readiness of the female as erotic collaborator, yet this very oppositionlessness is an opposition of a kind: a provocation all the more arousing in that it is the fleshy *manifestation* of absolutely static surrender. What the immediately ensuing lines focus as the question of how to "find out / The woman's part" (2.4.171–72) is an insurmountable problem on the level of the male looking for some evil "female" part in himself—but it is even more of an insurmountable problem for the male looking for the woman's part *in woman*. If the "woman's part" is dangerous (because it is sexual and cosmic impurity, the locus of the pure abyssing of truth and constancy), and if this part needs to be thought of as removable, the removability is ruined by the fact that the "part" is no part in any ordinary sense. The part is the whole, for the passivity that woman manifests in the seductive moment of her "fall" and betrayal is her being rather than her action, her passivity (nonresistance) rather than active transgression, her "reality" rather than a modification of it. Betrayal becomes the *truth* of woman, what she simply is. Her absolute passivity in the critical moment of seductive yielding collapses the difference (or the "visible" contrast) between her truth and her negation of it. The "woman's part" is thus in a sense "larger" than woman (larger than the whole it should belong to); for the "passive" potential for destructiveness stands out round woman like a negative aureole.

All this, of course, on the condition that one is not only jealous, but madly jealous. All this on the condition that, like Leontes, one has entered through jealousy the insanity of jealousy: a state in which the evil of woman is, literally, "nothing." Nothing is more infuriating than this "nothing" of woman; nothing is more infuriating than the fact that what darkens her is the absence of any obvious fault: that her fault essentially is that of lacking one; that her faultiness is so radical that it is part and parcel of her normal comportment rather than any dramatically special "extra activity." Nothing, in short, is more infuriating than the fact that her faultiness is her innocence.

The Winter's Tale is based on this "nothingness" of the sinfulness of woman—on this "sinfulness" of the nothing separating her guilt from her innocence. By merely being she radiates sin; by merely communicating she communicates seduction; by just being herself she shows the world her constantly ongoing betrayal of herself. Without doing anything wrong she does everything wrong.

"Nothing" and "everything" become strangely interchangeable. And there is nothing Leontes can do about this—unless he decides to do everything. Unfortunately, but not quite tragically, this is exactly what he does. The step is not tragic, his fall not tragical, because he is really not dialectically deceived, as Othello or Iachimo is. He simply *enters* the ontological undecidedness of "woman" from the wrong end: he makes the totalistically negative interpretation of the ontological undecidedness, creating "negative miracle." But precisely for this reason (the absolute proximity to the ontological interchangeability of value), miracle itself can spontaneously emerge from such a "false" reading. This is not simply to say that woman in familiar fashion can be satanic as well as paradisal, and that the superficiality of the male willingly moves at short notice from one view to the other—that idealization is at random totally negative or totally positive. It is instead to realize that the false/true dialectic no longer is truly operative as it is, for instance, in *Othello*. Leontes does not simply make a "wrong" reading of Hermione, and then find that the "right" reading restores her (and him) to some purified state of spiritual togetherness (in death or life). Such a "correction" of the "erroneous" reading does, to be sure, take place; Leontes does find out that he has been wrong and that Hermione has been "pure" all along; he does repent. But that repentance in no way whatsoever gives the drama the crucial energy of its theatrical power; on the contrary, his repentance and the dissipation of Hermione's proclaimed guilt do not stir us in the least. What we have to wait for, instead, is the belated occurrence of miracle; for only then will the *ontological* reversal of the dramatic presence of Hermione be actually felt as a materialized theatrical truth.

Thus, as I see it, the false/true dialectic does not engineer our real attention in *The Winter's Tale*. In *Othello*, the hero and the spectator have to move from a state of beclouded and incomplete truth (a state of falsehood) to a state of catharsis where the clear dividing line between the true and the false itself is celebrated as the luminous rod of justice and reason. But in *The Winter's Tale* there is no such transition from an ambiguous state to an unambiguous state (except on the secondary level of banal melodrama). On the contrary, the two extremes—negative miracle and miracle—are equally ambiguous, to an equal extent hypnotize spectatorial fantasy through pure oscillation. As I shall suggest, the glorious Hermione emergent at the end of the play is quite as enigmatic and "unbelievable" as the phantom of infidelity that Leontes at the outset creates with the eyes of a similarly "wondrous" attention. In the final analysis there is no "pure" Hermione at the beginning of the play, and no "pure" Hermione in the concluding magic; her "purity," at any rate, is quite different from that of Desdemona. Essentially, I would in fact argue, we are not here situated in a primarily moral universe, but on the contrary in one of ontological fascination. The two Hermiones are equally real and equally valid, as are Leontes' two interpretations of her: for they are energized by an ontological apperception of an indwelling instability in human reality, an instability whose poles are "optionally" true, and whose mutual conflict is resolved only by the whim of the creative eye itself. It may be that one of these visual creations (the negative one) is strictly that of Leontes, and that the other visual miracle (the positive one) is strictly that monitored by Shakespeare (or Paulina, if you like). But that difference between internal and external participants is exactly the kind of barrier that Shakespearean miracle tends to want to disassemble.

Beyond Imagination

Leontes' "nothing" is not simply any kind of "nothing"; nor is it simply any kind of jealous "nothing." It is, for the play as a whole, the nonfoundational foundation for miracle itself. In the "nothing" of this particular kind of jealousy (jealousy more jealous than the jealous, jealousy whose lack of ground is absolutely pure), Shakespeare *founds* the ground for what later will burst into the dramatic reality of miracle. That too will be based on "nothing."

But the base, in both cases, is not "nothing" from the viewpoint of Shakespearean craft. On the contrary, it is from that viewpoint everything. If "nothing" founds the negative miracle, and if "nothing" founds the positive miracle, and if these two miracles conjointly negotiate the temporal space of the drama as it slides from despair to hope, then the *linking* of the two miracles (negative and positive) is itself performed by "nothing." The use of the word *nothing* is curiously prominent in *The Winter's Tale*. (Italics mine, below.)

> With what's unreal thou coactive art,
> And fellow'st *nothing*
>
> (1.2.141–42)

> But of all, the burst
> And the ear-deaf'ning voice o'th'Oracle,
> Kin to Jove's thunder, so surpris'd my sense,
> That I was *nothing*.
>
> (3.1.8–11)

> But, O thou tyrant!
> Do not repent these things, for they are heavier
> Than all thy woes can stir: therefore betake thee
> To *nothing* but despair.
>
> (3.2.207–10)

> I have this intelligence, that he is seldom from the house of a most homely shepherd; a man, they say, that from very *nothing*, and beyond the imagination of his neighbours, is grown into an unspeakable estate.
>
> (4.2.37–41)

> What would he say? Or how
> Should I, in these my borrowed flaunts, behold
> The sternness of his presence?
> Apprehend
> *Nothing* but jollity.
>
> (4.4.22–25)

> My clown (who wants but something to be a reasonable man) grew so in love with the wenches' song, that he would not stir his pettitoes till he had both tune and words; which so drew the rest of the herd to me, that all their other senses stuck in ears: you might have pinched a placket, it was senseless; 'twas *nothing* to geld a codpiece of a purse; I would have filed keys off that hung in chains: no hearing, no feeling, but my sir's song, and admiring the *nothing* of it.
>
> (4.4.606–15)

> Here comes a gentleman that haply knows more. The news, Rogero?
> *Second Gentleman. Nothing* but bonfires: the Oracle is fulfilled; the king's daughter is found: such a deal of wonder is broken out within this hour, that ballad-makers cannot be able to express it.
> (5.2.20–25)

Looking at these units, we see that "nothing" is nearly always used in the thematized context of the experience or production of wonder. We also see, by recognizing the function of "nothing" in the first unit listed above, that "nothing" negotiates the inter-implications of negative and positive miracle discussed earlier. For jealousy too is a form of wonder. Jealousy is not simply something of the imagination but on the contrary, to echo Polixenes as quoted above, "beyond the imagination" (4.2.40). The "unspeakable state" (4.2.41) produced by such an exceeding of the powers of imagination is in the play's strongest staging of miracle a literal state of unspeakability. The experience of miracle in a sense requires the "knocking out" of the senses of the entire dramatic consciousness that is (or was) critically apprehending the story. This is the general phenomenon that we saw Shakespeare miniaturize a moment ago in the discourse of Autolycus. The purpose of his entertainment (on a vulgar and banal level) exactly parallels the purpose of Shakespeare (on the level of miracle play): to stun the audience. To deprive them of "hearing" and "feeling." To leave them "admiring the nothing of it."

> I would have filed keys off that hung in chains: no hearing, no feeling, but my sir's song, and admiring the nothing of it.
> (4.4.612–15)

The word or notion *nothing* is thus immensely important in *The Winter's Tale*, for it marks the hyperontological (non)area in which the play finds its metaphysical and spectatorial condition of possibility. Drama always involves making people believe in nothing: in illusion and mere showing. But here in the miracle plays, Shakespeare has pushed this situation to its limit. For here it is no longer merely the actual medium that is "nothing," but substance itself. The very story is from this viewpoint "nothing." And the audience has to be *stunned* into accepting "the nothing of it." Miracle is the performance of this "nothing," of the stunning, and of the general acceptance of its reality. But the fact that the entire story is "nothing" (and therefore radically in need of a miracle) does not only apply to the ballads of Autolycus and the tale told by William Shakespeare; it also applies to Leontes' jealousy. His story (that his wife is a whore) is also "nothing"; but, miraculously, he has been just as successful in making himself believe in it as Shakespeare has been in making the play believe in it.

It is important, in this general discussion of the role of "nothing" in *The Winter's Tale*, to understand the full implications of what I referred to a minute ago as the ability of jealousy/miracle to find a home for itself beyond the imagination. This means that jealousy/miracle is not something that is ever strictly *in* the imagination (as part of it, as "component" or imaginative item). That, in its turn, means that miracle in the final analysis is not imaginative at all. Miracle cannot be imagined; nor can radical jealousy/infidelity. It is precisely the swooning of the imaginative mind that puts Othello out (literally annihilates his imaginative faculties by producing an epileptic blackout). But this annihilation of the imaginative faculties is in a sense—and according to the logic of an unthinkable daring—exactly what Shakespeare devises for his entire drama when he assumes the aesthetic (and imaginative?) challenge of the miracle play. Perhaps for the first time he is creating drama without imagining it (that would account for a host of strange un-Shakespearean traits in the miracle plays). And perhaps, what is worse, he is asking us to *witness* a drama without imagining it. We create it in our minds without imagining it. Miracle is in this way not simply the ability to get seriously involved in a hyperimaginative occurrence at the end of the story; it is to cooperate with a theatrically foundational erasure of ordinary imaginative vision—and to let something finally appear as an object visible in that empty space.

From this perspective, in which we recognize the progressive emptying of imagination out of the Shakespearean miracle play, *The Winter's Tale* is a radically "unimaginative" play, piloted by a radically unimaginative hero. The emptying and absencing of imagination is not some "lack" of Shakespearean imaginativeness; on the contrary, the absence of imagination too has to be imagined. What could be more difficult to imagine? What could be more difficult to stage? What could be more hard to visualize on the boards of illusionist theater?

I will be suggesting later on that *Cymbeline* takes this dramatic possibility of the absencing of imagination to its logical extreme;

and I shall be arguing here in the current analysis that *The Winter's Tale* (like *Cymbeline*) problematizes and obstructs its potential for antiillusionist theater by hesitating between representational drama of an illusionist kind and the miracle play as disarranged illusion and disarranged illusionism.

In what way is Leontes unimaginative? Let me fire back an alternative question: In what way is he not *un*imaginative? Does he really *become* jealous—or is jealousy almost a type of decision? Does he slowly succumb to jealous insinuation, jealous suggestion, jealous torture, and jealous imagination? Or does he in fact somehow just make up his mind (a mind void of imaginative thinking), so that jealousy categorically becomes one with his male ego? Is not jealousy a category, here, rather than an emotion? Is not Leontes' jealousy quite irreversible precisely on account of this "abstract" and "categorical" aspect of its nature? No amount of emotional persuasion seems to be able to soften him. Pity, which he is ready to provide in gallons toward the end of the play, is quite unknown to him. Is this so because his jealousy is so intense, or is it so because his jealousy primarily is a category? Even Othello, the most jealous man of the universe, felt pity; indeed, he felt pity in the very throes of jealous climax. But Leontes does not seem to know that emotion until the rules of the game are changed and adjusted in order to suddenly let him "repent."

Leontes cannot *imagine* that he is wrong. The proof of his error has to be actual and physical. The Oracle itself cannot alter his mind; but its deeds can. In itself, as the suggestive power of its truth-speaking and oracular discourse, the Oracle cannot affect Leontes. It has no *imaginative* or *discursive* power over him in the way that the riddles of the Weird Sisters have power over Macbeth. Leontes is impressed by the Oracle only when it punishes him. His attitude to Paulina is basically of a similar kind. Only through punishment can she get through to him.

The animation of Hermione that functions as the play's terminal miracle can in a sense be seen as the restoration (even birth) of Leontes' imaginative faculty—but more importantly, perhaps. that animationist scene can be seen as further proof of his imaginative simpleness.

I am now ready to make a hyperontological definition of the dramatic situation as the play opens it: *Leontes can imagine nothing*.

But this definition cannot be treated lightly. It is not an empirical statement, but a hyperontological one. It does not only (or even primarily) mean that there is nó thing that Leontes can imagine; more than that, it first of all means that "nothing" is precisely what he *can* imagine. His whole jealousy-discourse comes into view in relation to this "nothing"; and as this nothing-discourse hits us, I permit myself to refer once more to the sizable list of "nothing" units discussed earlier. I assert again, then, that Leontes presences himself theatrically as one who can imagine nothing.

> Is whispering nothing?
> Is leaning cheek to cheek? is meeting noses?
> Kissing with inside lip? stopping the career
> Of laughter with a sigh (a note infallible
> Of breaking honesty)? horsing foot on foot?
> Skulking in corners? wishing clocks more swift?
> Hours, minutes? noon, midnight? and all eyes
> Blind with the pin and web, but theirs; theirs only.
> That would unseen be wicked? is this nothing?
> Why then the world, and all that's in't, is nothing,
> The covering sky is nothing, Bohemia is nothing,
> My wife is nothing, nor nothing have these nothings,
> If this be nothing.
>
> (1.2.284–96)

Wilbur Sanders argues that Leontes comes "dangerously close to buffoonery" in the scenes involving "comedy of the sexes";[31] but it could be argued that such a suggestion of buffoonery is vaguely present right from the outset. Is this discourse really designed to make us sympathize and provisionally identify with a man tormented by jealousy; or are we in fact expected to smile—smile awkwardly, but still smile? It seems to me that there is a certain amount of stylization in this discourse, and that the supposedly horrific "examples" of treachery identified here are faintly ludicrous: most of all, no doubt, "meeting noses" and "skulking in corners."

But in *The Winter's Tale,* Leontes' "ability" to imagine nothing is directly related to *the emergence of woman as nothing*. Again, both of these constructs open up a special type of "abrupt" theatrical attitude that is projected from Leontes onto the spectator. If Leontes, as I argue, can imagine *nothing,* and if the spectator as it were picks up this cue, then the audience's "ability" to imagine nothing in the theater joins up with that imaginative "emptiness" in the protagonist—thus clearing the way for the conjoint readiness for the "perception" of miracle. But since this "perception" of miracle also is a "perception" of woman (Hermione is killed *as* woman and is resuscitated *as* woman), the miraculously terminal envisioning of woman is also a "miraculous" perception of her as nothing. This phenomenon is what I intend to examine in what soon follows.

If miracle requires "de-imagining" the (ordinary) world, if it on various levels implies the surrender of our imaginatively illusionist faculties, then the advancement of *woman* as miracle is somehow going to involve the "de-imagining" of *her*. This, I will suggest, is what the play stages.

Hermione gets only seven lines after the middle of the play; in more senses than one, woman as fully-developed adult *disappears* from *The Winter's Tale*. But the terminal "miracle," by reinstating woman (and the imagining of her), does not automatically make up for this annihilation. The miracle itself cannot retrospectively alter the fact that woman has been nihilized on the level of dramatic imagination. The "female miracle" itself cannot obliterate the play's dominant imaginative obliteration of woman any more than Leontes' ridiculously belated softening and repentance can return to Hermione those sixteen years she lost through his totally inexplicable jealousy. On the contrary, as I shall argue, that "freezing" of woman remains active within the very thawing that supposedly recuperates her. The play at once recovers Hermione and infinitizes her nonrecovery, her nonrecoverability. (The wrinkles left in her terminal ideality indicate this "reserve" on the banal level of temporal alteration.)

Hermione is in this way rather different from Marina in *Pericles*. Marina is first of all a miracle, and only secondly a woman. This, curiously, is precisely why her femininity gets imaginatively preserved in *Pericles*. Marina is not subjected to the "nothing"-process (that of "de-imagining") that I have begun to outline in *The Winter's Tale*. This is so because miracle in *Pericles* is not hinged on the very conflict of the sexes that *The Winter's Tale* essentially maintains from beginning to end. Because woman from the outset is under siege in *The Winter's Tale*, and because the miracle is made *dependent* on this siege (miracle reverses the unhappiness that male prejudice sets in motion), the premiracle "void" that always has to forestructure miracle as its condition of possibility is in *The Winter's Tale* a distinctly female void, a distinctly feminine imaginativelessness—woman as "nothing."

Ontological Translation

The "nothing" of imagination is related to the "nothing" of flirtation. The opening of *The Winter's Tale* is constituted by this nothing. Flirtation is the immediate ground for Leontes' "jealousy." One nothing, in the play, leads to another. The final miracle puts an end to this process. But it also totalizes it.

Woman defines herself at the beginning of *The Winter's Tale* as the being that is capable of flirtation: that *is* flirtation. Her charm, indeed her power, is based on flirtation. The personality of Hermione grows straight out of her "innocent" flirtatiousness. She is coquettish-but-modest, yet at the same time modest-but-coquettish. The difference is nothing—and Leontes imagines this nothing. It is the very nothing he can imagine.

Flirting is nothing. It is harmless. But the nothing of flirtation is also something. It is the condition of possibility for Hermione's erotic appeal: what generally speaking delights everyone, including, up to a point, her husband. In the married woman, outward eroticism is and should be nothing/something. Otherwise she is "dead," without sex appeal (what the miraculously statuesque Hermione in the dramatic finale in a sense actually *achieves*). The married woman must behave erotically toward other men, otherwise she is frigid, made of marble. But the married woman must also be marblelike *in* her sex appeal. Nothing negotiates this difference. It is not even a difference.

Leontes, a man without imagination, can easily imagine this (non)difference, this erotically pivotal "nothing" of the sexual West, because culture imagines it for him. There is no part of his sexual culture that in the final analysis is not centered on this nothing-difference between serious and innocent flirtation.

There is no personality whatsoever in Leontes' "jealous" reaction to flirtation. His language and emotive profile conform to the mold of a precise stereotype. And it is meant to. This is why Shakespeare gives no real clue (but only trivial and false ones) to any secret vulnerability in the man that could—as in the case of Othello—account for his overpoweringly masculine reactivity. But in the same way, Hermione's flirtatiousness is nothing but its own stereotype. This stereotype, to be sure, is richly Shakespearean in its nuance and suggestiveness; but it is still a stereotype. Shakespeare does not say: "Here is a man; let us see him fall into the jaws of jealousy." Nor does Shakespeare say: "Here is a woman; let us now look at her as she comes to skirt the very boundaries of legitimate flirtation." On the contrary, Shakespeare says: "Here is jealousy." Period. "Here is flirtatiousness." Period.

A loss is created in this way. All of Shakespeare's imaginative power in a sense becomes provisionally useless and defunct. But a gain is also perceptible. For the first time, things like jealousy and flirtatiousness can be examined as such—that is, ripped from their human context (general as well as particular). This decontextualization (achieved here through stereotypicality) permits an "ontological" weighting of the phenomena—an inspection of *them* rather than of their effects and dramatic implications. Hermione's flirtatiousness and Leontes' "jealousy" have implications and consequences; and these effects can be dramatized. But I would not call the implications dramatic implications or dramatic consequences (as I would in the parallel junctures in *Othello*). It seems laughable to me to say that Hermione is absenced for sixteen years as a *dramatic consequence* of Leontes' "jealousy"; just as it seems laughable to me to say that Leontes' trumpeting "jealousy" is a *dramatic consequence* of Hermione's flirtatiousness. Nor is the resuscitation of the dead queen a "dramatic consequence." On the contrary, it is a miracle. A theatrical craftsman using that kind of gross and awkward dramatic causality would be a mere amateur, a spectacular bungler. Dramatic consequence is of no consequence at this stage in Shakespeare's career. But the nothingness of consequence—can that be dramatized? Let us hope, to begin with, that it cannot be imagined.

We turn now to Hermione's inaugural indiscretions. I shall start off by stating quite categorically that she immediately presences herself as someone far less idealized than the creature that emerges in statuesque sublimity in the finale. She is shown displaying a sophisticated form of seductive flirtation and erotic insinuation—all the while supposedly inquiring into the innocent boyhood frolics of her husband and his friend Polixenes:

Polixenes. We were as twinn'd lambs that did frisk i'th'sun,
And bleat the one at th'other: what we chang'd
Was innocence for innocence: *we knew not*
The doctrine of ill-doing, nor dream'd
That any did. Had we persu'd that life,
And our weak spirits ne'er been higher rear'd
With stronger blood, we should have answer'd heaven
Boldly "not guilty," the imposition clear'd
Hereditary ours.
Hermione. By this we gather
You have tripp'd since.

Polixenes. O *my most sacred lady,*
Temptations have since then been born to's: for
In those unfledg'd days was my wife a girl;
Your precious self had then not *cross'd the eyes*
Of my young play-fellow.
Hermione. *Grace to boot!*
Of this make no conclusion, lest you say
Your queen and I are devils. Yet go on;
Th'offences we have made you do, we'll answer
If you first sinn'd with *us,* and that with us
You did continue fault, and that you slipp'd not
With any but with *us.*
Leontes. Is he won yet?
Hermione. He'll stay, my lord.
Leontes. At my request he would not.
Hermione, my dearest, thou *never* spok'st
To better purpose.
Hermione. *Never?*
Leontes. Never but once.
Hermione. What! have I twice said well? when was't before?
I prithee tell me: cram's with praise, and make's
As fat as tame things: one good deed, dying tongueless,
Slaughters a thousand, waiting upon that.
Our praises are our wages. You may ride's
With one soft kiss a thousand furlongs ere
With spur we heat an acre. But to th'goal:
My last good deed was to entreat his stay:
What was my first? It has an elder *sister,*
Or I mistake you: O, *would her name were Grace!*
But once before I spoke to th'purpose? When?
Nay, let me have't: I long!
Leontes. Why, that was when
Three crabbed months had sour'd themselves to death,
Ere I could make thee open thy white hand,
And clap thyself my love; then didst thou utter
"I am yours for ever."
Hermione. 'Tis Grace indeed.
Why lo you now; I have spoke to th'purpose twice:
The one, for ever earn'd a royal husband;
Th'other, for some while a friend.
Leontes. *(Aside)* Too hot, too hot!
To mingle friendship far, is mingling bloods.
I have *tremor cordis* on me: my heart dances,
But not for joy. This entertainment
May a free face put on, derive a liberty
From heartiness, from bounty, fertile bosom,
And well become the agent; 't may, I grant:

> But to be paddling palms, and pinching fingers,
> As now they are, and making practis'd smiles
> As in a looking-glass; and then to sigh, as 'twere
> The mort o'th'deer—O, that is entertainment
> My bosom likes not, nor my brows. Mamillius,
> Art thou my boy?
>
> (1.2.67–120; emphasis added)

The dramatic situation is based on the tension between the status of woman as an ontological creature and the status of woman as a social creature. I suggest that this difference (ontological versus social) is a clue to the "psychology" of the play. The friendship-versus-sex problematic created by the mixing of children's love with adult love has *immediately* caused Leontes to view the whole situation in a quasi-metaphysical context: the scene becomes a sort of tableau of the Fall of Man, and Hermione, *through that tableau,* comes to be visually situated in a center that is an abyss.

No imagination at all is needed for this visualization of her as sinful. As soon as the paradox of female sin/purity itself makes itself conspicuous—which it does through the ability of Hermione to bridge and negotiate the opposites of sex and friendship—Leontes can turn to any random sequence of human gestures and translate them into the semiotics of fall and jealousy. There is nothing Hermione can do at this point that will not function as exemplum in that Fall of Man tableau. Even the act of conforming to Leontes' commands (those directing her to persuade Polixenes to prolong his stay) will suggest nonconformity; even the signs that she is exclusively his and no one else's will appear as signs indicating looseness and lasciviousness. In this mood of his, which from the outset is that of ontological confusion rather than private jealousy, he himself "supplies" the signs required for the illustration of the abyss/tableau. Unlike Othello, who has a scarcity of incriminating signs at his disposal—his fate almost boils down to the whereabouts of a handkerchief—Leontes drowns in "signs" of infidelity: signs that he voluntarily multiplies into overabundance in the process of translating the world itself into fall and fallenness. He almost seems to want to plunge himself into this abyss, to *feel* that unthinkable distance between boyhood/friendship and maturity/guilt.

Any jealous man can of course in this way multiply the "circumstances" of supposed infidelity; any man can "read" the comportment of femininity in terms of the comportment of fallenness. But Shakespeare has not simply focused a jealous man in a jealous man-to-woman situation; on the contrary, he spends very little time and energy on any delineation of the intimacy of the rapport between Leontes and Hermione. Shakespeare has instead situated the jealous predicament inside the frame of the Fall of Man tableau we have discussed. Shakespeare has deliberately started off with a rather detailed and elaborate picture of pre-Fall friendship (that between the boy Leontes and the boy Polixenes), and he has quite carefully positioned the ex nihilo jealousy of Leontes in relation to that innocence. We can see this stress on the Adamic paradigm by rehearsing some of the crucial lines in the passage cited a moment ago:

> what we chang'd
> Was innocence for innocence: we knew not
> The doctrine of ill-doing, nor dream'd
> That any did.
>
> (1.2.68–71)

The problem, in a nutshell, is that there is a difference between falling and not-falling also when one is clearly on the farther side of that difference: as mature woman, Hermione wavers between innocence and guilt (for Leontes), in spite of the fact that she is already "fallen" and "guilty" through the fact of her humanity. From the ontological (rather than the social) viewpoint, it is thus odd to hear Polixenes address her as "O most sacred lady" (1.2.76)—ontologically, that line jars with everything that so far has been suggested about the fall and about adulthood. Indeed, that "sacredness" of Hermione jars dramatically with the tenure of her discourse, which is electrically charged with nonsacred implication and "harmless" provocation. She does not dream of ill-doing (of hurting her husband, his feelings, or their marriage); yet there is an ocean of difference between the absence of the thought of such ill-doing and the absence of evil identified by Polixenes in reference to boyhood: "we knew not / The doctrine of ill-doing, nor dream'd / That any did" (1.2.69–71). Although Hermione is *socially* and factually just as far from ill-doing as the frolicsome young princes were far away from ill-doing in their childhood games, she is not at all *ontologically* as far-removed from ill-doing as they were. On the contrary, her entire discourse is from the ontological view (the one centered on the status of man's being/fallenness) perfectly crammed with the insights of carnal knowledge and cosmic "ill-doing."

What Leontes thus cannot accept (cannot ontologically stomach) is her selling of herself as "innocent." Although he himself encourages and propels the very ultrafriendliness that she manifests (toward Polixenes), and although Leontes somehow knows that there is no evil or sly calculation behind her display of social warmth, he instinctively feels that there is a weird chasm between this version of "friendship" and the one experienced with Polixenes in boyhood. Hermione, without mocking, seems to mock that friendship. "Innocence" in the adult world is already something noninnocent in relation to the honest play of children. This heightened purity that is achievable only in preadult friendship is of course foregrounded explicitly in the passage we have been reviewing: "Had we pursu'd that life . . . we should have answer'd heaven / Boldly 'not guilty,' the imposition clear'd / Hereditary ours" (1.2.71–75).

What happens in the dialogue between Hermione and Polixenes is that "temptation" gets disarranged through the interconfusing of two meanings: an ontological one and a social one. The lines that immediately follow clarify this suggestive undecidedness:

> *Hermione.* By this we gather
> You have tripp'd since.
> *Polixenes.* O my most sacred lady,
> Temptations have since then been born to's: for
> In those unfledg'd days was my wife a girl;
> Your precious self had then not cross'd the eyes
> Of my young play-fellow.
> *Hermione.* Grace to boot!
> Of this make no conclusion, lest you say
> Your queen and I are devils.
>
> (1.2.75–82)

Hermione, the "sacred lady," has given way to "temptation" *by simply being a woman.* Meeting a man at all is from this ontological viewpoint the succumbing to temptation and the trespassing into the Adamic world of ill-doing. Such innocent-yet-guilty transgression is signaled by the unit "cross'd the eyes" (1.2.79). When the adult (and therefore sexual-and-sinful) woman lets her eyes be *crossed* by the adult (and therefore sexual-and-sinful) man, she irrevocably enters a world beyond innocent play. Yet in persuading Polixenes to prolong his stay in Sicilia, Hermione appears to *have* to resuscitate that world of innocent play. She *has* to play with Polixenes (to generate enough charm to make him change his mind), and she *has* to make that play innocent play. She is forced to interact with him precisely on the level formerly established between the boy princes; her attitude, *socially*, to Polixenes, becomes indistinguishable from Polixenes' boyhood attitude to Leontes. She has to consider him as "my young play-fellow" (1.2.79). Thus, in sum, Hermione has to enact on the level of social reality a "pure" playing that Leontes (and everyone else) knows is a mere chimera on the level of ontological reality.

What radicalizes this tension between ontological guilt (which Hermione never can avoid) and social guilt (which Hermione must and does avoid) is the seemingly overdemonstrative intensity of the queen's erotic rhetoric. Her almost shamelessly sexual type of public imagination appears to be grounded in a purity of erotic loyalty and self-confidence that is almost a defiance: "cram's"; "make's / As fat"; "You may ride's"; "With spur we heat"; "when?"; "let me have't: I long!" (1.2.91–101). The sexual electricity of these words can be picked up without any straining of the imaginative faculties; indeed, as I have already suggested, Leontes lacks any developed imagination.

We cannot stress too much, then, this need for the critic to separate social guilt and ontological guilt. When Hermione speaks those words, she is perfectly lily-white from the social viewpoint (on the dialectical level where her words have meaning in relation to social relations, including her relation to Leontes); but when she speaks those words, she is not at all lily-white on the ontological level. On that special level, the one crystallized by Shakespeare in the play's opening, it is impossible for Hermione to recover the "not guilty" (1.2.73) that is the condition of possibility for truly innocent play. Ontologically, Hermione can never play innocent. Socially, she can.

It should be emphasized that the kind of difference we are discussing here (social versus ontological) should not be taken lightly as some notion of an abstract kind about "original sin." To say, merely in a generally airy fashion, that the opening scenes touch the question of "original sin" is not very helpful. For the notion of original sin is a commonplace, and so is the notion of the relation between jealousy and original sin. But the Shakespearean treatment of these two notions in *The Winter's Tale* is by no means commonplace; nor is Hermione's way of intertwining these ideas. What is subtle in her (and Shakespeare's) discourse is the usage of a special angle that disarranges the opposition between the ontological and the social. Hermione's ontological guilt *becomes* social guilt (through the "socialization process" of her flirtatious discourse), just as her social innocence almost *becomes* ontological innocence. It is this "hypocrisy" of her discourse (metaphysical rather than private) that in the final analysis rouses Leontes' "jealousy" and our unease. It is not that the heroine is ambiguous or undecided, but that she mixes two types of indecision to the point of abyss, vertigo, and imaginative paralysis. There is indecision between one indecision and another: between social ambiguity and ontological impurity.

I have said that Leontes tries to clear up this supplementary ambiguity (the one *between* the two ambiguities) by translating Hermione's essentially ontological (and universal) fallenness into a social fallenness. Crudely, he translates the impurity of "woman" into the impurity of "Hermione." If Leontes can view Hermione's ontologically disturbing oscillation as a social rather than cosmic phenomenon, he can start shouting at it, he can keep it at a safe distance. He can, in fact, objectify it. Hermione progressively emerges (through his accusations) as a socially negative creature: bad wife and bad mother. When Paulina and her quasi-feminist allies begin to want to reverse this negativity, they do not alter the social (rather than ontological) emphasis. On the contrary, they maintain the social type of "reading" of Hermione—viewing her affairs as dialectical affairs, viewing her restoration, ideally, as the outcome of a successful dialectic (facing man dialectically, woman retorts, delivers a crushing and fatal counterblow).

Thus the "socialization" or "deontologization" of Hermione leads to a strange situation in which the social level of her dramatic presence is at once totalized and annihilated. On the one hand, she is now *thought* as a social creature (negatively by Leontes, positively by Paulina); on the other hand, she is socially banished—for sixteen years she becomes a social nobody, a social blank. But this situation is a form of dramatic stalemate: a situation where Hermione is the object of a brief "sociological" dispute between dialectical man (Leontes) and dialectical woman (Paulina), but where there is no way out of sociological one-dimensionality in general. The "translation" of Hermione into an exclusively social (and ontologically dead) figure has, as it were, become infinitely successful. However much Leontes repents, and however much Paulina goes on prodding him, action remains stereotypical. The only way out of this dead-end street is the miracle itself. Only miracle reverses the ontological-into-social "translation" that Leontes set in motion. Only miracle can *restore* Hermione as an ontologically all-powerful being—the kind of being she was, in an altogether different mode of difficulty, from the outset. Only miracle recuperates at once Hermione as ontologically living creature and the ontological dimension as such. Only a miracle saves us from one more act of bickering between Paulina and Leontes, or one more act of (fairly ineffectual) "repentance." As a thing socially dead, Hermione can be saved by Paulina; as a thing ontologically dead, she cannot be saved at all. But she can be resurrected.

I have emphasized that in both of these processes of translation (that from the ontological into the social and that from the social into the ontological) the *imagination* is put out of action, operative relevance, or theatrical primacy. Accusing Hermione, reading all her "playful" behavior as sinning: this required no special effort of the imagination. On the contrary, a deadening of Leontes' sensibility was involved in this process. He does not experience heightened awareness through jealousy, as Othello does; he does not refine his own powers of human sensibility through inner torment. Instead he grows blunt, coarse, categorical, and almost ludicrously vulgar. But the pure reversing of this deadening of Hermione/Leontes—the miracle itself—does not require imaginative effort either. On the contrary, *it* provides all the imagination/imagining—is the visible and ongoing *fact* of hyperimaginative reality. It would be impossible to avoid witnessing/imagining the miracle of the resuscitation of Hermione, because it comes across as a visibility that is more obvious than the obvious. This law that I am identifying—that miracle in some way presupposes the putting aside of the imaginative faculties—can be understood by considering the hypothetical existence of a person who had no imagination whatsoever. To this human being, every single phenomenon in the universe would appear as a miracle. Each moment and object of perception would be utterly miraculous.

Generally speaking, then, *The Winter's Tale* moves from (1) an ontological/sociological state of ambiguity in the opening scenes to (2) a middle region of "flat" merely-social dialectic, and then (3) finally on to a hyperontological reinstatement of the ontological: a miracle that does not only restore the ontological but also heightens it into apotheosis; a transubstantiation that does not only restore woman to the complexly suggestive region of her ontological richness but also heightens womanhood itself into a brief vision of inexplicable glory.

As I shall argue in a moment, however, the price that woman has to pay to attain the level of "miracle" is in a sense extravagant. But before I open that particular inquiry, I would like to finalize the analysis of the logic of Leontes' "jealousy."

> Mamillius,
> Art thou my boy?
> *Mamillius.* Ay, my good lord.
> *Leontes.* I'fecks:
> Why that's my bawcock. What! hast smutch'd thy nose?
> They say it is a copy out of mine. Come, captain,
> We must be neat; not neat, but cleanly, captain:
> And yet the steer, the heifer and the calf
> Are all call'd neat.—Still virginalling
> Upon his palm!—How now, you wanton calf!
> Art thou my calf?
> *Mamillius.* Yes, if you will, my lord.
> *Leontes.* Thou want'st a rough pash and the shoots that I have
> To be full like me: yet they say we are
> Almost as like as eggs; women say so,
> (That will say any thing): but were they false
> As o'er-dy'd blacks, as wind, as waters; false
> As dice are to be wish'd by one that fixes
> No bourn 'twixt his and mine, yet were it true
> To say this boy were like me. Come, sir page,
> Look on me with your welkin eye: sweet villain!
> Most dear'st, my collop! Can thy dam?—may't be?—
> Affection! thy intention stabs the centre:
> Thou dost make possible things not so held,
> Communicat'st with dreams;—how can this be?—
> With what's unreal thou coactive art,
> And fellow'st nothing: then 'tis very credent
> Thou may'st co-join with something;
>
> (1.2.119–43)

The editor of the Arden edition, J. H. P. Pafford, paraphrases the concluding part of this speech as follows: "Can your mother (be faithless)? Is it possible? Lustful passions: your intensity penetrates to the very heart and soul of man. You make possible things normally held to be impossible just as dreams do. How can this be? Lust causes one to associate in the mind with persons who are purely imaginary, who do not exist at all, therefore it is very credible that the most unthinkable lustful association can take place between real people."[32] This will do as paraphrase, but I am not quite sure that the lines are reducible to a disquisition on "lust" and "real people."

"Something" does not first of all mean "real people." It first of all means "something." And "something" is an ontological unit. It relates itself—ontologically—to its partner, "nothing." "Nothing"/"something" *together* ("coactive," "fellow," "cojoin") form an ontological nexus. The emphasis ("be") is on being. The emphasis, in other words, is ontological:

> —how can this be?—
> With what's unreal thou coactive art,
> And fellow'st nothing: then 'tis very credent
> Thou may'st co-join with something;
>
> (1.2.140–43)

This passage, far from primarily being the idea of an empirical constellation of possibilities, is the creation (by Shakespeare) and intuition (by Leontes) of a pure abyss. In the unimaginable depths of this abyss, "nothing" and "something" are radically coimplicative, and "something" is strongly the actual (or likely) outcome of "nothing." For the spectator, and probably for Leontes, the general effect is a vertiginous indecision in which the airy "nothing" (not) imagined by the suspicious mind is indistinguishable from its object of inquiry, from the zone of erotic fantasy where woman's passion is supremely real, but only in terms of a discursive charm and a physical flirtation that are "unreal." Generally, here, to be "coactive" with what's "unreal" (1.2.141) is not only to be fantastical in the (female) act of imaginative passion, but to be fantastical in the (masculine) faith in such a seductive abyss. Leontes can "imagine" the imaginative unthinkability of infidelity; he can "imagine" the "unreal" quality of seductive infatuation. Yet at the same time this "imagination" of his is no real imagination at all—but on the contrary something that pulls up this side of imagining things, becoming itself also the very "nothing" that the impossibility of infidelity *is*. The impossibility of infidelity for Leontes also becomes the impossibility of imagining it. Or to rephrase that: the impossibility of the possibility of infidelity also becomes the impossibility of its *imaginative* possibility. It is this seductive abyssing of possibility/impossibility that in the final analysis causes "affection" to generate an "intention" that "stabs the centre" (1.2.138). The stabbing of the center is no mere psychological emotional, or empirically marital entity. For the "centre" itself is no empirical entity. "Centre" here is center *as such*. It is each and every center (centeredness in general) that is at stake, and it is this universalization of decentration that creates the immense scope of the sense of existential swoon. "Affection" is by implication just as much the feelings of Leontes for Hermione as the supposed feelings of Hermione for another man. "Affection!" (1.2.138) is ultimately a universal category, and thus what "stabs the centre" is also a universal threat. The world itself hangs in the balance through Hermione's "infidelity." The play's final restoration of her and her fidelity thus also restores the world we live in.

As we faintly perceive in the passage recently quoted at some length, Leontes in a sense has an originary intuition of the emptiness ("nothing") of his jealousy. He senses that believing his own quick jealousy presupposes some sort of faith in an airy nothing. This at first leads him, for a second, to withdraw thought from its hostilities. But then it strikes Leontes that seduction itself presupposes "nothing"—that it itself materializes its substance out of nonsubstance, the "reality" of seductive fascination out of the "unreality" of its dreaminess. Leontes is permitted to think according to a logic that *equates* love and the suspicion of it. His suspicion *of* a love affair gets legitimized by the ontological "void" central to love itself (its quality of dreamy self-fabrication). In the manner of "an eye for an eye," Leontes can *counter* the autogenerative nature of love ("With what's unreal thou coactive art" [1.2.141]) with the autogenerative intensity of his own hatred of the autogenerativity of love. He places his accusations firmly in the foundational ground of "nothing"—knowing that this "nothing" is precisely what always will find a seductive echo in love itself (on account of the immateriality and volatile evasiveness of "affection").

The Petrification of Miracle

In order to clear the way for a hyperontological analysis of miracle itself in *The Winter's Tale*, I am here going to give an "exaggerated" feminist reading of the play. *First* woman is allowed to display the various charms that men relish: she is erotic, enticing, seductive, fascinating. *Then*, because woman's femininity has shown itself to be a little too feminine, woman is imprisoned, banished, and put away forever. *Finally*, after sixteen years, woman is released from her imprisonment—emerging chaste, glorious, and erotically spotless. She is now as unambiguous as the Rock of Gibraltar, and her chastisement into befitting silence is broken only by one or two tender words of reconciliation exchanged with the now-happy husband.

This reading, I grant, is a form of caricature; but I think we need to think through the implications of such a perspective before moving on.

In particular, such a reading might facilitate a sighting of some of the worst forms of patriarchal prejudice besetting the play. To give an example, let me quote what the Arden editor has to say in reviewing the famous exchange between Perdita and Polixenes on the matter of the naturalness of flowers and horticulture (I return to this passage later on).

> Polixenes' wider and more philosophical grasp of the principles befits him: but Perdita's resolute sensitiveness and feminine refinement about anything that might savour of sophistication or unchastity befits her. The argument does her no less honour than it does Polixenes, though, *qua* argument, he has the better of it.[33]

The Winter's Tale thematizes the *perfect* woman. Feminine transcendentalism being a natural structural dimension of the miracle play, this in no way causes surprise. We have already beheld Shakespeare's presencing of Marina as miracle, and in *Cymbeline*, Imogen is discovered in the cave (by Guiderius, Arviragus, and Belarius) on such terms:

> *Belarius.* By Jupiter, an angel! or, if not,
> An earthly paragon! Behold divineness
> No elder than a boy!
>
> (3.7.15–17)

I observed some time ago that the feminine transcendentality is more than an idealization. In fact, as my review of *Pericles* tried to suggest, miracle and idealization are quite different things. *The Winter's Tale* does not quite hold apart these opposites. Hermione promotes miracle as well as humanist ideality. She thus comes to *humanize* miracle; she threatens to become an odd entity that we might call "humanist miracle"—something poised in an awkward limbo between Renaissance imagination and medieval faith. She is miracle-as-protagonist. Marina, altogether more free, never carried this burden of being center and protagonist. Her miraculousness therefore is all the more persuasive—for a miracle never comes from the center. Nor does miracle strictly speaking come from the margin. It comes from the outside. Or more radically, it comes from nothing. The Renaissance, by always doing away with "nothing" (by always dramatizing, humanizing, and appropriating it) automatically does away with miracle too.

Hermione in one sense does come from nothing (and this fact alone ensures the possible materialization of her as dramatic miracle): she returns from death, absence, and nothingness. She makes an *appearance* that (for spectator as well as hero) is the experience of the miraculous itself. But she can never move as Marina can move (she is as it were made aesthetically rigid and inflexible by the very stoniness of her supposed being), for she centralizes miraculous experience in the preexisting mold of conventionalized patriarchal ideology. She is "perfect woman" not only in the sense of being miraculously restored to human life, but by conforming perfectly to an idealist stereotype. She is from this viewpoint rather disturbing: the very objectification of woman that masculine culture traditionally has projected in the ideology of the West. She is perfect as perfect object, ideal as ideal thing. Her objectification is the tripartite progression I have already mentioned: (1) sex-object utilized by the progressive male for the purposes of social display, (2) sex-object imprisoned and annihilated for the purposes of masculine totalitarianism, and (3) miraculous reutilization of this butchered sex-object as transcendental signified. Somewhat ruffled by this treatment, but by no means lacking in stoic composure, woman not only endures her degradation into objectification, imprisonment, and nothingness, but also endures the idealization of this degradation. Perhaps that is part of her miraculousness (in a positive as well as negative sense): that woman miraculously survives an idealization of her that strictly speaking is a mockery of the ideal.

What I am outlining, here, is thus not only a petrification of woman in *The Winter's Tale,* but a petrification of miracle. The petrification involves a process of idealization and a type of idealization that I have been viewing as aesthetically and experientially "incompatible" with the strong sense of miracle (that given in *Pericles*).

Now this "decline" of miracle, its gradual absorption into the traditional molds of humanist drama and its gradual secularization into theatrical "effect"—these things can be interpreted as signs of Shakespeare's inability to make significant progress inside the framework of the miracle plays as such; but these signs of the "weakening" of miracle can *also* be interpreted as indications of an awareness in Shakespeare that miracle really needed to somehow "integrate" itself with sublunary theatrical requirements. One miracle play *(Pericles)* is in a sense enough. Not enough for a medieval writer of miracle plays, but enough for a Renaissance dramatist making a living in the first decade of the seventeenth century. In the predominantly theological scenario of medieval playwriting, one miracle play justified the next: an abundance of miracles illustrated miraculousness as such, the general principle of it. But for Shakespeare's more secularist sensibility, the *miracle* of a miracle play could not serve the purposes of such representationalism. It is not, to return to Wilson Knight, that the "great artist" cannot successfully "repeat himself";[34] but that miracle itself, in order to be miracle, cannot become part of any repetitiousness or too-conscious manipulativeness. Miracle, and the miracle of woman, are obviously the functions of a technological manipulativeness in the later miracle plays of Shakespeare. For Shakespeare, now, the miracle does not come from nothing; it comes from Shakespeare. *The Tempest,* as I have argued from the outset, totalizes this "Shakespeareanization" of the miracle play: totalizing Shakespeare but at the same time obliterating play as miracle play.

My main point now, however, is that the "weakening" of miracle (through its humanization and centration) in no way amounts to a weakening of the general potential for dramatic innovation. By deemphasizing the nonhumanist ("medieval") aspects of the miracle play, Shakespeare on the one hand deprives himself of certain imaginative and spiritual possibilities, but on the other hand acquires a new set of options and signifying potentials.

Forgetting the "unkind" reading of *The Winter's Tale* for a moment, then, we might say that the task of presencing Hermione as a combination of miracle and traditional idealization amounts to an aesthetic and imaginative challenge: for Shakespeare, but also for the audience (a still somewhat medieval constellation of minds).

In the "straight" miracle play, the challenge would have simply been that of having woman come alive again; but the challenge in *The Winter's Tale* is that of making the objectification of woman come alive—as woman, but also—wonder of wonders—as objectification.

What is thrown into quaint, suggestive outline through these accretions of all-too-human ingredients in the spectacle of miraculous presencing is the role played by Perdita, Hermione's daughter. She is miraculously saved from the cruelties of

Leontes' "jealous" wrath. Believed to be sired by Polixenes, she narrowly escapes fire (2.3.95, 133, 140), prison (2.2.28), and lethal exposure to the elements (2.3.175).

Like Hermione, Perdita is shaped by the play's traditionally idealizing energies into an emblem of woman-as-perfection. But the idealizations of the two women are opposites. One depends on the ontological, the other on the social.

We can understand this splitting by recalling the originary status of Hermione in the play. There, I argued, her erotic poignancy was at once social and ontological. My entire analysis of the opening of the play was based on this identification of the tormentingly "dual" quality of Hermione's flirtatiousness: it suggested a disarrangement of the difference between the social and the ontological (between social guilt and original sin), and it was the disarrangement itself that Leontes could not cope with. It was the disarrangement of the opposition itself that created "jealousy." But as indecision (neither social nor ontological, but both) woman is a *permanent* source of discomfort—not only for the theatrical character Leontes, but also for the men in Shakespeare's audience. A way of becalming the *tremor cordis* produced by female indecision in general is therefore that of artificially separating the ontological magnetism of woman from her social magnetism. This is precisely what *The Winter's Tale* does. And through Perdita, it can do so simultaneously on two levels: on the universal one of woman and on the particular, character-bound, and personality-bound one of Hermione.

On that first, universal, level, two quite different beings emerge in the latter parts of the play. One of them is called Perdita, and henceforth is there to incarnate the social magnetism of woman. The other one is called Hermione, and henceforth is there to incarnate (or disincarnate) the ontological magnetism of woman. Two zones are created: that of pastoral bliss and that of ontological resurrection. Both of these zones involve the sense of the miraculous; for both females return from the area of the "eternally lost." Yet the zones, precisely by reassuringly separating what is inextricably intermingled in woman (the social and the ontological) achieve their dramatic potencies only at the price of some degree of artificiality—whether pastoral or sculptural.

But if this separation takes place on a general and universalist level of dramatic persuasion, so that the inaugural complexity of woman becomes the idyllic noncomplexity of her two terminal forms of erotic perfection, it also takes place *in* Hermione herself.

The division ontological/social, which "purifies" her originary duplicity, takes place *in* her being, indeed *in* her character. This is the price the play asks Hermione to pay for the continuance of her part in it (the woman's part). It is a price that she pays as woman, but also as character. As woman, she has to abandon her personality (what personality has a statue? how much is left of the originary Hermione once the stoning of woman in the play is triggered and completed?)—but as character she is also stoned to silence (receiving a bare seven lines for the "glorious" part of her stoned mode of presence). Perdita, we now see, is a (biological, dramatic, and aesthetic) modification of Hermione. Perdita, as subcomponent of Hermione, too is imprisoned, banished, annihilated. As Hermione's daughter, she "survives" those sixteen years of Hermione's own incarceration by being at large in the world as a Hermione-that-is-not-Hermione. As an infinitely sweet and touching creature of *pastoral* flirtatiousness, Perdita can perform all the erotic enchantments cooperatively displayed by Hermione in the social opening of the play, *without* provoking the dreaded *tremor cordis* that hits the male (hero, critic, spectator) as soon as the ontological and the social are presenced in their natural (feminine) mixture.

Divided, Hermione can now no longer harm the male, hurt his feelings or his pride. As Perdita (Hermione turned "innocent," doll-like, and adolescent), Hermione's social self is without ontological admixture (without the stain of original sin). "Boyhood," as idealized by the originary fraternity of Polixenes and Leontes (itself a form of miniature pastoral), now resurfaces as girlhood. As Perdita, "Hermione" can now assert herself erotically without asserting herself; she can flirt endlessly—and only evoke the *unreserved* admiration of the complacent male (character, spectator, critic). Her innocence masquerades as the equivalent of Hermione's innocence—but of course is no such thing. There is no ontological problematic buried inside Perdita's innocence—for, unlike the originary Hermione, she does not live in the world, but in pastoral. In fact Perdita is not even capable of innocence, as Hermione is; for to exist in pastoral (a world of social courting without ontological foundation in the abyss of our fallenness) is to be unable to choose between the ideal and its ruination. Perdita is not capable of any acts of innocence, for she *is* innocence.

The Hermione that is not Perdita (the part of the ur-Hermione that has not been pastoralized) is now an exclusively ontological remainder. One half of the ur-Hermione (Perdita) discourses prettily in the courtly world of pastoral idyllicism; the other half (Hermione) of the ur-Hermione, the one deprived of social agility (now exclusively the feminine property of Perdita), henceforth *is* all that was ontological in the ur-Hermione—and as such simply *awaits* the only moment of action that can give her a voice (miracle as ontological or hyperontological occurrence). The name "Perdita" (Lost One) is from this critical perspective poignant. She is on the level of empirical events the Hermione that is recovered from loss; but on a different level she is the very vanishing of Hermione from Hermione: the loss of Hermione, the radical expenditure of woman in the one-dimensional prettinesses of pastoral beautification.

Fortunately, of course, Shakespeare's genius never permits us to really lose Perdita as a strong artifact. But the play's recuperation of Perdita from pastoral abstraction and idyllic commonplace is not the only "recovery" that seems to materialize. On the outskirts of the play, quick possibilities vanish and go—most of them faintly suggestive of either loss or reappropriation. This tendency in the play toward the recirculation of "dead" and bygone material can perhaps be glimpsed at the moment when Florizel eloquently places Leontes in the provisional and imaginative position of a young lover. Asked to recall the passions of youth, Leontes faces Perdita much as he once faced Hermione: as admirer. This ("incestuous") moment in which father almost comes to court daughter is "internally" electrified by the kind of proximity between Hermione and Perdita that I have called attention to—Perdita is a "lost" Hermione, a shadow-Hermione who lacks what in Hermione herself was overrich (femininity as equivocation). Significantly, Paulina (ever on the outlook for dialectical contrasts and dialectical differences) rushes in to clarify the supplementary perfections of her mistress, Hermione's superiority over her daughter.

Leontes. You are married?
Florizel. We are not, sir, nor are we like to be:
The stars, I see, will kiss the valley's first:
The odds for high and low's alike.
Leontes. My lord.
Is this the daughter of a king?
Florizel. She is,
When once she is my wife.
Leontes. That "once," I see, by your good father's speed,
Will come on very slowly. I am sorry,
Most sorry, you have broken from his liking,

Where you were tied in duty; and as sorry
Your choice is not so rich in worth as beauty,
That you might well enjoy her.

Florizel. Dear, look up:
Though Fortune, visible an enemy,
Should chase us, with my father, power no jot
Hath she to change our loves. Beseech you, sir,
Remember since you ow'd no more to time
Than I do now: with thought of such affections,
Step forth mine advocate: at your request,
My father will grant precious things as trifles.

Leontes. Would he do so, I'd beg your precious mistress,
Which he counts but a trifle.

Paulina. Sir, my liege,
Your eye hath too much youth in't; not a month
'Fore your queen died, she was *more* worth such gazes
Than what you look on now.

Leontes. I thought of her,
Even as these looks I made.

(5.1.202–27)

From the immediate viewpoint of dramatic meaning, Leontes' "attentions" toward Perdita are of course meant to suggest the resemblance between Perdita and Hermione. His admiration of Perdita is implicitly his admiration of Hermione. But as Paulina senses, the situation is reversible. The danger is that Hermione eventually will look like a copy (and a flawed one) of Perdita. The function of Paulina, in addition, is vaguely metadramatic: she always appears as a figure semiextraneous to the dramatic action, as if her main purpose is not to take part in that action but to ensure its smooth onwardness. Paulina is there to see that the right character encounters the right fellow-character at the right moment and with the right response. Even at the very climax and termination of the play, she is busy with the minute regulations of "proper" social intercourse. In the current scene, it is as if Leontes threatens, *as character,* to become a bit too hypnotized by the beauty of Perdita. Her beauty thus somehow has to be delimited, reduced, and bracketed. But that process, in the terminal stages of the dramatic action, is obstructed by other theatrical requirements that in fact demand of Perdita that she retain the purity of her beauteous perfection. What is created in this way is what we might call the problem of the *relativity of perfection* in the play. This relativity is by no means a side issue, a construct of "marginal" interest. On the contrary, the "relativity of perfection" is what *The Winter's Tale* from the outset speaks. But let us return first to the question of the "likeness" between Hermione and Perdita. If Hermione is of stone, if she in some uneasy sense is petrified woman rather than woman, does that petrification also affect Perdita? Is Perdita too stoned in/by the play? I think the answer is no. I shall try to clarify this matter by first pointing to the discursive preparations for the miraculous unveiling of Hermione as living artifact and statue:

> *Leontes.* O Paulina,
> We honour you with trouble: but we came
> To see the statue of our queen: your gallery
> Have we pass'd through, not without much content
> In many singularities; but we saw not
> That which my daughter came to look upon,
> The statue of her mother.
> *Paulina.* As she liv'd *peerless,*
> *So her dead likeness,* I do well believe,
> *Excels* whatever yet you look'd upon,
> Or hand of man hath done; therefore I keep it
> Lonely, apart. But here it is: prepare
> To see the life as lively mock'd as ever
> Still sleep mock'd death: behold, and say 'tis well.
> I like your silence, it the more shows off
> Your wonder: but yet speak; first you, my liege.
> Comes it not something near?
> *Leontes.* Her natural posture!
> Chide me, *dear stone,* that I may say indeed
> Thou art Hermione; or rather, *thou art she*
> In thy not chiding; for she was as tender
> As infancy and grace. But yet, Paulina,
> Hermione was not so much wrinkled, nothing
> So aged as this seems.
>
> (5.3.8–29)

If we for a moment manage to wrench ourselves out of the hypnotic grip created by Shakespeare's dramatic spell and instead consider this scene from the viewpoint of some mode of critical detachment, we see that *Leontes addresses Hermione as stone* ("dear stone"). This address is not wholly disengaged from the kind of patriarchal attitudes that we discussed earlier: the tendency to *behold* the seductive "perfection" of woman only when an extreme objectification keeps it at a safe distance—almost a safe aesthetic distance. To aestheticize the undecidedness of woman is from this viewpoint simply one of several possible reifications. Stoned to stone, Hermione certainly does retain some human remainders, some tokens (the wrinkles) that she is not all stone: that an underlying humanness and human vulnerability qualify the idealization. But the aesthetic hypnosis is so overpowering that we, like Leontes, are quite ready for a moment to see those wrinkles too as part and parcel of "perfection"—whether it is the unusually delicate handicraft of the sculptor or the skilled imaginative precisions of William Shakespeare. The main hyperontological potency of the scene, however, emerges from the crucial lines spoken by Paulina:

> As she liv'd peerless,
> So her dead likeness, I do well believe,
> Excels whatever yet you look'd upon
>
> (5.3.14–16)

The hyperontological conundrum, here, is that "dead likeness" in several important ways is originary. On the banal level of mere reference, this means that the statue/imitation of Hermione for a second or two looks more real and lifelike than Hermione herself. On a more suggestive and uncomfortable level, however, it means that Hermione is more like her likeness than herself—that the idealizing petrification of woman "excels" her by being more "true." The truth of woman here becomes her ability to coincide perfectly with her ideality and her idealization—but thus also with her objectification and terminal stoniness. What is brought alive is not woman but her death. What she *ought* to perfectly resemble is her own "dead likeness." In fact, crudely and cruelly speaking, Leontes can only love Hermione as stone: as "perfection" so close to stone that its difference from stoned perfection is marginal (a wrinkle or two).

Imitation, in this way, can be sensed as preceding identity: for there is little in identity itself (Hermione as conforming purely to her idea) that is not coactive with its imitative heightening. Hermione thus *excels herself*. As a superb likeness of a "dead likeness" (5.3.15), as the living incarnation of the dead *as* dead, she comes into full and satisfying (masculine) view as the silent and passively beautiful ideal she ought to have been from the outset.

What in a sense gets animated at the end of the *The Winter's Tale* is thus not merely what formerly was living, any person we could understand within the reality-principle as a believably lifelike female, but also the deathlike mask and frozen specter of such a being. The statue, to be sure, is a "dead likeness" of an undead queen; but the statue, on the sensual level of Shakespeare's linguistic flotation, is also the dead likeness of dead likeness itself—the perfect coinciding of the objectified woman and the objectification, the "perfect" coinciding of objectification with itself. Normally we do not have an objectification at hand as a pure object; but here we do. Here there is for a moment no space or difference between objectification and object: between the *reality* of the object as object and the *notion* of the object as pure idea (miracle and/or objectification). In a terminal sense, Hermione is from this perspective rather sexless, the ungendered and frigid personification of the stony effigy she was supposed to have been buried in.

The play's positive and poetically generous treatment of Perdita is perhaps a structural consequence of this strange petrification. In spite of all the discursive efforts to equate Perdita with Hermione, to make Perdita's perfection a mere reflection of Hermione's, perfection in Perdita escapes from such dialectical mimesis. That supplementary charm or perfection in Perdita is furthermore no mere function of the pastoralism that threatens to choke her with its artificiality; instead that special charm seems to grow out of her ability to evade the dialectic of perfection and petrification.

Perdita is the dead likeness of Hermione, we grant. But Hermione is already herself the dead likeness of Hermione. According to the "laws" of the thinking of the play, according to its sensation of ontological necessity (that all motion falls forward to the miracle that must retrospectively illuminate it), Hermione *must* coincide with "Hermione"—the miracle and the ideal are one, revelation and beauty concur purely. As identity, Hermione finalizes her presence as the fortunate and happy congruity of her own being. She is thus "peerless," and exactly according to the self-congratulatory rationale of "grave and good Paulina," because she in the final analysis only is allowed to compete with her own ideal petrification. But if she in this way, as I argued above, is always already the imitation of her identity, Perdita, a subsidiary "dead likeness," cannot *imitate* that imitation-into-identity. On several occasions, Shakespeare's language makes Perdita "compete" with Hermione (as beauty and ultimate ideal); but since idealist competition has already run itself to the extreme limit of the possible in Hermione's "dead" likeness to her own (dead) likeness, there is nothing that Perdita really can *add* to this abyssing of likeness to the point of death (to the point of the touch of stone). Perdita is freshly perceived at the farthest possible distance from effigy and petrification, and at no moment do we conceive her in terms of stasis or patiently endured paralysis.

Marbling

It is now time to finalize our discussions of *The Winter's Tale* by means of a supplementary turn of the screw. Really, what I have been saying about the terminal monumentalization of Hermione in the play is that it amounts to (1) a miracle, (2) an idealization, and (3) an objectification. Marbled into deathlike frozenness, Hermione is miraculously reclaimed from negativity. But the marbling of woman is in a sense also irreversible—the "miracle" preserves and guards the very marbling it seems to negate. The marbling of woman is itself objectified into immaculate artifact and "beauteous thing." The petrification of woman is not alleviated but only dramatized to its limits.

But I have also suggested that the play in Perdita touches a more convincing glimpse of the miraculous. She is in no way involved in any real miracle; she is not, like Marina, the source of a truly visionary ecstasy. Yet by being miraculously recovered (from the desert), she carries with her some luster suggestive of the felicity of miracle. As character, she in a modest way is felicity itself.

Yet the appeal and likableness of Perdita, I have argued, are not merely a function of the sweet poetry she is permitted to speak and personify. I think there are other reasons. One, I believe, is that she creates a sense of imaginative freedom by countering the strongly centristic motions of the play—its overpowering tendency to anthropologize the miraculous (whether negative or positive) and make man (or woman) its center. If the play thus has its dramatic outskirts, and if the "desert" is part of such a far-distant margin of all-too-centered theatrical persuasion, then the ability of Perdita to cast her own (and rather different) spell is a function of her ability to *remain* in the desert where she should have been completely lost.

The play "saves" her from the desert (from being eaten up by a bear); but the play does not immediately recenter her in the monolithic space of monumentalized recovery. On the contrary, the *territory* of Perdita remains alien to the territory of centered recovery. She makes a recovery, but not in the center. She recovers, but not for the sake of the center. She enjoys recovery in terms of play and deferred exile rather than in terms of static belongingness and transcendental presence. The statue of Hermione becomes a statue of miracle itself, miracle as statue. Thus miracle in *The Winter's Tale* becomes a transcendental signified, an almost phallic erection of the traditionally idealist kind. As statue and monument, whether inanimate or "living," Hermione puts an end to play. With the emergence of statue/stone/idealization *as* Hermione, the play has to terminate. But no such feelings of fixed transcendental terminalism are experienced with Perdita. Lightfooted and gay, she is the affirmation of recovery rather than the recovery of recovery. In this way, at least for me, Perdita comes closer to Marina than Hermione ever could—she comes closer to that pure mixing of poetry and miracle that *Pericles* alone among the miracle plays maintains as sustained dramatic emotion. The originary desert (she is ontologically speaking born there) that frees Perdita from suffocating belongingness and oppressive human dialectic is in this way compatible with the ocean that always encircles Marina as home without solid foundation. Unlike Hermione, Perdita is not grounded in the ground of centered belongingness itself. She may marry, may conform in all kinds of ways to the expectations generated by "home"; but the lightness of her step does not ground her in the ground; whereas, in the cementation of her statuesque capacity for inflexible suffering, Hermione as statue and marble becomes the very animation of the ground itself—the ground *as* living humanity.

We may understand this difference between Hermione (on the one hand) and Marina and Perdita (on the other hand) by considering the way critics have reviewed the protagonists of *Pericles* and *The Winter's Tale*.

Wilbur Sanders admires Hermione. Her presence is one of feminine stoicism, what Sanders applauds as her "brave magnanimity."[35] Hermione has the classical virtue of being able to solidify into pain-absorbing statue in situations of crisis. "Harrowed but calm, displaying a kind of serenity in her very anguish, she manages, somehow, to continue caring for Leontes."[36] No distinction is made between classical virtue and virtue proper to a miracle play (the kind of virtue displayed throughout *Pericles* by Marina). This difference, I may add, in the final analysis boils down to a difference between a masculine sense of virtue (the classical scheme) and a nonmasculine sense of virtue (the nonclassical scheme). What happens in enthusiastic celebrations of Hermione as a female equipped with the full armor of classical "magnanimity" is that criticism unthinkingly translates masculine virtue into a reassuring feminine counterpart. Female virtue is in such a scheme simply the feminization of a virtue that is typically masculine. I am not saying that it is wrong to identify Hermione's virtue as classical virtue; but I am saying that it is superficial to congratulate the drama in a one-sided fashion for having utilized that particular notion of virtue. Marina eschewed such masculine ideology and could negotiate the pure sense of miracle through that very evasion. She circumnavigates the facile formula "pain-and-reward." She does not demonstrate a knowing patience, but one that is so pure that she does not even know that it *is* patience.

Let me clarify the difference between the two virtuousnesses by quickly returning to Pericles, Marina's father. He is a key to all those moments of poetic glory in *Pericles* that Wilson Knight identified in terms of "feminine transcendentalism." Hermione moves us in her own way, is a "miracle" in her own right. But she cannot generate the quasi-mystical sense of "soft" miracle: the sense that the core of reality itself is radiance. Hermione's softness, a dialectical softness directly produced by the reversibility of the opposition soft/hard, has stone for its condition of possibility. The core is solid, it is not light itself.

In a review that I very much admire, J. M. S. Tompkins points out that *Pericles* does not foreground "the theoretical 'invulnerability' of Senecal man."[37] Tompkins gives the outline of a mode of patience that is not ontologically compatible with the "brave magnanimity" discussed a moment ago by Sanders as the central virtue of Hermione.

> What [Shakespeare] shows us is not the Stoic discipline under grief. . . . Pericles is no Stoic; there is no theoretical stiffening in his attitude, nor does he take Fortune's buffets and rewards with equal thanks, or call contempt of pain his own. He is wounded to the quick, yet "gentle." . . . There is no human clamour to match the sea's outrage.[38]

The main difference between *The Winter's Tale* and *Pericles*, then, is that the former play does not produce its visionary light from "man's sense of his subordination in a world of mysterious forces."[39] Instead we begin with raw passion, caused, as in *Lear*, by a provocation that is fundamental and real only in the high-strung egocentricity of a masculine whim. *This* tempest then tosses us through a dialectic of retribution and suffering. What is inexplicable is not the cosmos, but the idiosyncracies of an imperially positioned male; the originary enigma is almost reducible to a mannerism, the quirks of a slightly twisted and prejudiced personality. Pericles does not stand for such a patriarchal centering of the problem of suffering; and this difference, opening the gates of the unique "feminine transcendentalism" of the play, distinguishes him from most other Shakespearean heroes. Tompkins again:

> All the other heroes are dominated, as Elizabethan tragic heroes are bound to be, by impulse, passion, resentment, leading to physical and spiritual violence. They have moods of weary suffering, but this is not patience but numbness and melancholy. They recognize their deprivation. They cry out for patience, like Lear—"You heavens, give me that patience, patience I need!"—and recognize it enviously in others, like Hamlet.[40]

The "theoretical stiffening" mentioned by Tompkins (above) as the classical and Stoic reactivity of Senecal man seems to me to be reflected in the entire visionariness of Hermione—a rigidity that is not only physical and stony, but also spiritual and inward. It is true that she is "soft" compared with the relentlessness of grave and good Paulina, but her softness is quite compatible with that relentlessness. In her very self-silencing, self-petrification, and self-annihilation, Hermione inadvertently subscribes to the ideology of "theoretical stiffening." No such classical rigidity engineers the life-styles of Perdita and Marina.

Hermione thus falls outside the zone of strong feminine transcendentalism. This transcendentalism is no softening of the male; indeed, as originary softness without dialectical profile, this softness is a softening of nothing. *Of* nothing. And of *nothing*.

The hyperfeminine in *The Winter's Tale* is related to its hardness as well as its softness—and to the difference that spaces out that opposition. We can approach an understanding of that source of contradiction and play by considering one of Perdita's most celebrated moments of theatrical persuasion. This is the scene where she debates with Polixenes on the subject of nature-versus-art. Patriarchal criticism of the kind I have refuted tends to blandly inform us that there is no true "profundity" at stake in the philosophical dialogue between Perdita and Polixenes.[41] I would argue, on the contrary, that this dialogic piece is a crucial cornerstone in the entire structure of the play—and that Shakespeare in more ways than one knows this.

Polixenes. Shepherdess—
A fair one are you—well you fit our ages
With flowers of winter.
Perdita. Sir, the year growing ancient,
Not yet on summer's death nor on the birth
Of trembling winter, the fairest flowers o'th'season
Are our carnations and streak'd gillyvors,
Which some call nature's bastards: of that kind
Our rustic garden's barren; and I care not
To get slips of them.
Polixenes. Wherefore, gentle maiden,
Do you neglect them?
Perdita. For I have heard it said
There is an art which, in their piedness, shares
With great creating nature.
Polixenes. Say there be;
Yet nature is made better by no mean
But nature makes that mean: so, over that art,
Which you say adds to nature, is an art
That nature makes. You see, sweet maid, we marry
A gentler scion to the wildest stock,
And make conceive a bark of baser kind
By bud of nobler race. This is an art
Which does mend nature—change it rather—but
The art itself is nature.
Perdita. So it is.
Polixenes. Then make your garden rich in gillyvors,
And do not call them bastards.
Perdita. I'll not put
The dribble in earth to set one slip of them;
No more than, were I painted, I would wish
This youth should say 'twere well, and only therefore
Desire to breed by me. Here's flowers for you:
Hot lavender, mints, savory, marjoram,
The marigold, that goes to bed wi'th'sun
And with him rises, weeping: these are flowers
Of middle summer, and I think they are given
To men of middle age. Y'are very welcome.
(She gives them flowers)
Camillo. I should leave grazing, were I of your flock,
And only live by gazing.
Perdita. Out, alas!
You'd be so lean that blasts of January
Would blow you through and through. Now, my fair'st friend, *(To Florizel)*
I would I had some flowers o'th'spring, that might
Become your time of day; and yours, and yours,

(To Mopsa and the other girls)
That wear upon your virgin branches yet
Your maidenheads growing: O Proserpina,
For the flowers now that, frighted, thou let'st fall
From Dis's waggon! daffodils,
That come before the swallow dares, and take
The winds of March with beauty; violets, dim,
But sweeter than the lids of Juno's eyes
Or Cytherea's breath; pale primroses,
That die unmarried, ere they can behold
Bright Phoebus in his strength (a malady
Most incident to maids); bold oxlips and
The crown-imperial; lilies of all kinds,
The flower-de-luce being one. O, these I lack,
To make you garlands of; and my sweet friend,
To strew him o'er and o'er!
Florizel. What, like a corpse?
Perdita. No, like a bank, for love to lie and play on:
Not like a corpse; or if—not to be buried,
But quick, and in mine arms. Come, take your flowers:
Methinks I play as I have seen them do
In Whitsun pastorals: sure this robe of mine
Does change my disposition.

(4.4.77–135)

This passage, a small miracle that in itself is a beautiful intermixing of the natural and the artificial, is of course at once an affirmation and a negation of what Perdita ideologizes as the superiority of nature over art. Only through the artificiality that permits aesthetic and mythological distancing ("Dis's waggon," "Juno's eyes," "Phoebus in his strength," "Whitsun pastorals") does Perdita's lyricism come over *naturally* as a celebration of nature. The cultural (hence nonnatural) points of learned reference "cool" rhetoric; yet this cooling is precisely what gives a clear edge to the emotional warmth that carries across to friend, lover, and spectator.

In addition, we notice that the presencing of erotic compliment and sexual suggestion reactivates moments of earlier dialogue between Hermione and her admirers. Hermione's feigned erotic alarm is now matched by that of her daughter:

Camillo. I should leave grazing, were I of your flock,
And only live by gazing.
Perdita. Out, alas!

(4.4.109–10)

Socially speaking, Perdita's "Out, alas!" is the equivalent of Hermione's "Grace to boot!" (1.2.80) pronounced as a reaction to Polixenes' reference to marriage as an instantiation of the rehearsal of original sin. But Shakespeare has of course removed the possibility of sexual tension in the dialogue between Perdita and Polixenes by deliberately pastoralizing it as a discursive tableau, and (more importantly) by spacing out the difference between the young female and the mature male as a generation gap. The "middle age" of Polixenes (4.4.108) is not only something positive (what gets him the special flowers "naturally" associated with such a golden mean), but also an ontological screen that protects Perdita from serious erotic dialectic. Polixenes is too old to compete—in pastoral—with a Florizel, just as Perdita is too young to hover in that special zone of sexual indeterminacy monitored by Hermione in the opening scenes. There it was an equality of age (the projection of Leontes/Polixenes as twins) that permitted Hermione to achieve a sense of oscillating interchangeability.

But the flower passage is interesting not only in its peculiarities and details, but also in its thematic and ontological generality. It is, once followed from beginning to end, a miniature version of the hyperontological motion of the whole play: a socioontological conundrum and irresolvable difficulty that quickly shoots into structural innocence by means of an idealized simplification. At first there is a conceptual paradox that seems to be in need of analytical elucidation. Then there is a smoothing-over of this difficulty through the emotional discharge of Perdita's (and Shakespeare's) poetic effusions. Yet that simplification (the poetic tableau of nature as innocent positivity) is on closer inspection itself qualified by the details and linguistic particularities of its texture.

According to Polixenes, the supplement is originary. The supplement that adds itself to nature by marking an addition totally outside nature is already in nature as something natural: "so, over that art, / Which you say adds to nature, is an art / That nature makes" (4.4.90–92). Artificiality here is something at the heart of the universe, the very core of what is natural. But this notion is of course precisely what the play as a whole asserts on its intellectual level: first through the intermixing in Hermione of social innocence and ontological fallenness, finally through a statuesque and ultraartificial immobilization of Hermione that itself comes to life. In that last ontological drama, there is not the sensation of an exterior artificiality being removed from Hermione as cover and veil. There is no discovery/unveiling in that sense; no "natural" Hermione "below" the supplementary surface of her sculptural artificiality. Instead artifice opens up, as she comes alive, from inside toward outside: as if what is artifice and aesthetic immobility in her itself starts to move; as if she is not a woman externally masquerading as artifice, but an actual artifice parading as woman. As the quite art-ificial result of Shakespeare's art this in the final analysis is what she actually is.

To speak of the "marbling" of Hermione is thus an enterprise of tantalizing complexity. From the "feminist" perspective recently opened, that marbling is an actual petrification—the irreversible transformation of the living sexual flesh of woman into its frigidly "preserved" and conserved (masculine) ideality. But "marbling," any good dictionary will tell you, is also something other than the homogeneous solidification of something into a seamless marble solid; it is a distribution of the systems of difference and play—so that to speak of the "marbling" of meat is to identify the intermixture of fat and lean strands in the texture of a steak. Difference itself is what creates "marbling." But this type of marbling (most conspicuous in the "wrinkles" of Hermione, the nonideal "remainder" of the ideal) is precisely what the flower passage itself highlights when it starts off from the "piedness" (4.4.87) of "streak'd gillyvors" (4.4.82) to quickly unconceal (and conceal) the all-important ideological notion of the inextricable and irreducible marbling of nature: not simply its constant drift toward artifice, culture, and exterior supplement, but also its constant tendency to reinclude what it excludes by patterning the exclusion into the beauteousness of artificial inclusion.

3
Miracle in Abyss

Miracle and Overdraft

Miracle in Shakespeare is a quasi-religious experience, and a miracle play is in the Shakespearean corpus a play that aesthetically speaking depends on such a felt sensation. *Pericles* is almost unthinkable as a play separable from its intermittent mystical consciousness; *The Winter's Tale* is almost unthinkable in a state of separation from its terminal revelation and from the peculiar awe made possible by that showing. By contrast, *Cymbeline* is not organized in a directly aesthetic relation to a crucial sighting of miracle.

Miracle in *Cymbeline* does not function as miracle. In *Cymbeline*, the miraculous is absorbed by plot, author, and structural blueprint. Although the plot uses miracle, miracle does not redeem and save the plot. On the contrary, the plot itself saves the plot, the plot itself goes out of its way to show that the plotting can handle plot. Miracle does not work a miracle *for the play.* Miracle does not "need" to save the plot; strong miracles are superfluous. Or else miracle is unable to save the plot; miracles in *Cymbeline* want to be strong but turn out weak.

According to the norms I am setting here, what a play needs if it is to count as a strong Shakespearean miracle play is a miracle that is absolutely decisive in shaping our whole aesthetic enjoyment of the drama. *Cymbeline* lacks such a miracle. Yet strangely, or perhaps for this very reason, *Cymbeline* is strewn with "wonders" that seem to want to attempt the miraculous—wonders that seem at once aware of the glory of miracle and aware of their own invalidity as functioning miracles.

Your average miracle play may be a play sporting a miracle or two; but a Shakespearean miracle play is a play *handed to you* by the possibility of miraculous recovery itself. This recovery somehow involves recovering the play as such: from failure, from boredom, from the nonmiraculous . . . from itself. *Cymbeline* is from this particular viewpoint a "dead" play, a false miracle play—the shadow or mockery of such potent drama. There is no priceless "religious" ecstasy in *Cymbeline*—but there are many efforts (of doubtful sincerity) to stage such an ecstasy. Where miracle reveals, *Cymbeline* simply discovers. Wonder, in this hypersecularized world, is the wonder of discovery—not wonder itself. Characters are impressed or overimpressed. They are startled. They announce their enthusiasm. But they do not share with us what we share with Pericles or with Leontes.

This flattening of miracle in *Cymbeline* is a function of the bias already touched in my previous references to *The Tempest:* the gradual appropriation of feminine transcendentalism by the authorial forces of all-powerful patriarchy. Leontes could have come to dominate *The Winter's Tale* as Prospero dominates *The Tempest*—but feminine counterforces (by no means exclusively the property of Paulina and "feminism") prevent the totalization of such a takeover. He becomes, in his own pathetic way, "secondary"—like Pericles. The male is in different ways softened into awareness, contemplation, respect, silence, humility, and wonder.

In *Cymbeline*, "feminine transcendentalism" never really gets a chance. There is contest, dialectic, battle, revenge, negotiation, settlement, accounting, economy. (The final handing-out of dues to Rome is an agile theatrical U-turn worthy of a Gorbachev.) While the dramatic tension between Polixenes and Leontes in *The Winter's Tale* never is allowed to develop into a central rivalry and play-length power struggle, the contest between Posthumus and Iachimo centralizes dialectic as such in *Cymbeline*. But this story of masculine pride (in *Pericles* elegantly distanced into the archaic horizon of courtly tilting) is by no means an isolated phenomenon. On the contrary, the structure of masculine hierarchization obsessively (and foolishly) returns to "degree" and the question of prestige. "Degree" is far more important than miracle in *Cymbeline*. In fact, the play actually thematizes "degree" *as* miracle: degree is sold to us as the miraculous itself. In *Cymbeline* the most frequent miraculous happening, indeed showing, is that performed through the ability of high birth to manifest its innate superiority over the common. Cymbeline's sons, Guiderius and Arviragus, are themselves small "miracles": reared in the mountains, they inadvertently keep revealing their hidden breeding—all to the sweet pleasure of Belarius, their benevolent guardian. He admires the princes for their uncanny ability to spontaneously exhibit the noblesse of their unknown father, King Cymbeline. (Notice the use of the verb "to miracle.")

> *(Aside)* O noble strain!
> O worthiness of nature! breed of greatness!
> Cowards father cowards, and base things sire base;
> Nature hath meal, and bran; contempt, and grace.
> I'm not their father, yet who this should be,
> Doth miracle itself, lov'd before me.—
>
> (4.2.24–29)

This wonder at the miraculous workings of proper blood is, as we perceive in the following extract, made to intermix and blend with the general sense of amazement in the face of a world full of wondrous and enigmatic occurrences:

> O thou goddess,
> Thou divine Nature; thou thyself thou blazon'st
> In these two princely boys: they are as gentle
> As zephyrs blowing below the violet,
> Not wagging his sweet head; and yet, as rough,
> (Their royal blood enchaf'd) as the rud'st wind
> That by the top doth take the mountain pine
> And make him stoop to th'vale. 'Tis wonder
> That an invisible instinct should frame them
> To royalty unlearn'd, honour untaught,
> Civility not seen from other, valour
> That wildly grows in them, but yields a crop
> As if it had been sow'd. Yet still it's strange
> What Cloten's being here to us portends,
> Or what his death will bring us.
>
> (4.2.169–83)

This slant given to wonder/miracle is of course banal, and repeated as often as it is in *Cymbeline*, it is tedious. The poetry, moreover, is mediocre: "wonder" does no great miracle for language. Unfortunately, this third-rate realization of miracle and the language of miracle also extends to what might have become a central visionary tableau in the play, the Jupiter Vision. Here we are miles away from miracle as "feminine transcendentality." If, as some critics have argued, the Jupiter Vision is the miraculous moment of revelation in *Cymbeline*, "miracle" here is masculinity itself—the prototypical showing of the godhead as masculinity and of masculinity as godhead.

Jupiter descends in thunder and lightning, sitting upon an eagle: he throws a thunderbolt. The Ghosts fall on their knees.

Jupiter. No more, you petty spirits of region low,
Offend our hearing: hush! How dare you ghosts
Accuse the thunderer, whose bolt (you know)
Sky-planted, batters all rebelling coasts?
Poor shadows of Elysium, hence, and rest
Upon your never-withering banks of flowers:
Be not with mortal accidents opprest,
No care of yours it is, you know 'tis ours.
Whom best I love I cross; to make my gift
The more delay'd, delighted. Be content,
Your low-laid son our godhead will uplift:
His comforts thrive, his trials well are spent:
Our Jovial star reign'd at his birth, and in
Our temple was he married. Rise, and fade.
He shall be lord of lady Imogen,
And happier much by his affection made.
This tablet lay upon his breast, wherein
Our pleasure his full fortune doth confine,
And so away: no farther with your din
Express impatience, lest you stir up mine.
Mount, eagle, to my palace crystalline. *(Ascends.)*
Sicilius. He came in thunder; his celestial breath
Was sulphurous to smell: the holy eagle
Stoop'd, as to foot us: his ascension is
More sweet than our blest fields: his royal bird
Prunes the immortal wing, and cloys his beak,
As when his god is pleased.
All. Thanks, Jupiter!
Sicilius. The marble pavement closes, he is enter'd
His radiant roof. Away! and to the blest
Let us with care perform his great behest.
(The Ghosts vanish.)
Posthumus. (Waking) Sleep, thou hast been a grandsire, and begot
A father to me: and thou hast created
A mother, and two brothers . . .
. . . . A book? O rare one,
Be not, as is our fangled world, a garment
Nobler than that it covers. Let thy effects
So follow, to be most unlike our courtiers,
As good as promise.

(*Reads*) When as a lion's whelp shall, to himself
unknown, without seeking find, and be embrac'd
by a piece of tender air: and when from a stately
cedar shall be lopp'd branches, which, being
dead many years, shall after revive, be jointed to
the old stock, and freshly grow, then shall
Posthumus end his miseries, Britain be fortunate,
and flourish in peace and plenty.
'Tis still a dream: or else such stuff as madmen
Tongue, and brain not: either both, or nothing,
Or senseless speaking, or a speaking such
As sense cannot untie. Be what it is,
The action of my life is like it, which
I'll keep, if but for sympathy.

(5.4.93–151)

With the significant exception of the last six lines, this entire section is worthless—linguistically, poetically, theatrically, intellectually, emotionally, spiritually. Out of context, this language would be identified by few people as interesting, enriching, or Shakespearean. Yet the last six lines are clearly Shakespearean. They are compressed into imaginative suggestion without intellectual limit. Those lines are Shakespearean because (1) they were probably written by Shakespeare and (2) because they are characteristic of Shakespeare's intellectual presence and dramatic style: there are echoes of *Macbeth* and anticipations of *The Tempest*.

But what interests me most, again, is Shakespeare's attitude to his own writing in the Jupiter Vision—if, indeed, it is his "own." It could fail to be his own either because most of the Vision is the work of an alien hand (preceding or supplementing Shakespeare's primary contribution), *or* because Shakespearean writing in parts of the late plays is not quite Shakespearean. That is basically what I am constantly returning to as the crucial question of "recovery." Shakespeare may well have had to recover or supplement work of inferior quality done by partners or apprentices; but in some (important) sections of the late plays he may have had to recover and supplement work/writing/drama completed *by himself*—not a month or a year ago, but a minute ago, a second ago.

Such a situation could be caused by the dramatist's new tendency to move too far out into the "exterior" regions of writerly experimentation: his need then to suddenly pull back and make sense of his drama, indeed his writing. (Those last six lines look very much like traces of such a process.) Thus Shakespeare *could* in his late period often have found himself in a position of "estrangement" vis-à-vis his own writing, and he *could* have wanted to occasionally break that estrangement by suddenly reverting to his familiar verbal resourcefulness. It is possible, in other words, that Shakespeare in the late plays is frequently indulging in the deliberate or semideliberate act of "un-Shakespeareanizing" his own art, of abdicating not from the theater but from imagination and full linguistic drive. This, as I have said before, may have been a predicament caused by new aesthetic or professional concerns, or it may simply have been caused by some loss—or at least widening—of normal creative concentration. We will never know, and it is pointless to speculate at length. What we do need to firmly recognize, however, is precisely what dishonest critics persistently refuse to recognize: that there is a strange line of demarcation in many of the late plays between writing that is good and writing that is bad—indeed, between drama that is good and drama that is bad. I cannot imagine that an artist of Shakespeare's caliber could have failed to be aware of the materialization of such a line of aesthetic demarcation.

Now my point is that this aesthetic dividing-line (between the worthless and its other) is often very sharp in the late plays, as we saw in the final part of the long passage just cited from *Cymbeline*, and that Shakespeare in his *successful* miracle plays manages to make that line itself part of the miraculous process. *The transition between substandard writing and strong writing becomes absolutely coextensive with the transition between a world of lost hope and a world of wondrous recovery.* The miracle that takes place "in" the play (a character's jolt from apathy to ecstasy) is virtually indistinguishable from the miracle "of" the play: its sudden acquisition of an excess of imaginative and creative energy. This process, we have already seen, is at its clearest in *Pericles*, where it takes place on the largest possible scale. The first acts are pretty dead, and then Shakespearean writing "rescues" the entire play. But that rescuing, there, becomes more than rescuing, more than the restoration of the substandard to the standard—more even than the restoration of the substandard to Shakespearean standard. For what gets written in *Pericles* is not (in those final three acts) simply a normal Shakespearean piece of writing, but that writing taken to the level of miracle. Miracle, from such a viewpoint, is not simply, for writing, what it writes, but what writes it. Shakespeare creates miracles in *Pericles* (as he does in *Cymbeline*), but miracles also create Shakespeare in *Pericles*: create a writer who is no longer simply "turned on" by inspiration—but by wonder and miracle—by the sighting of the possibility of the most difficult recovery. Such a writer does not only make a recovery: he witnesses it. Possibly, he also wonders at it.

What are we specifically referring to here? To a sensation produced by a particular kind of writing in Shakespeare's miracle plays, and to that sensation as a force that has invaded the dramatic sensibility of the spectator. What is this sensation? It is exactly what John Danby identifies in discussing the special quality of the moments of wonder in *Pericles*.

> The swimming suggestiveness of phrase . . . brings Shakespeare nearer to the romantics of the nineteenth century than to his contemporaries in the seventeenth. . . . Shakespeare's late verse is now, comparatively, a friable thing. Its aura of suggestion is shadowier than can be tabulated in terms of pun, or ambiguity, or multiple meaning. It is really an expansion of meaning beyond that which is immediately relevant or required, a constant quickening of the listener to have feelings immediately available, and a constant sudden overdraft on these.[1]

This commentary in itself perhaps looks rather "swimming" and romantically nebulous; but examined closely, it amounts, I think, to one of the most sophisticated and precise definitions ever made of Shakespeare's late writing. We can see how Danby's "expansion" and "overdraft" work even in those concluding lines of the Jupiter Vision: a poetic feeling is "immediately available"—but it comes from nowhere, except from some sudden source of verbal glory inexplicably uncovered in the poet's wandering attention.

As "overdraft" (Danby's term, above), such "expansion" of excessively immediate meaning is perhaps only possible against a background of lost, depleted, or absent meaning. Miracle, in other words, as I have already tried to suggest, depends on the preexistence of some form of emptiness or nothingness. In simple terms, this preexisting nothingness (or nonsignifying void) may simply be hopelessness: only when hope is abandoned utterly is the sighting of miracle structurally possible. But the "nothingness" necessary for miracle as a condition for its possibility is on the aesthetic and creative level something more complex and elusive. For you to be able to make a miracle of the very text you are writing, of the very drama you are imagining, it is somehow necessary that there be some radical flaw at hand: in your attention, in the plot, in the characters, in the movement, in the language, in the general feeling, in intensity, in color, whatever. "Expansion" in the miracle play *as miracle* is thus no ordinary expansion "of" meaning, but on the contrary the sudden arrival of meaning itself. Meaning lands like a spacecraft, suddenly is there in front of you, as UFO: alien, complex, full of dreaming more awake than reality. Meaning arrives from "nowhere." We thus see that Wilson Knight intelligently conjectures that in *Pericles* the peculiar beauty of the poetry *requires* some form of absence or inadequacy as generic condition of possibility: "Nowhere else does Shakespeare's sea-poetry move with quite so superb an ease; . . . as though . . . his deepest genius were enjoying a liberty hitherto unknown. Perhaps only whilst desultorily working over an old plot in which he scarce half-believed could such unsought-for excellence have matured."[2]

One is perhaps reluctant to admit the thesis that half-belief in a foundational plot needs to be seen as a result of being overly relaxed ("desultorily working"); but it is nevertheless obvious that the word *half-believed* accurately depicts the mood of the late plays: no spectactor "believes" in Pericles as he believes in Othello or Hamlet; Shakespeare himself can hardly have been as much under the skin of Pericles as he was under the skin of Othello or Hamlet. But what happens in the miracle plays is that some compensatory dash of genius suddenly becomes necessary for the purpose of recovering the play as an emotional and experiential whole: something drastic is needed to secure for the spectator the feeling that he has actually witnessed a rounded play, and to secure for the dramatist the feeling that he has actually written one (or even that he is writing one).

There comes, then, in the miracle plays, a moment (which I would not call a moment of crisis) where the "deadness" or inertia of the dramatic material suddenly itself lets the dramatist (and therefore also the spectator) glimpse the possibility of some unexpected glory. The question of the authorship of the "dead" parts of the miracle plays is from this viewpoint fairly academic: in *Pericles* it does not in the final analysis matter whether Shakespeare was or was not instrumental in the creation of the first two (linguistically substandard) acts. The answer to that question is very interesting from the scholarly viewpoint; but the question, or problem, is not actually going to *worry* any serious Shakespeare critic. What matters, as Kermode points out, is that

"Shakespeare's *interest* begins, substantially, with the third act."[3] This, in its turn, means that Shakespeare can become interested in something that, up to a point, does not really heat him up at all. Or it can mean that Shakespeare for a while works with a specific attitude (to his own writing, to the drama, to the story, to the characters, to the audience, to the medium, to language, to himself, to possibility); and that at some breaking point that attitude gives way to something else: possibly to another attitude, but more likely to the vanishing of "attitude" altogether. For "attitude" is a form of distancing, and miracle, precisely by implementing the type of unusual "immediacy" discussed by Danby above, dissolves distance.

Returning now to the Jupiter Vision in *Cymbeline*, we see that the crossing of the line of demarcation between the prosaic and the poetic (apathy and engagement) is there *not* accompanied by the sense of the miraculous. Miracles "in" the play are not miracles "for" the play. Nothing really happens to characters or words through contact with miracle as episode. On the contrary, episode remains episode, just as the Vision remains mere vision—indeed, just as Jupiter's Vision remains Jupiter's. Vision is not in any rich sense the visionary.

We may, if we like, try to overcome this negative appraisal by saying that the vision is confined by no means to Jupiter, but on the contrary to Posthumus, who is supposed to be experiencing it. But although Pericles and Posthumus have similar "visions" monitored from above as special "states" operative in their dazed consciousnesses, Posthumus cannot be filled with the visionary as Pericles can. This is partly so because Pericles is shown as a cosmic figure, a universal wanderer charged with the negativity of eternal human suffering—and Posthumus is no such figure of cosmic proportions. Posthumus is from this viewpoint far too human (far too much of an ordinary character of the illusionist type) to be capable of absorbing visionary purity. The mind of Posthumus is always too much of a plenary theater. It is not suited for the admittance of wonder as something truly foreign and astonishing. Nothing could astonish Posthumus *more* than what has already astonished him in human terms: the possibility of Imogen's infidelity. All supplementary "wonders" in the play fade by comparison.

This impotency in *Cymbeline*—one made more conspicuous for every "miracle" that vainly tries to fertilize it—seems to be actually mirrored in those concluding lines of the Jupiter Vision already reviewed. Magnificently, almost, those lines discuss the "nothing" that needs to be "in" the story for miracle to be able to work its belated wonders on creativity and drama. Yet that "nothing" in *Cymbeline* in a sense never moves out of the region of nothing: and the lines, reprinted below, seem to recognize this. Out of nothing comes nothing: and this time without the implicit accoutrements of bittersweet existential nostalgia (*King Lear*) or miraculous dumbness (*Pericles*). The play (or writing, if you like) almost seems to pity its own voidness, or to want to tenderly recognize such voidness in modest terms of mere "sympathy."

> 'Tis still a dream: or else such stuff as madmen
> Tongue, and brain not: either both, or nothing,
> Or senseless speaking, or a speaking such
> As sense cannot untie. Be what it is,
> The action of my life is like it, which
> I'll keep, if but for sympathy.
>
> (5.4.146–51)

The experience of Vision here leads to a drastic sense of uncertainty; and this uncertainty, as dominant emotion, is nothing that miracle will ever dissipate in *Cymbeline*. Only plot will do that. Posthumus, like the rest of us, will come to know everything worth knowing about the "mysteries" of his world; but he will never come to know the mystical as such.

Unrecognized Miracle

It must be said, then, that the Jupiter Vision does nothing for *Cymbeline*. (The similarly all-powerful "Oracle" in *The Winter's Tale* threatens to claim an equally centristic power for itself, and thus to overorganize the drama noetically in corresponding fashion.)

My overall purpose, however, is not to join the chorus of critics voicing the insufficiencies of *Cymbeline* or to pay any special attention to the quarrel over the "successfulness" of the play. What interests me is (1) the manner in which *Cymbeline* deviates structurally from the strong miracle play (*Pericles, The Winter's Tale*) and (2) the way in which *Cymbeline* utilizes the structural mechanisms surrounding the possibility of the dramatization of miracle in order to create its own "equivalent" of a miracle—a perverse form of "miracle" that I shall presently be identifying as "unrecognized miracle." Unrecognized miracle is a "miracle" that is recognized neither by the spectator nor by the protagonist participating in its action. "Unrecognized miracle" is not *there,* as it were, except in the perspective opened by perversity, or perverse seeing. Such perverse seeing is to a certain extent what the critic himself brings along to the play: what the play yields once looked at from the "perverse" perspective. On the other hand, however, *Cymbeline* itself is stuffed with perversity—and stuffed (like *Troilus and Cressida*) with encouragement that is perverse, encouragement to view action and episode from the *viewpoint of the perverse.*

Understanding that kind of perversity in *Cymbeline* requires first of all an understanding and appreciation of what in that play amounts to a sense of irreducible ugliness. This irreducible ugliness, in a sense operative already in *King Lear,* is almost thematized in the play. It culminates in the scene where Imogen finds the beheaded villain Cloten dressed up as her lover Posthumus. She falls on the corpse in the tragic ecstasy of an absolutely sincere adoration. (In passing, I call attention once more to the forestructuring role played by the word *nothing.*) We are now in the Welsh mountain cave inhabited by the princes and their guardian; Arviragus has previously carried in the supposedly dead body of Imogen, and Belarius, more recently, has placed the headless body of Cloten (killed as an intruder) close to Imogen.

Imogen. O gods and goddesses!
(Seeing the body of Cloten.)
These flowers are like the pleasures of the world;
This bloody man, the care on't. I hope I dream:
For so I thought I was a cave-keeper,
And cook to honest creatures. But 'tis not so:
'Twas but a bolt of nothing, shot at nothing,
Which the brain makes of fumes. Our very eyes
Are sometimes like our judgements, blind. Good faith,
I tremble still with fear: but if there be
Yet left in heaven as small a drop of pity
As a wren's eye, fear'd gods, a part of it!
The dream's here still: even when I wake it is
Without me, as within me: not imagin'd, felt.
A headless man? The garments of Posthumus?
I know the shape of's leg: this is his hand:
His foot Mercurial: his Martial thigh:
The brawns of Hercules: but his Jovial face—
Murder in heaven! How—? 'Tis gone. Pisanio,

All curses madded Hecuba gave the Greeks,
And mine to boot, be darted on thee! Thou,
Conspir'd with that irregulous devil, Cloten,
Hast here cut off my lord. To write, and read
Be henceforth treacherous! Damn'd Pisanio
Hath with his forged letters (damn'd Pisanio)
From this most bravest vessel of the world
Struck the main-top! O Posthumus, alas,
Where is thy head? where's that? Ay me! where's that?
Pisanio might have kill'd thee at the heart,
And left this head on. How should this be, Pisanio?
'Tis he, and Cloten: malice and lucre in them
Have laid this woe here. O, 'tis pregnant, pregnant!
The drug he gave me, which he said was precious
And cordial to me, have I not found it
Murd'rous to th' senses? That confirms it home:
This is Pisanio's deed, and Cloten—O!
Give colour to my pale cheek with thy blood,
That we the horrider may seem to those
Which chance to find us. O, my lord! my lord!
(Falls on the body.)
(4.2.295–332)

If we for a moment bracket the emotional context as given by the plot (a decontextualization persistently encouraged by the play itself), we see that this scene in fact is a recognition scene: "I know the shape of's leg: this is his hand: / His foot Mercurial: his Martial thigh: / The brawns of Hercules" (4.2.309–11). But the recognition is as it were incomplete. This is not mainly so because the headless body is not Posthumus (it is Cloten), but because the head is missing. It is true that the missing head, if supplied, would close the gap between heroine and audience: she too would realize that Posthumus is not dead at all. But the missing head does not simply have that kind of function on the hyperontological level. There, on the contrary, the missing head is what *enables* this scene to be a "recognition scene." Recognition here, no less transcendental than any other recognition from the viewpoint of ecstatic transport in the subject, is not recognition lacking a head, but on the contrary *headless recognition*. The recognition scene itself is headless, and the missing head has to be there, as missing, to complete that mutation of recognition itself. From this hyperontological perspective, just about everything and everyone is headless here: the scene, the body, love, Imogen, Posthumus, Cloten, the spectator, language, art . . . Shakespeare. "To write, and read / Be henceforth treacherous!"

(4.2.316–17). What is grotesque is no longer securely the "subject matter" of the artifact; it has become, instead, the perfume of a general perversity invading also the exterior conditions of art: artist, audience, medium, the integrity of a craft. "O! / Give colour . . . That we the horrider may seem to those / Which chance to find us" (4.2.329–32). But who are those that chance to find this oddly transcendental (or transcendentally odd) couple if not all the spectators? We find them "horrider" (more horrid than the horrid), because the horrible here can no longer play a dialectical game with its opposite: with transcendental beauty. It is not only that Imogen actually soils herself (personally and aesthetically) by becoming too intimate with the most detested man in her life; and it is not only that a transcendental aesthetics is here charged with the stench of constructional and emotional impurities. It is that writing itself, here, as a transcendental activity, is a questionable, perhaps for a moment even detestable, business. When the author permits Imogen to move around *looking* for Posthumus' missing head, he not only drags her into a region of theatrical and linguistic vulgarity, he also makes sure that the transcendentality of high aesthetic suggestion itself gets vulgarized: "but his Jovial face— / Murder in heaven! How—? 'Tis gone" (4.2.311–12). "O Posthumus, alas, / Where is thy head? where's that? Ay me! where's that?" (4.2.320–21). Drama is looking for its head here. And so is language.

The spectator, himself headless, is of course entitled at this point to go on admiring all that is felicitous in the language of Shakespeare and in the motion of the dramatic artifact. As critic, he is even entitled to smooth over the obscenities thrown at him here, and to distance the grotesque as motif, imagery, "style," or whatever. Yet what Shakespeare in this passage has coined as the "irregulous" (4.2.315) is in the final analysis not only an attribute of Cloten's, but of art and writing themselves in *Cymbeline:* what the Arden editor glosses as the "absence or disregard of rule." Drama is here not only irregular but irregulous; not only law-defiant but "lawless."[4] To be without a head does not mean to break the law. It means to lack knowledge of it—at least until the time of the restoration of the head. (Posthumus/love eventually regains its head, and so, if you like, do art and linguistic integrity.)

The Arden editor correctly identifies this soliloquy of Imogen's as "the finest thing in the play."[5] What I am analyzing as "perverse miracle" in this scene thus needs to be reviewed with a considerable amount of critical seriousness. It may well be that many a spectator experiences the scene on the banal level of what the Arden editor calls the "farcical" or "ludicrous";[6] but any alert critic looking for a structural clue to *Cymbeline* and to the late plays in general cannot treat its bizarreness merely as something intellectually "light";[7] nor can we make the comfortable assumption that Imogen's grotesquely mistaken adoration of the villain's sensual-but-headless outline is "soon forgotten" because Shakespeare "resolves" the hideousness with characteristic "grace."[8] I see no "grace" here at all, least of all "grace liberating the spirit of comedy."[9] Comedy is present (the corpse is not that of Posthumus, mistaken identity calls for laughter), tragedy is present (Imogen's inner pain is that of genuine despair), and the macabre is present (Imogen actually does search for the missing head, she actually does moisten her face with the blood of the man who wanted to rape her)—but these three things (comedy, tragedy, and the grotesque) do not intermix so as to neutralize one another on a "higher" level of aesthetic resolution.

What actually is negotiated on the hyperontological level may now perhaps be grasped by first reconsidering the words spoken by Imogen upon waking up in the Welsh cave, once a tranquil protective womb but now the locus of a horrid, monstrous, and headless invader. (A psychoanalytical reading is at this point helpful.)

I'll lie down and sleep.
But, soft! no bedfellow?[10] O gods and goddesses!
(Seeing the body of Cloten.)
These flowers are like the pleasures of the world;
This bloody man, the care on't. I hope I dream:
For so I thought I was a cave-keeper,
And cook to honest creatures. But 'tis not so:
'Twas but a bolt of nothing, shot at nothing,
Which the brain makes of fumes. Our very eyes
Are sometimes like our judgements, blind. Good faith,
I tremble still with fear: but if there be
Yet left in heaven as small a drop of pity
As a wren's eye, fear'd gods, a part of it!
The dream's here still: even when I wake it is
Without me, as within me: *not imagin'd, felt.*
A headless man? The garments of Posthumus?
I know the shape of's leg: this is his hand:
His foot Mercurial: his Martial thigh:
The brawns of Hercules

(4.2.294–311; italics mine)

I repeat: this is a *recognition scene*. It matters little, on the hyperontological level of suggestion now reaching the spectator, that the object of recognition is missing/absent/mistaken. What matters in a recognition scene in Shakespeare's late plays is recognition as such. As such, recognition has certain (dramatic and hyperdramatic) properties. These properties, the "interior" qualities of the recognitional moment, are what get focused in late-Shakespearean drama. In the early comedies, recognition serves plot; in the late plays, plot serves recognition. Thus recognition is no longer a mere question of identifying someone, discovering the true presence or identity of another person. On the contrary, recognition itself has to be discovered. The object and person of recognition can, as we see in *Cymbeline*, actually be forgotten or bracketed for the moment. In fact, once adopted, this technique of foregrounding recognition at the expense of the presence of the recognized moves most easily into its systems of creative totalization and dramatic perfection when identity in the normal sense is out of play. Imogen's ability to *recognize* Posthumus is in a strange way more prominent, as will-to-recognize, in a scene where Posthumus is absent than in a scene (given later) where he is present. Nowhere is Posthumus recognized *more* by Imogen than in this scene where he is effaced by Cloten, and where his missing head is Cloten's missing head. When Imogen looks around to find and replace the head of Posthumus, she is really looking around for the head of Cloten—she is really about to reattach *it*. But this macabre quest for the reassemblage of identity (a reassemblage that only promotes the further disarrangement of identity) is not, as I have said, primarily focused on identity, but on reassemblage itself. Shakespeare seems to be willing to go exceedingly far to ensure this superiority of recognition over presence, of the recognitional ecstasy over the recognized person. Thus he actually *alters* the physiognomy of Cloten, so that the various idiosyncratic features of his body truly become identical with those of Posthumus.

This move is quite ridiculous and irrational from the viewpoint of plot, psychology, and human probability. Moreover, it is aesthetically grotesque to create a villain who is physically speaking the identical twin of the hero, and to create a heroine who is so lacking in the powers of physical discrimination that she mixes up the body of her unique lover with the body of the most eminent lout in the country. But in the late plays, Shakespeare seems willing to take all kinds of risks in order to shift the question of identity from the locus of character to the locus of ecstatic recognition. Even in the cases of Marina and Hermione, it can be said that the recognition of recognition is more important than the recognition of person, identity, or presence. What makes Marina and Hermione objects of glory for the person recognizing them is not simply their identity as it preexisted the moment of recognition, but the "light" of recognition itself. As ecstasy, recognition sheds light not only on the one recognizing a presence but also on the object being recognized. Human identity "partakes" of a hyperidentity generated by recognition as recognition. When I meet a person I have missed for several years, what "lights up" the occasion is not simply the inner factualness of the other person's human identity, but the light of recognition itself.

In her sensitive discussion of the nature of recognition in the late plays, Inga-Stina Ewbank correctly remarks that *Pericles* displays a linguistic power in which Shakespeare gets "as close" as he ever did to "expressing the inexpressible."[11] Ewbank also points out that dialogue in the recognition scene "*creates* character."[12] This notion, in its turn, is structurally related to a sensation identified by Anne Barton (also discussing *Pericles*): that "Shakespeare appears to be using Marina less as a character than as a kind of medium, through which the voice of the situation can be made to speak."[13] But what is this *voice of the situation?* It is the voice, in the scenes involving the sense of miracle, of recognition itself. If the situation is recognition, and if the situation has a "voice," then recognition itself must have a "voice." But this is exactly what I am saying about the "perverse" recognition scene in *Cymbeline* (the one involving the wrong object for the right sense of recognition): that here the ecstatic recognition formula of the late plays is rehearsed, but this time with a *totalized* sense of the superiority of the voice of the situation over the situation, of voice over substance.

Barton argues that "*Cymbeline,* in its final scene, deliberately treats its plot material as unreal."[14] And I would like to extend that statement so as to make it applicable to other parts of the play. The "recognition scene" just reviewed is a good example of such an unrealizing of plot for the sake of the foregrounding of the "voice" of the moment. The moment *itself* can of course have a "voice" (distinguishable from the discourse of characters) only if the characters somehow are voiceless. (We are back here in the issue of "muteness" focused in our early discussions of *Pericles*.)

This displacement of "voice," which is a general possibility rather than a general phenomenon in late-Shakespearean drama, is related to a process of abdication, in which language progressively decides to loosen itself from the requirements of meaning. Barton touches this issue: "A number of critics have felt that Shakespeare, in his Last Plays, destroyed that close relationship between language and dramatic character which had seemed the permanent achievement of his maturity."[15] "It is not easy," she observes, "to see why a dramatist who had so triumphantly [affirmed] verbal expression . . . should suddenly decide to sacrifice the accomplishment."[16] But this "sacrifice" of expression and verbal triumph is what I have all along been focusing under the rubric of "muteness": that "voice," in the ordinary sense, is often put out of proper action in the late plays. "Over and over again, Shakespeare jettisons consistency of characterisation because he is more interested in the impersonal quality of a moment of dramatic time."[17] Webster's dictionary defines the noun *jettison* as "a voluntary sacrifice of cargo to lighten a ship's load in time of distress." And we have seen how the evacuation of Thaisa from the distressed ship in *Pericles* amounted, quite literally, to this very sacrifice. But that sense of the sacrifice of a specific character/person in the late plays also slides over into the intermittent presence of a general sacrifice of character and person—or of their "voice." In a sense the beheading of Cloten/Posthumus (which is also the grafting of the cutting of the one onto the cutting of the other) is such sacrifice, such jettison. A headless character is the very guarantee of muteness, and the *recognition of such a headless person* promises in a priori fashion to be reflected in the muteness of the most astonished "silent wonder." No wonder could be more silent, more wondrous, than that of the character Cloten, headlessly and mindlessly "absorbing" the praise and adorations of Imogen. (What is more characteristic of Cloten throughout the play than his mindlessness and headlessness? What is more natural for him than headless love?)

Ewbank decides to frame her discussion of recognition and language in the notions of unity, presence, and identity. In *Pericles,* Shakespeare makes the discovery "of a peculiar oneness of plot, character and language."[18] "His art lies in making style and subject one."[19] In the case of Marina, "the real miracle lies in what and who she *is*."[20] I think it is fair to say that this impression is generally speaking accurate, certainly with respect to *Pericles* taken as an isolated instance of the language of recognition. Things become a bit more complex, however, as soon as we wish to find a theory for recognition as such in the late plays. In

Pericles, Ewbank observes, the dialogue between the hero and his daughter "enables us to share in the interaction of two minds, in the movement towards mutual discovery, and in the arrival at full recognition, with all that it means."[21] At the same time Ewbank has just said that Pericles and Marina do not have "anything like the fullness of Lear and Cordelia," and that, as we have seen, "dialogue in this scene *creates* character."[22]

The contradiction, then (in Shakespeare rather than Ewbank) is that we get "full recognition" between characters who, as characters, do not have "anything like . . . fullness." Recognition creates the characters, but also the fullness. Moreover, recognition creates a *full* dialectical intercognition between characters that, a minute before the recognition, were not full at all—either as characters or as persons. There is a thin two-dimensional thing walking around called "Pericles," and there is a fragile and incomplete (certainly not "full") daughter of his needing to be recognized: but in the recognitional movement the energy of recognition actually gives radiant substance to those half-empty molds of human presence. *What* the two recognize in each other, paradoxically, is the fullness they never have had—at least not for the spectator. Fullness is in this way retrospectively created; and "voice" is given belatedly by recognition to characters who have really lacked ordinary dramatic voice from the outset.

Ewbank's statement, cited a moment ago, that Marina's "real miracle lies in and what she *is*" now becomes somewhat problematical. In order to be able to recognize something, I must situate myself in relation to an object that preexists my act of recognition. But here in late-Shakespearean recognition, the object (or at least its fullness) is *created* by the recognition that encompasses it. This means that recognition and its object are somehow "simultaneous" in miraculous recognition as outlined by Shakespeare. Thus recognition is not re-cognition at all. It is not the resuscitation of a cognition: both cognition and recognition are of a piece. Perhaps that, in Shakespearean miracle, is what is most miraculous.

Within the givens of this general Shakespearean mechanism, recognition is at once unstable and stable. In the case of Marina, as Ewbank has observed, there is primarily a dominant sense of balance and ontological centering. Marina *is* Pericles' daughter—and that fact in itself is pivotal. Pericles is overcome by a fact. In *Cymbeline,* however, Shakespeare has exploited the opposite potential in the peculiar mechanism of his recognition device: the simultaneity of the emergence of recognition and the emergence of its sudden object is a simultaneity that can be taken to the creative, experimental, and logical limit where recognition moves ecstatically through the negative outline of its opposite (Cloten instead of Posthumus). Imogen *recognizes* an object ("I know the shape of's leg: this is his hand: / His foot Mercurial: his Martial thigh" [4.2.309–11]) and is not merely deceived by an outer garment; but our impression of a consolidation of the sense of recognizant accuracy is in uncanny fashion fused with our own prior noetic certainty that Imogen's ecstasy is operative outside the bounds of empirical reality. An invisible screen has materialized between miracle on the stage and miracle as a possible happening in the audience.

What we have said so far on the subject of "recognition" in the "headless" scene of *Cymbeline* can from the viewpoint of narrowly empiricist criticism simply be written off as a question of knowledge: Imogen does not know what the audience knows. Unfortunately, however, the empirical viewpoint explains very little in the higher regions of Shakespearean signification. What the hyperontological perspective permits us to understand, it seems to me, is the peculiar ontological complexity of "recognition" as a dramatic device in the last plays. If the supreme dramatist of our civilization in one of his last plays fabricates a scene involving the question of recognition, and if the commentator in the most scholarly established edition of that play views that scene as one of centermost dramatic importance, then we cannot lightheartedly assume that recognition here is something banal—involving the mere "either—or" of correct-versus-incorrect knowing. Least of all can we cling to such a neat assumption while knowing that recognition as such is at stake for Shakespeare in most of his late plays. It is hardly likely that recognition is something ontologically poignant in *Pericles* and *The Winter's Tale*, and then *not* something ontologically poignant in that astonishingly perverse recognition scene between Imogen and Cloten/Posthumus.

What this issue boils down to, essentially, is the question of representation. Ewbank's commentary has already called our attention to this. In an unprecedented fashion, Shakespeare gets close "to expressing the inexpressible."[23] Wanting to express the inexpressible is wanting to represent the unrepresentable. For Ewbank this involves wanting to shortcut representation (an interesting notion that I shall be returning to), to have presentation (or presencing) without *re*-presentational work. Through an uncanny "literalness"[24] ("My name is Marina") there is a meeting of the strange and the true, a "peculiar closeness of word and fact."[25] It is clear, however, that "literalness" as such cannot create the sense of miracle, least of all in the Shakespearean sense. Shakespeare certainly uses "simple words" in the ecstasy of Pericles, words that "simply refer";[26] yet it is clear that simple empirical reference and stylistic literalness cannot by themselves produce language as miracle, or the sense of it. To be very literal and referentially simple ("My name is John") in itself produces no miraculousness, but the very opposite.

Clearly, then, something exceedingly sophisticated is going on in the miracle plays, something that makes the naiveté of their linguistic representationalism not simplicity but the semblance of simplicity. I have already outlined the condition of possibility for such late-Shakespearean sophistication (simplicity-as-sophistication, sophistication-as-simplicity) by discussing the dexterous aesthetic moves through which Shakespeare founds his miraculous ecstasies on the absencing of foundation or ground. I have called attention, in other words, to various types of negation and sacrifice (similar to those made by great chess players in order to gain a sudden advantage many, many moves later) that prepare the ground for miracle by removing ground: sacrifice of meaning, "voice," fullness, identity, expression, all dramatic "law." It is through this process, in my view, that the experience of miracle operates, not only through the assertion of fact, the establishment of "pure," immediate reference. During miracle, Shakespeare's words *seem* to be (re)presenting a recovered object, and they seem to be identical with the triumphant presencing of that object; but what the words really try to represent is the unrepresentable itself. This unrepresentable thing, far from being the object/person of recovery/recognition, is the ongoing sensation of miraculousness. If the problem is that of "expressing the inexpressible," and if the artist really accepts that challenge as such, he cannot circumnavigate the difficulty by presencing an object or person that represents the inexpressible. On the contrary, he has to find out what the inexpressible *is*. And the inexpressible, unlike a person/object, is in the final analysis not reducible to "is." A miracle may be based on a fact. But it itself is not a fact. Least of all is its sensation a factual sensation.

Headlessness

Ewbank, of course, is not saying that miracle is mere fact; she is calling attention to an awesome linguistic pruning that in *Peri-*

cles makes the language of wonder strangely transparent: as if Shakespeare, just by pointing at reality, could make us sense some strange potency for the wondrous in it. In a way, this impression of naiveté is operative in the crucial "recognition scene" in *Cymbeline* too. The scene, I hope, is one we are learning to recognize:

> O gods and goddesses!
> *(Seeing the body of Cloten.)*
> These flowers are like the pleasures of the world;
> This bloody man, the care on't. I hope I dream:
> For so I thought I was a cave-keeper,
> And cook to honest creatures. But 'tis not so:
> 'Twas but a bolt of nothing, shot at nothing,
> Which the brain makes of fumes. Our very eyes
> Are sometimes like our judgements, blind. Good faith,
> I tremble still with fear: but if there be
> Yet left in heaven as small a drop of pity
> As a wren's eye, fear'd gods, a part of it!
> The dream's here still: even when I wake it is
> Without me, as within me; *not imagin'd*, felt.
> A headless man? The garments of Posthumus?
> I know the shape of's leg: this is his hand:
> His foot Mercurial: his Martial thigh:
> The brawns of Hercules: but his Jovial face—
> Murder in heaven! How—? 'Tis gone.
>
> (4.2.295–312)

This scene, I claim once more, is a recognition scene—and it is a recognition scene in the vicinity of the region of Shakespearean miracle not in spite of its missing object, but because of it. The object of recognition is always in abyss prior to strong miraculous experience in Shakespeare's last plays. This is "perverse" miracle: that Cloten, headless as usual, should be adored by Imogen in an ecstasy accelerating through the tender viewing of headlessness itself. A further term I have used is "unrecognized miracle." As miracle, recognition is based on nonrecognition. As recognition, nonrecognition itself is the wondrousness. The moment is not visionary, but it is potentially visionary, structurally visionary. Imogen may be transported into ecstatic grief; but the real ecstasy belongs to Cloten. He has no visionary moment, but he *would* have had one, had he known what Imogen had in store for him on the transcendental level of erotic adoration. That he has no head at this moment only adds to the wondrousness of this unlikely—this impossible—scene: that Imogen should love him, love him without a head, adore him without a head . . . go looking for his head. We do not need to recognize the validity of all of this; it is, as I have said, *un*recognized miracle. An unrecognized miracle, in the strong sense, needs to endure as unrecognized—needs to always be sure of only being partly recognized. The only figure who would wholly have recognized this miracle as miracle is a fool. "Cloten."

Of course much of the soliloquy, but not all, flirts with the foolish; notice the play of the gods: "foot Mercurial," "Martial thigh," "Jovial face." Mercury, Mars, Jupiter. But Jupiter is missing (though we recognize him in the Jupiter Vision). Jupiter is murdered; there is chaos in heaven: "but his Jovial face— / Murder in heaven! How—? 'Tis gone" (4.2.311–12). The Jovial face, the face of Jupiter, is gone: the body of the god (adored by Imogen) is without a head, without a godhead, without a god. And what replaces the head?—the god? Nothing. The head of the god is gone forever. On the empirical level of interpretation that is what defers miracle (the stereotypical restoration of Posthumus to Imogen); on the hyperontological level of interpretation, the absence of the head prematurely negotiates miracle itself—but as perversity, its only strong form in *Cymbeline*.

Nothingness is not only the void left by the head, but is in the soliloquy what Imogen refers to as "a bolt of nothing, shot at nothing" (4.2.300). This nothingness first points to the now-dreamlike world of Welsh mountains and idyllic cave-keeping. But for the spectator (and perhaps for Imogen too), it is the very contrast between the rustic idealism of the cave and the grotesque brutishness of the headless lover that triggers the general sense of "nothing, shot at nothing." One unreality faces another. Wales now seems unreal, and so does the experience of perceiving a headless corpse as her "bedfellow" (4.2.295).

But if the two unrealities are equal in one sense, they are unequal in a more important sense. Both unrealities are referred to in terms of dream (4.2.300, 306), yet one of them (cave-life) feels like something imaginative (the past as paradisal fiction), while the other feels like something *not* imaginative:

> The dream's here still: even when I wake it is
> Without me, as within me: *not imagin'd*, felt.
>
> (4.2.306–7)

On the simple level of paraphrase and empirical psychology, signification is banal enough: This nightmare is real whether my eyes are shut or not, whether I am dreaming or awake. But on the hyperontological level, one dealing with the ontological abyss of the entire drama, the *absence of imagination* is by no means a trivial thing, even when occurring only on the level of minute linguistic detail. This minute linguistic unit ("not imagined") reverberates against the emotional frame of the entire scene: that fascination, throughout, is somehow negotiated by imagination's absence. (Cannot Imogen—or even Shakespeare—make something better of headlessness than *this*?)

Imogen is fascinated by the body of "Posthumus" (Cloten); we too are fascinated—almost paralyzed—by the body, but also by her fascination. Yet the spell that in this way is produced is not cast by the manufacturing imagination but by its imbecilic annihilation. Imogen seems to be unable to perform the most ordinary reading of reality, and this unreaderliness seems to spread everywhere. Idiotically, she fondles the various parts of the villain's body, lingering lovingly over details reminding her of the precise gallantries of his physical charm. Cloten, thanks to this odd "recognition," emerges for a moment as a sort of horizontal equivalent of the miraculous statue in *The Winter's Tale*. In an uneasy interlude—at once furtive and extended—Cloten is grotesquely "heroic": half hero, half mummy; a body without a head, but also the transcendental body of headlessness itself.

This queer miraclizing of Cloten is not imagined by the play. On the contrary, it is negotiated through a general draining of imaginative richness.

Normally, what is real in a play is what is imagined—what it imagines and what gets imagined in it. But this play seems to want to move toward a site where there is a complication of this traditional sense of imaginative representation. Imogen again: "not imagined, felt" (4.2.307). Reality, starkly, is what is not imagined, not what is imagined. But this "principle" may be regarded in an encompassing way as somehow crucial for the entire structuration of the last plays: *feeling something without imagining it*.

"Imbecility," here, is no longer a personal and merely-private characteristic, but a hyperontological mode. Imogen and Cloten are *joined* on this level. Cloten's inability to think is not merely a stupidity in him; it is a form of ontological victimization that he personifies. His inability to think is not simply his lack of intelligence, but his lack of imagination. On the empirical level it is infinitely unbefitting that Imogen should love a headless Cloten, but on the hyperontological level this tenderness for the headless is perfectly befitting—almost a work of art. It is the triumph of the absence of Cloten's head over Cloten. It is the triumph, *literally*, of unimaginable love.

Shakespeare, I have remarked, has already prepared us for this unimaginable transcendentality by showing us that Cloten is a man entirely incapable of imaginative thinking. We only have to look at his negative fascination with Imogen's phrase "his mean'st garment" to gauge this radical unimaginativeness. Imogen ridicules Cloten by infinitizing the status of Posthumus:

> *Imogen*. He never can meet more mischance than come
> To be but nam'd of thee. *His mean'st garment*,
> That ever hath but clipp'd his body, is dearer
> In my respect, than all the hairs above thee,
> Were they all made such men. How now, Pisanio!
>
> *(Enter Pisanio.)*
>
> *Cloten*. "His garment!" Now, the devil—
> *Imogen*. To Dorothy my woman hie thee presently.
> *Cloten*. *"His garment!"*
> *Imogen*. I am sprited with a fool,
> Frighted, and anger'd worse. Go bid my woman
> Search for a jewel, that too casually
> Hath left mine arm: it was thy master's. 'Shrew me,
> If I would lose it for a revenue
> Of any king's in Europe! I do think
> I saw't this morning: confident I am.
> Last night 'twas on mine arm; I kiss'd it:
> I hope it be not gone to tell my lord
> That I kiss aught but he.
> *Pisanio*. 'Twill not be lost.
> *Imogen*. I hope so: go and search. *(Exit Pisanio.)*
> *Cloten*. You have abus'd me:
> *"His meanest garment!"*
> *Imogen*. Ay, I said so, sir:
> If you will make't an action, call witness to't.
> *Cloten*. I will inform your father.
> *Imogen*. Your mother too:
> She's my good lady; and will conceive, I hope,
> But the worst of me. So I leave you, sir,
> To th'worst of discontent. *(Exit.)*
> *Cloten*. I'll be reveng'd:
> *"His mean'st garment!"* Well. *(Exit.)*
>
> (2.3.131–55)

The iteration of the "garment" unit is meant to suggest the thick-headedness of Cloten as well as the intensity of his private astonishment and sexual humiliation. Yet the iteration passes energetically and obstinately beyond that point—almost becomes more ludicrous than the character speaking it. We feel here that Cloten has difficulties *imagining* the scope of his erotic defeat: he has never imagined such a possibility, and he *goes on* being unable to do so.

Cloten's ridiculously overdetermined decision to at all cost negotiate his revenge through Posthumus' suit appears to demonstrate that he has actually understood the full implications of Imogen's verbal assault; but the ever-renewed obsession with the word *garment* might also suggest a continued inability to imagine the challenge in signifying proportion to its context. Cloten plods abstractly on inside the empty snowballing of *garment*—until *its* imagination (the word's own power and theater) seduces the villain into a ludicrously stereotypical and simpleminded revenge drama. The word *garment* has itself imagined this theatrical scenario. What Anne Barton discussed some time ago as the shifting of voice from character to situation (giving the impersonality of the moment itself a voice in the late plays) is here taken a step further: not only the moment but the *word* has a voice of its own. This voice/word (word-as-voice, voice-as-word) is what dominates and empowers action here. *Garment*.

So absent is Cloten from his own (revenge) play, here, that he has to remind himself ("which, as I say," below) of its inventive factualness. His imagination is similar to that of soccer hooligans: he can "imagine" and "create" the extreme possibility of gross destruction precisely because imagination and creativity are utterly exterior things, functions of the preexisting symbolic order of dialectical myth (winner takes all) rather than of imaginative innerness as such:

Cloten. Wilt thou serve me?
Pisanio. Sir, I will.
Cloten. Give me thy hand, here's my purse. Hast any of thy late master's garments in thy possession?
Pisanio. I have my lord, at my lodging the same suit he wore when he took leave of my lady and mistress.
Cloten. The first service thou dost me, fetch that suit hither, let it be thy first service, go.
Pisanio. I shall, my lord. *(Exit.)*
Cloten. Meet thee at Milford-Haven! (I forgot to ask him one thing, I'll remember't anon) even there, thou villain Posthumus, will I kill

> thee. I would these garments were come. She said upon a time (the bitterness of it I now belch from my heart) that she held the very garment of Posthumus in more respect than my noble and natural person; together with the adornment of my qualities. With that suit upon my back, will I ravish her: first kill him, and in her eyes; there shall she see my valour, which will then be a torment to her contempt. He on the ground, my speech of insultment ended on his dead body, and when my lust hath dined (which, *as I say,* to vex her I will execute in the clothes that she so prais'd) to the court I'll knock her back, foot her home again. She hath despis'd me rejoicingly, and I'll be merry in my revenge.
>
> (3.5.121–47)

Cloten's imaginative voidness (his uncontextualized situatedness with respect to Imogen, spectator, and himself) makes him oddly pliable for the purposes of "perverse miracle." His inability to imagine either hate or love makes him not only headless but mindless—and therefore, like a teddy bear, the possible object of unconditional "love" itself. When Imogen admires him as headless trunk and mindless corpse, and when she fondly fingers the heroic properties of his physical outline, then she is, as I have already claimed, somehow materializing the very erotic hope that the swaggering villain once proposed for himself: "With that suit upon my back, will I ravish her: . . . there shall she see my valour" (3.5.138–40).

Cloten is a mutation: "his honour / Was nothing but mutation" (4.2.132–33). But the mutation is on the hyperontological level not simply a degradation and negative perversity. As mutation, Cloten *fits* a transcendental "world" where love and recognition are themselves mutations. He is dead, to be sure; cannot "experience" Imogen's (misdirected) tenderness. But *we* can feel her loving hands on him. As "unrecognized miracle," the scene negotiates a sensation that is sensually real in the theater; yet sender and receiver are both absent from the signifying dialectic of love as "true communication."

In sum, something is "going on" between Cloten and Imogen on the play's own level of thinking (not to be confused with its imaginative center)—something that transcendentally speaking ought to worry Posthumus much more than the supposed erotic transactions between Iachimo and Imogen. Surely the spectator is in *some* way affected by the closeness between the death of Cloten and the death of Imogen (experienced by everyone as factual a moment before the recognition scene). Guiderius enters carrying Cloten's head (4.2.112) and a moment later (4.2.195)

Arviragus enters carrying Imogen's body. Conjointly situated in a mythlike landscape of fabulous grottoes, the two deaths cohabit a realm of shared theatrical vision where the spectator, without imagining anything at all, is witnessing an almost occult unfolding of empty mystifications.

The Resemblance of Miracle

Not long ago, I defined Shakespearean miracle hyperontologically by stating that recognition and its object are "simultaneous." Miracle does not simply restore an old version of Marina or Hermione: miracle actually creates those figures insofar as they are dramatically and imaginatively "complete" beings. Recognition is not merely a reproduction of cognition (of what once upon a time already has been in full view). The bedfellow of this structure is a parallel mechanism: as recognition and cognition are choreographed into simultaneity, so are representation and presentation. This structure is something we already have glimpsed in the cave scene where Imogen mistakenly falls in adoration on the body of the headless villain: there comes a point in the drama where the difference between resemblance and identity no longer really counts. In *The Winter's Tale* the resemblance of Hermione (the statue) becomes Hermione—and the "new" Hermione, the one born in miracle, carries with her into her new light some significant traces of her resemblance, her representation. She is a strange synthesis of the artificial and the natural, of representation and presence—of art and nature, if you like. The empirical and emotional conditions are quite different in the "unrecognized miracle" in *Cymbeline;* yet I would suggest that "recognition" there in an important sense (at least for the spectator) is generated by the same uncanniness: that the representation of Posthumus (i.e., Cloten) for a moment *is* Posthumus. I need to emphasize here that I am not speaking metaphorically, that I am not referring to an ordinary "as if" structure. When I say "is" I mean is. For half a minute Imogen is not operative in the normal, representational, ironic "as-if" world: limb for limb, instead, Cloten actually is Posthumus, feature for feature she actually recognizes *him*. In *The Winter's Tale,* in the same way, we for half a minute actually witness the mobile livingness of the *representation* of Hermione. We "recognize" a statue come alive rather than a woman come alive.

Cloten only has to utilize the crudest possible representational device (Posthumus' "garment"), a deliberately unspecified and nondescript disguise, for the representational thing to take power over language, identity, and action—and for him to merge with the represented. This abyssing of the difference between identity and representation, with specific reference to borrowed garments, can also be observed in *The Winter's Tale,* where Autolycus deceitfully and playfully refers to himself as an other and then suggests that this other ("Autolycus") has forced him to wear the garments he is wearing. Representation and identity are here circulated so as to be set in abyss.

> *Autolycus.* Some call him Autolycus.
> *Clown.* Out upon him! prig, for my life, prig: he haunts wakes, fairs, and bear-baitings.
> *Autolycus.* Very true, sir; he, sir, he: that's the rogue that put me into this apparel.
> (4.3.97–101)

Here the representational skewing is light, compatible with comedy; in the "recognition scene" in *Cymbeline* such skewing is *almost* compatible with comedy. What we are faced with, here, is a manipulative skewing of dialectic in general at crucial points in the last plays. And I think Anne Barton accurately identifies the crucial skewing mechanism when she discusses the last plays in terms of the mutation of antithesis (dialectic).

> Throughout his writing life, Shakespeare displayed a marked predilection for analysing situations by way of contraries or antitheses. Dualities and polar opposites are striking features of his style, superimposed upon the individual verbal habits of particular characters: darkness and light, frost and fire, summer and winter, love and hate. Elizabethans, trained as they were in the discipline of formal rhetoric, often thought in such patterns. With Shakespeare, however, certain words seem to summon up their opposites almost automatically, as the result of an ingrained habit of mind almost more than from the requirements of a particular situation or rhetorical pattern. This is the case especially with the true-false antithesis, as even a quick glance at the two words in the Shakespeare concordance will reveal. They are surprisingly constant companions. In the Last Plays, however, *something odd seems to happen to antithesis generally,* and to the true-false figure in particular.[27]

This notion of the breakdown of antithesis is operative in the structures I have discussed in terms of their transvaluation: representation-versus-identity, recognition-versus-object. Also dumbness and miracle are to be considered in relation to this demolition of dialectic. An apathetic deaf-mute like Pericles does not live in a dialogic world prior to miracle; nor is the father-versus-daughter ecstasy really a dialogic ecstasy. There is a dialogue and there is recognition, but there is not dialogic recognition. There is not dialectic. There is miracle. This uncanny dissipation of the sensation of antithesis was also functional, as we saw some considerable time ago, in the "comparisons" that *The Winter's Tale* tried to draw between mother and daughter. The mother/daughter relationship could not be placed in a satisfying dialectical mold because the daughter, as dead likeness of her mother, was already a dead likeness of a dead likeness. *In* Hermoine there already preexisted all the dialectical comparisons that the play (or thinking) could handle. All potential dialectic and comparation appeared to be internal to Hermione: as a crossover between life and its opposite, being and nothingness, or indeed the possible and the impossible, "she" had no really reflexive exterior outline at the end of the play. And that is a consequence of Shakespeare's miracle effect. Ewbank shows that this breakdown of antithesis is operative on the language/reality interface. In the ecstasy of *Pericles* words do not only tell "of" the reality they are supposed to be depicting: "The science of language would suggest that Pericles's words, like Marina's just quoted, are 'models' of an underlying reality. Our experience in the theatre is that they *are* reality."[28] In the perverse world of *Cymbeline* this erasure of antithesis from the interbalancing of thesis-versus-antithesis creates a persistent "lopsidedness" in our intellectual impression of the action.

The most fantastic instance of this, no doubt, is the occasion when General Caius Lucius bravely offers to ransom Imogen (disguised as boy) and takes it for granted—according to the humane logic of dialectical charity—that Imogen will do the same for him. Yet Imogen is not willing to be antithesis to his thesis, not even in matters of life and death. And she does not bother to give a serious excuse or explanation for her one-sided behavior:

Lucius. This one thing only
I will entreat, my boy (a Briton born)
Let him be ransom'd: never master had
A page so kind, so duteous, diligent,
So tender over his occasions, true,

So feat, so nurse-like: let his virtue join
With my request, which I'll make bold your highness
Cannot deny: he hath done no Briton harm,
Though he have serv'd a Roman. Save him, sir,
And spare no blood beside.

Cymbeline. I have surely seen him:
His favour is familiar to me. Boy,
Thou hast look'd thyself into my grace,
And art mine own. I know not why, wherefore,
To say, live boy: ne'er thank thy master, live;
And ask of Cymbeline what boon thou wilt,
Fitting my bounty, and thy state, I'll give it:
Yea, though thou do demand a prisoner,
The noblest ta'en.

Imogen. I humbly thank your highness.

Lucius. I do not bid thee beg my life, good lad,
And yet I know thou wilt.

Imogen. No, no alack,
There's other work in hand: I see a thing
Bitter to me as death: your life, good master,
Must shuffle for itself.

(5.5.83–105)

This abrupt dismissal of the General—and of what seems to be his life—is perhaps nothing to worry over: Imogen has more important things to attend to, and the huge "wondrous" denouement she is about to trigger will make a happy world for everyone to live in. Yet the spectator cannot avoid having this impression of dialectical incompletion added to all the other instances of improper balance already accumulated in the play. The *cutting* of dialectic (the removal of antithesis from thesis) is callous enough ("your life, good master, / Must shuffle for itself") to become a theatrical effect; and since being in the theater in an important way is experiencing a sequence of effects, Imogen's peculiar gesture becomes an item contributing to the impression of a general skewing.

It is possible, of course, to sense the workings of Shakespearean irony in the dialogue cited above. But irony and miracle, as I have claimed from the outset, are not quite compatible. It is this flirtation with irony (and sometimes with ordinary dramatic imagination, especially on the level of plot) that "disqualifies" *Cymbeline* as a strong miracle play. The comic and the miraculous cannot together create a miracle play. They can certainly create a play—*Cymbeline*—but that play will not be able to use its moments of "miracle" for the ecstasy of miracle—for miracle itself. Instead of miracle, we get "discovery," "surprise," and wonder as theatrical commonplace. In *Cymbeline* miracle is dead. I quote at some length from the "miraculous" denouement of the play to clarify the nature of miracle as dead miracle. (Posthumus has still not identified the "page" as Imogen, and he still believes that she is lost forever.) Notice how the play here apologizes for its own improbabilities. Our passage, however, starts with the strong moment in which Shakespeare has his unknowing hero strike the woman he loves:

Posthumus. The temple
Of Virtue was she; yea, and she herself.
Spit, and throw stones, cast mire upon me, set
The dogs o'th'street to bay me: every villain
Be call'd Posthumus Leonatus, and
Be villainy less than 'twas. O Imogen!
My queen, my life, my wife, O Imogen,
Imogen, Imogen!
Imogen. Peace, my lord, hear, hear—
Posthumus. Shall's have a play of this? Thou scornful page,
There lie thy part. *(Striking her: she falls.)*
Pisanio. O, gentlemen, help!
Mine and your mistress: O, my lord Posthumus!
You ne'er kill'd Imogen till now. Help, help!
Mine honour'd lady!
Cymbeline. *Does the world go round?*
Posthumus. How comes these staggers on me?
Pisanio. Wake, my mistress!
Cymbeline. If this be so, the gods do mean to strike me
To death with mortal joy.
Pisanio. How fares my mistress?
Imogen. O, get thee from my sight,
Thou gav'st me poison: dangerous fellow, hence!
Breathe not where princes are.
Cymbeline. The tune of Imogen!
Pisanio. Lady,
The gods throw stones of sulphur on me, if
That box I gave you was not thought by me
A precious thing: I had it from the queen.
Cymbeline. New matter still.
Imogen. It poison'd me.
Cornelius. O gods!
I left out one thing which the queen confess'd,
Which must approve thee honest. "If Pisanio
Have," said she, "given his mistress that confection
Which I gave him for cordial, she is serv'd
As I would serve a rat."

Cymbeline. What's this, Cornelius?
Cornelius. The queen, sir, very oft importun'd me
To temper poisons for her, still pretending
The satisfaction of her knowledge only
In killing creatures vile, as cats and dogs
Of no esteem. I, dreading that her purpose
Was of more danger, did compound for her
A certain stuff, which being ta'en would cease
The present power of life, but in short time
All offices of nature should again
Do their due functions. Have you ta'en of it?
Imogen. Most like I did, for I was dead.
Belarius. My boys,
There was our error.
Guiderius. This is sure Fidele.
Imogen. Why did you throw your wedded lady from you?
Think that you are upon a rock, and now
Throw me again. *(Embracing him.)*
Posthumus. Hang there like fruit, my soul,
Till the tree die.
Cymbeline. How now, my flesh, my child?
What, *mak'st thou me a dullard in this act?*
(5.5.220–65)

Certain images and lines are beautiful. But I think most commentators would agree with the view that miracle here, although striving toward the ecstatic, is not the ecstasy it is in *Pericles,* or indeed *The Winter's Tale.* Shakespeare tries to complete an intricate puzzle and a strong miracle at the same time—and the former interferes with the latter. Indeed "miracle" is in a sense almost exclusively the wonder produced by the ingenuity of the puzzle. The embarrassment at having to do so much last-minute "fixing" is shifted over from the artist onto the characters—just as the incredulousness of the spectator in apotropaic fashion is shouldered by unbelieving asides spoken by Cymbeline. The players themselves are on the verge of becoming unbelieving spectators—not of a miracle but of an intricate theatricality. The king laments that he is "a dullard in this act" (5.5.265); but as several critics have remarked, he is a dullard throughout the play. The queen has not really fared much better, and her death, acknowledged by Imogen as something that has made her "sorry" (5.5.270), is tagged by Cymbeline as something of considerable unimportance: "O, she was naught" (5.5.271).

In this way, undecidedly poised between comic play and miracle play, *Cymbeline* generally speaking reverses the flow and direction of the mystical. In drama acknowledging miracle as mystical ecstasy *(Pericles)*, miracle does not really "explain" the mystical, but instead finalizes it, monumentalizes it *(The Winter's Tale)*. Icon. Vision. Artifact. A new love. But *Cymbeline* does not quite know the trick of withholding imaginative fullness and then releasing the dams of the imagination in one single ecstatic burst (recognition as ecstasy). Instead *Cymbeline* mixes imaginative and antiimaginative techniques, comic wonder and miraculous wonder. It is of course impossible to know if this mixing is the deliberate result of an aesthetic experimentation or simply the artistic chaos created by the difficulties of a new dramatic challenge. Indeed, these two main alternatives might both be operative. We cannot know, in other words, whether *Cymbeline's* tendency to laugh at its own miracles is a strength in it or a weakness, the consequence of the fact that the artist now has "miracle" at some safe aesthetic distance or the consequence of the fact that he cannot always call forth miracle at short notice—that miracle is disappointingly difficult to produce by means of sheer dramatic willpower or sheer professional know-how.

There are signs, however, that the "excuses" made in *Cymbeline* are excuses *for* the play. King Cymbeline is openly amused not only at the impotencies of its miracles but also at the impotencies of its plot (a plot idealized by some critics as one of the seven wonders of the world). The ability of Belarius, Guiderius, and Arviragus to single-handedly defeat the Roman army is no miracle of any quasi-religious order, but certainly a wondrous and ludicrously improbable event from the viewpoint of martial art and dramatic construction. As the dramatist realizes, the feat is almost a joke (and a bad one). Therefore the apotropaic technique is used again, projecting the incredulousness of the spectator into the ironic commentary that is made to take place on the level of character and dialogue:

Lord: This was strange chance:
A narrow lane, an old man, and two boys.
Posthumus. Nay, *do not wonder at it: you are made*
Rather to wonder at the things you hear
Than to work any. Will you rhyme upon't,
And vent it for a mock'ry? Here is one:
"Two boys, an old man twice a boy, a lane,
Preserv'd the Britons, was the Romans' bane."
Lord. Nay, be not angry, sir.
Posthumus. 'Lack, to what end?

> Who dares not stand his foe, I'll be his friend:
> For if he'll do as he is made to do,
> I know he'll quickly fly my friendship too.
> You have put me into rhyme.
>
> (5.3.51–63)

The Arden editor provides this commentary:

> The whole force of Posthumus' remark . . . lies in the fact that the Lord is a foppish courtier who dabbles in verse (hence the rhymes that follow) and who was created rather to wonder at warlike ballads than to perform warlike deeds. Posthumus, then, scornfully tells him not to wonder at fact since he was born to wonder at fiction.[29]

An alternative interpretation is also possible: the Lord on this particular occasion is forced to abandon the (literary) creation of wonders in order to instead admire the wondrous achievements of others. By saying "do not wonder at it," Posthumus means "do not start your aesthetic kind of wonderment." "This historical event is not asking you to work any literary miracles/wonders, but to actually silence yourself in real wonder": you are made [by the military achievement] / Rather to wonder at the things you hear / Than to work any.

The general effect that Shakespeare produces, in any case, is that our attention is diverted from the emptiness of the play's own literary "wonder" (the absurd military fairy tale). Instead we are made to focus the bravery of the British fighters, a thing of such unquestionable importance that *no* aesthetic rationale of a literary kind should at all be allowed to interfere with wondrous admiration. The Lord, provisionally the prototypical inventor of unlikely "wonders," for a moment carries the entire burden of creative and poetic superficiality.

Aqua Vitae

The question of the aesthetic and theatrical fragility of *Cymbeline* has really brought us back in full-circle fashion to the issue that from the outset permitted us to inspect *Pericles* from a hyperontological perspective: the question of recovery. Miracle in *The Winter's Tale* alters the aesthetic and ontological status of the play; *Pericles* without its moment of ecstatic recognition is not a play at all, not anything really worth showing an audience. Shakespeare recognizes miracle as a matter of life and death for the play, for its ability to survive and make a lasting impression. He knows, in writing that final miracle in *The Winter's Tale,* that he is changing the entire fate of the play, not merely its structure. He knows, when animating *Pericles* with the lifeblood of his own poetry, that he is giving the "kiss of life" to what easily could be mistaken for a corpse.

Such a general perspective on the miracle plays in this way forces us to engage honestly with the question of failure. Numerous critics evade that type of honesty, finding "failure" and "Shakespeare" to be a metaphysical contradiction that upsets their conception of the world. How could the world's greatest dramatist finally have come to the verge of total failure?

But what kind of hero is Shakespeare? Is there not a heroism that needs to face the reality of failure too? And how could any sincere reviewer of the late plays ever avoid staring this issue straight in the face?

I have not discussed the current plays as failures. But I am going to complete a discussion already opened in this book long ago: that of thinking of the late plays in relation to failure. This relation is operative on various levels, all along the spectrum from minute linguistic detail to encompassing ontological frames. Let me begin by quoting a critic who actually decides to sink *Cymbeline.* I do not support his view, but I am citing it for the purpose of perspective and intellectual context. Johnson's view is familiar. Look now, for a change, at Hazelton Spencer's commentary:

> Of all the completed plays of Shakespeare's unaided authorship, this seems to me the poorest. . . . Cymbeline is every inch not a king. Cloten is uncertain whether to provide a role for the clown, the first heavy, or the leading juvenile. Posthumus Leonatus, the principal tenor, is simply incredible; compared with him, Beaumont and Fletcher's Philaster is positively a hero, and they give him more effective arias to sing. The mountain princes, though mere bundles of instinct, are fairly amusing cubs; but they are a poor substitute for Nature's dwarfs in the folk tale, and theirs is a fake primitivism since Papa Belarius is always on the job baby-tending his Noble Savages. Philario is a cipher. Iachimo is little more; and Shakespeare's failure to characterize him wrecks the play, as a comparable Iago would have wrecked *Othello.* Caius Lucius is just another imperturbable empire-builder. Pisanio and Cornelius, those bright vague angels of good works, are as characterless as the villain. . . . [Imogen] is, of course, a clumsily and carelessly executed Snow-White. . . .
>
> [Shakespeare] seems to be writing *Cymbeline* half asleep. . . . For

> the trouble with this play is mainly that Shakespeare lets poetry and artful characterization alone, and confines his attention almost exclusively to plot. . . . That my sentiments are shared by many lovers of Shakespeare I have no doubt; but the prevailing note of the critics is one of praise and, for Imogen, of ecstasy.[30]

Although this commentary is exaggerated, it is impressive. It is impressive because its sincerity does away with a characteristic hypocrisy automatically triggered by the study of anything in Shakespeare that is questionable. We too easily find excuses for Shakespeare, grateful as we are for having received from him the greatest gifts that literature can furnish. I think, in other words, that we *first* have to measure up a play like *Cymbeline* against ordinary Shakespearean norms, and that we *then* need to make an intellectual and evaluative judgment that starts out from some understanding of the difference between orthodox and unorthodox approaches to Shakespeare. Spencer does not do that. He takes the first step only and never bothers to question his own premises. The always-enthusiastic Shakespeare critics do not even do that. They pretend that a play like *Cymbeline* is still real within the fixed norms of Shakespearean orthodoxy, and with that wrong set of premises still attempt to create the illusion that Shakespeare is managing splendidly. The former error, that of Hazelton Spencer, is to cry "failure," and to stop at that. The latter error is to cry "success," and to stop at *that*. I wish to dismantle this opposition, and to see the success/failure issue as a real device within the plays themselves. It is a structural—and indeed creative—tension.

Hazelton Spencer, we saw, complained that *Cymbeline* was written by a Shakespeare "half asleep." But if Shakespeare was "asleep" (and I have my doubts) that is not exclusively a negative event. To have the greatest dramatist in the world writing a play *while asleep* is a perfectly fascinating situation. Very much depends, of course, on what one means by "sleep." For Hazelton Spencer, sleep here seems to be a mere blackout. But what I have referred to in earlier discussions as the withholding of imagination in the miracle plays is in a sense precisely a sleep, a state in which "normal" functions are put out of action in order to let others take over. If sleep in this manner of speaking should amount to inadequacy and insufficiency, then waking from that sleep is the miracle itself: that a dramatist writes something in his sleep, wakes up, and then finishes off the business in the most startled state of pure amazement. What better mood for the creation of miracle?

The same type of argument could be turned against a further criticism of Shakespeare forwarded by Hazelton Spencer: "in *Cymbeline* he votes himself a holiday from the exacting requirements of art."[31] Many interesting things happen on a holiday!

Perhaps Shakespeare needed a holiday at this point. Perhaps *art* needed a holiday. And miracle (not altogether incompatible with holi-days) is perhaps not entirely, or even mainly, a question of art. This line of thought brings us straight up against the notion of failure as something larger than a mere aesthetic danger. Shakespeare could not have gone on writing more *Hamlets, Lears,* and *Macbeths*. But such inability is not a question of a mere exhaustion of nervous energy; it is a question of the impersonal mechanisms of aesthetic logic. I will try to explain that.

Shakespeare is consistently developing, is a man incapable of stasis and stagnation; one cannot swallow Danby's view that Shakespeare's intellect itself went into retirement: "Up to 1606 Shakespeare was growing. His works are an existential record of his growth. After that time all his work seems to be that of a man who has got things finally clear and is no longer worried. Not only are things clear, they are almost cut and dried."[32] If Shakespeare instead actually goes on developing in very significant ways, then it is clear that it is precisely this developmental urge that will *not* permit him to go on writing another *Hamlet*, another *Lear*, and another *Macbeth*. In fact, to ensure a real breakaway, Shakespeare will have to radically alter not only the human visions and artistic procedures of his works, but also some of their "natural" premises. Such a sea-change is functional on some of the levels we have been considering, especially that of "representation."

Critics tend to think of this kind of structural change in the mature Shakespeare as a gentle swing of a positive kind: as if Shakespeare woke up one day with a different human outlook (softened, as it were), and as if he decided to navigate his genius so as to align it with such an existential shift. I think this comfortable assumption is potentially misleading—and, what is worse, that it obscures the entire question of "failure" in late-Shakespearean writing. Not that I want to drag Shakespeare into the gloom of the unsuccessful, but that I want to forward a sense of the *success* of the miracle plays as somehow being dependent on "failure." That dependency on failure is not an empirical dependency. For the failure is not an empirical failure. "Failure" here, rather, is a form of negative resource: some sense of radical lack that is urgent enough to produce an abundantly overcompensatory counterdrive.

The "impersonal" forces of aesthetic logic mentioned a moment ago operate here in the conclusive "paradigm shift" of Shakespeare's career through the fact that a *further* development of the intensities unleashed in the great tragedies would lead to breakdown: not human breakdown (though that is possible) but aesthetic breakdown. As Theodore Spencer argues, we can perceive traces of this phenomenon in *Timon of Athens*.

> The story of Timon, the open-hearted and over-generous spendthrift who turned into a violent misanthrope and fled from human society when he lost his money and found that none of the people who had profited by his generosity would come to his aid—this story, handed down from Lucian and Plutarch, was an Elizabethan commonplace, and as such was likely sooner or later to be dramatized. And it obviously called for a denunciation of mankind. But neither of these things completely accounts for the fact that Shakespeare decided to dramatize it toward the end of his tragic period, nor do they account for the kind of savage relish with which Shakespeare's Timon attacks human nature. It is difficult to resist the conclusion that the old misanthropic story was at this time sympathetic to Shakespeare, just as, if we accept the view that the play as we now have it is all his, it is difficult not to conclude that he abandoned it because he saw that the story could not, from its very nature, be turned into a first-class play.[33]

This commentary is interesting, and *Timon* certainly is disturbing in a strange way. But Spencer perhaps underestimates the aesthetic nature of the "blind alley," just as he perhaps overestimates its psychological nature (full misanthropy):

> In a sense *Timon* may be regarded as the climax of Shakespeare's presentation of the evil reality in human nature under the good appearance. . . . Perhaps it was because Shakespeare was aware that he had started down a dramatic blind alley that he left the play unfinished—in trying to account for what he did it is always wise, since we are dealing with so consummate a craftsman, to suggest technical explanations first. But few Shakespearean critics, and I confess I am not among them, have resisted the temptation to go further, and to see in the fact that Shakespeare left *Timon* unfinished an indication of a change in Shakespeare's attitude toward the nature of man. Sir Edmund Chambers, one of the most cautious of scholars, has even suggested that at this time in his career, Shakespeare had a nervous breakdown, and that thereafter the intensity of the tragic vision was physiologically impossible; it was more than Shakespeare could stand.[34]

Although I am prepared to appreciate the relevance and possibility of both of these alternatives (the technicist one and the psychological one), I refuse to see them as truly separable. It seems to me that the "blind alley" that Shakespeare gets trapped in during the late-tragic period is a psychological trap produced by an aesthetic attitude, just as it is an aesthetic trap produced by a psychological attitude. Shakespeare has simply looked "into" man for too long. This into-ness in itself is bound to lead to "misanthropy" in the long run—just as a man staring at his body for ten years might end up with a pretty shabby notion of the "filth" of existence. *Timon* seems to be the end of the line here, for all sense of horizon other than the horizon of man is out of focus. The "paradigm shift" opening the world of the last plays is from this viewpoint an abandoning of "into-ness" and of "man"—and thus also a gazing at humanity through its horizons. Only by *ceasing* to gaze at man can Shakespeare begin to perceive humanity again: what it is to be alive, to dream, hope, endure, and be happy.

What I have wished to call attention to, here, is not a debate between psychological Shakespeare criticism and technicist Shakespeare criticism, but the potential importance of the idea and possibility of failure. To leave a play unfinished is, in one way or another, a failure. And to write a play as one-sidedly obsessed with evil as *Timon* is is also a mode of failure.

Now if, as I suspect, Shakespeare needed to start from scratch again—develop a new dramatic rationale, without "man" as centered innerness—then he cannot have been unaware of the risks involved. A "consummate" player who no longer is going to base his game on his best stroke is going to be aware of things "missing" in his new achievements. He is even going to have moments of regret, moments when he longs to be back in that more familiar world of full human characterization and full human "inquiry." He is going to wonder whether a play without "into-ness" really works. Up to a point he is going to trust his new rationale; beyond that point he is not.

The question of "recovery" is crucial in this context. Recovery is a rubric for the entire new way of writing, because that writing amounts to a decision to fight oneself out of the "blind alley" discussed by Spencer. But "recovery" is also a danger: the dramatist will often be tempted to "recover" what is going wrong in the new rationale by means of a device that really belongs to the old rationale. Furthermore, the sense of recovery promoted *in* the plays by the new rationale ("miraculous recovery") is going to be looked at as something that itself needs to be amended, indeed recovered.

Any objective investigator will find that the miracle plays of Shakespeare are perfectly crammed with the idea of recovery. Miracle, although in itself all-powerful, is only one type of recovery in an entire array of recoveries. Recovery is indeed so overdetermined in the late plays that it begins to be looked at ironically. It risks becoming something ridiculous when the thing it recovers is absurd in the first place. We witness such an effect in the humor of *The Winter's Tale*, where Autolycus maliciously frightens the Clown with a deliciously grim picture of human suffering:

> *Clown*. Has the old man e'er a son, sir, do you hear, and't like you, sir?
> *Autolycus*. He has a son, who shall be flayed alive, then 'nointed over with honey, set on the head of a wasps' nest, then stand till he be three quarters and a dram dead; then recovered again with aqua-vitae or some other hot infusion; then, raw as he is, and in the hottest day prognostication proclaims, shall he be set against a brick wall, the sun looking with a southward eye upon him, where he is to behold him, with flies blown to death.
> (4.4.783–93)

In this way, the comic parts of *The Winter's Tale* stand playfully free from the main intellectual powers of the drama; yet those powers, organized largely by the hyperontological concept "recovery," also participate in the molding of the most innocent forms of play. The picaresque fortunes of unimportant characters are intertwined with those of grander figures. Rogues and balladmakers too get involved in "wonder," either through plot or through language. Thus we see toward the end of *The Winter's Tale* that the play's desire to use apotropaic screens to anticipate the disbelief of an unfavorable audience is a drive utilizing previous "comic matter." Trivial wonder on the level of comic subplot now actually helps trivial wonder on the level of the main plot to look *less* trivial. As in *Cymbeline*, what is structurally marginal and banal tends to magnetize things that risk looking banal in the central sections of the play. Comic "wonder" purifies more serious wonder by absorbing traces of superficiality in serious wonder. Notice how the play tries to cover its improbabilities:

> *First Gentleman*. I heard the shepherd say he found the child.
> *Autolycus*. I would most gladly know the issue of it.

First Gentleman. I make a broken delivery of the business; but the changes I perceived in the king and Camillo were very notes of admiration: they seemed almost, with staring on one another, to tear the cases of their eyes: there was speech in their dumbness, language in their very gesture; they looked as they had heard of a world ransomed, or one destroyed: a notable passion of wonder appeared in them; but the wisest beholder, that knew no more but seeing, could not say if th'importance were joy or sorrow; but in the extremity of the one it must needs be.

(*Enter another Gentleman.*)

Here comes a gentleman that haply knows more. The news, Rogero?

Second Gentleman. Nothing but bonfires: the Oracle is fulfilled; the king's daughter is found: such a deal of wonder is broken out within this hour, that ballad-makers cannot be able to express it.

(*Enter a third Gentleman.*)

Here comes the Lady Paulina's steward: he can deliver you more. How goes it now, sir? This news, which is called true, is so like an old tale that the verity of it is in strong suspicion.

(5.2.6–29)

This tendency of the play to constantly show that it is aware of its own improbabilities is operative, we have seen, also in the very terminal miracle that restores Hermione to life: "we are mock'd with art" (5.3.68). We saw there, however, that Shakespeare generated a strange energy that dissipated such play-internal scepticism. The *visual* reality of Hermione is in itself strong enough to marginalize a spectatorial disbelief that haunts the very unveiling of the centermost mystery:

That she is living,
Were it but told you, should be hooted at
Like an old tale: but it appears she lives

(5.3.115–17)

"Failure" here seems to me to be structurally linked to miracle according to the law of what almost looks like a necessary reciprocation: only by coming *so* close to something "hooted at" does the play actually achieve an unprecedented type of spectatorial surrender. The audience is silenced by having its "hooting" shifted from the noisy zone of the spectators to the silent zone of visionary disclosure. They are coaxed into the unprotesting mood that Paulina cleverly generates in Leontes, causing him to finally accept a role as *pure* spectator: "I am content to look on" (5.3.92). The appeasement of the leading player is also the appeasement of an audience. Hermione becomes visionary for both. She moves hypnotically through a silence that is also a simultaneity, a sharing of sudden faith.

At other moments in *The Winter's Tale*, however, the play's belief in its own reality is perhaps doubtful. "Time" ends the chorus introducing act 4 in the following manner:

> Of this allow,
> If ever you have spent time worse ere now;
> If never, yet that Time himself doth say,
> He wishes earnestly you never may.
>
> (4.1.29–32)

This is too much for Wilbur Sanders:

> How arch can you get? I don't much like it when authors, who have spent a great deal of ripe consideration on their own creations, turn round and invite an audience to treat it all as "a waste of time." It's either a failure of nerve that'd be better suppressed, or it's cheaply disingenuous and (possibly) fishing for compliments. . . . It's this air of offhand effrontery that makes me reluctant to read any very deep significance into Time's jingling pronouncements.[35]

Sanders refuses to take the speech of Time seriously. "Shakespeare is fooling about."[36] "If this is the best means Shakespeare has at his disposal to help him over a hump in his story, he's in pretty bad shape."[37] This type of quick intolerance is fairly misdirected, however, and is only operative on a level where one understands the play atomically—bit by bit, line by line, speech by speech. The speech of Time is of course not a trivial thing in the play; and the notion of "failure," almost consciously foregrounded here by the play itself, needs to be perceived within the mode of general dramatic awareness that I have tried to map recently: a delicate zone of attention where we are almost *meant* to understand disaster as a "partner" of wonder also on the rhetorical and aesthetic levels.

The Ecstasy of Telling

Appreciating Shakespeare's miracle plays requires a special type of tolerance—the very tolerance missing in the criticism of

"Time" above. This tolerance involves a peculiar readiness not to expect everything to be "imaginative," least of all imaginatively "full." Critics equating *all* of Shakespeare with "imagination" are bound to find crucial parts of the miracle plays "inferior"; those plays simply do not operate mainly through "imagination." Instead they operate through telling. The less imagination you have in a story, the more telling you have in it, pure telling. The supposedly "trivial" lines spoken by "Time" above are an example of this sudden emphasis on telling-as-telling; such lines "test" the spectator's ability to attend to telling as such, to abandon most other types of attentive criteria. In its purest form, time is itself this thing: telling without imagination. We can never be sure that time is always going to imagine reality, make it "full"; but we can always trust time (whether inside or outside the theater) to be a teller. Time tells us something (presents a new event/moment) whether this thing is imaginative or unimaginative, whether imagination can handle it or not. Life is full of incidents and periods that are not "full," not filled with meaning or imaginatively interesting "matter." But that kind of onwardness too needs to be recognized as real. Also the trivial lines spoken by time *count*.

The miracle plays of Shakespeare can in this way be understood in relation to the interaction of three things: imagination, telling, and miracle.

As a truly moving miracle play (and indeed a great success in Shakespeare's lifetime), *Pericles* offers a clue to the conditions of possibility for high-intensity miracle. Here events are deliberately told *instead* of imagined. Telling is emphasized, imagination is deemphasized. In all dramatic invention, of course, imagination is active and instrumental, the prime mover. Now according to Shakespearean standards, there is not *much* imagination/invention in *Pericles*. But there is very much telling. This distribution can partly, but only partly, be explained by the supposed prior involvement of a "collaborator." This collaborator, let us say, was a "teller" (acts 1 and 2), and Shakespeare then does his best to "elevate" telling to the level of full imaginative drama (acts 3, 4, and 5). But Shakespeare might have realized that doing his "best" (in imaginative terms) would be to ruin what the play already had going for itself as a "non-imaginative" artifact. Telling still dominates over imagination in the concluding acts.

Unfortunately, many well-meaning critics fail to appreciate this deliberate Shakespearean withholding of imaginative power, or its strategic significance. Instead one enthusiastically works a hermeneutic criticism on units of drama that need to be *left* as pure telling: as things just told. This "imaginative fallacy" (that narrated units always conceal deep-lying imaginative "truths") is, as I said in my opening remarks, particularly conspicuous in vulgar psychological criticism—vulgar in proportion to its ingeniousness.

In *pure telling,* as we know from observing children listening to the soothing syllables of a good-night story, there is created a narcotic sense of "empty" appeasement. This is the mystical window to the oblivions and miracles of night. The child listens, and listens "attentively." But it is doubtful whether imaginative participation is the key factor. Telling is. The sleepy child listens not only to the story but to the telling. And there is a part of the telling of the story that, as telling, has nothing whatsoever to do with the story. The story may be positive or negative. But the telling as such is always positive. The story may be disturbing or soothing. But the telling as such has been soothing. In this way, in pure telling, there is an "emptying" of the mind. This is what the sleepy child appreciates most. Not because the child wants to be emptied; but because it wants to become the pure recipient of unconditional telling.

The preeminence of telling—its ascendency over story, meaning, listener, language, and teller—is a function of a radically holistic process, a pure mobility. Telling is nomadic. In *Pericles* it is ultranomadic. It must move from episode to episode, always reminding the listener of the drive of the telling itself, its sensual, "pulling" onwardness. But the episodic here is not to be thought of as a fragmentation: for while story in a sense disintegrates, telling unites with telling. Telling becomes absolutely "whole," its own process and purpose, because it never gets bogged down in individual imaginative alleyways. Telling is unbroken.

The strange livingness of Marina is made miraculously possible by this ability of telling to move quickly "past" imagination, ahead of its deliberations and colorific contortions. Pericles encounters numerous obstacles on his *via dolorosa;* but the listener listening to telling does not meet any obstacles at all. He travels light; and he meets Marina in the most unburdened of moments. No Hamlet-like introversion clouds pure seeing; no Othello-like despair dims the screen of "outward" perception.

What Marina emerges from is not a story in which she has been imagined but a telling in which she had not been imagined. She has no foundation in imagination—*and does not exist there.* That is her freedom. But also ours. That, in a sense, is her miracle. As her father no longer carries "Marina" as an imaginative possibility in his wandering semblance of consciousness (the loss of hope is also the loss of the habit of imagining what hope hopes to recover), so we are never permitted to fully imagine Marina until ecstasy suddenly makes her mere presence an artifact. Prior to miracle, Marina lacks a foundational status as "full reality" in the mind of spectator or protagonist. Pericles can no longer imagine her. But her sudden ability to turn up does not in itself remedy this crisis. (His) imagination itself has to turn up. We assist him in this enterprise. We "call forth" Marina out of the imaginative abyss, out of the watery wastelands of telling; but we also assist imagination itself. This midwifery is a collective enterprise; it involves Pericles, Shakespeare, spectator, critic, reader, actor. Yet imagination is not the midwife, or even the birth. Imagination is instead the object—exquisitely feminine—that miracle delivers.

What has to be called into view in miracle, I have shown, is not only the empirical object but the mental activity (imagination) required for the materialization of true apperception. This applies (in an act of theatrical simultaneity) for spectator as well as protagonist: the stage must deliver not only an object/person miraculously recovered from danger or death; the stage must also deliver the special imaginative suddenness that has to unexpectedly emerge "inside" the beholder. Shakespeare demonstrates this nonempirical, double, and transcendental aspect of miracle by delineating Pericles' apperception of Marina/miracle as a two-stage process. The first phase is an empirical one: Marina is presenced. But this is not enough. Pericles' senses are still sheepish, still "unimaginative." He must be woken, *as* Pericles/imagination, to complete the miracle. Miracle becomes wonder of the highest order only if its factualness is paralleled by an inward flushing of the imaginative faculties.

Miracle that does not implement such transcendental apperception remains at the empirical level of "surprise" and "delightful thrill." Empirical miracle, soon to be institutionalized in the mystique of Jacobean masque, is essentially the agent of an ontology of extreme showing and extreme spectacle. Empirical miracle is empirical wonder, and the exceptional happiness it creates is an empirical happiness. In this way, a person who has lost a dog might the next week weep for joy and be ecstatic upon the chance retrieval of the loved pet—calling such bliss, indeed, a "miracle." But what Shakespeare produces in *Pericles* and *The*

Winter's Tale is not reducible to such empirical fortune or such empirical delight. What is at stake is a sudden enrichment on the level of transcendental apperception.

* * *

In my concluding remarks, now, I would like to call attention to a feature of the last plays of Shakespeare consistently stressed in this investigation: their heterogeneity. Helpful on some occasions, the general notion of "the romances" often obscures this heterogeneity. At the beginning of his study of the last plays, Howard Felperin asks: "What are we to make of romance as a literary genre?"[38] I try to avoid simplifying that type of question, because I do not think play-external knowledge too quickly should predetermine our ideas of what a play actually is up to. Watching a late-Shakespearean play and "knowing" that it is a "romance" (and indeed knowing very much about the history of romance) is certainly going to help you detect a lot of interesting romance-oriented detail; but it is also going to blind you to other possibilities. For me, each of the so-called romances is an utterly individual play, and the constructional differences separating those plays from one another are radical. Writes Felperin: "The obvious affinities of the miracle play with Greek romance make it easy to recognize as a version of romance."[39] I do not want to "make it easy" to recognize one thing as the "version" of something else. On the contrary, I want to make the recognition of the plays difficult. First because I do not believe in the ideology of easy recognition; second because I think that Shakespeare deliberately wanted to mock or defer such easy generic recognition-thinking; third because recognition, as we have seen, is promoted by the plays themselves as something complexly mystical and strange—"easy" only to the superficial intellect.

At the end of his career, Shakespeare discovered (or had to discover) a newness. This newness did not have a single effect, nor did it come down from the sky as a single thing-in-itself. Shakespeare's final newness therefore does not create a sweet array of pleasing effects, a beautifully satisfying spectrum of stable possibilities. On the contrary, as final repositioning in relation to his own art, late-Shakespearean newness creates an instability.

If "newness," as I believe, is for late-career Shakespeare very much a reflection of the sense of the miraculous, then the new is by no means a resuscitation of the old, a "recycling" of bygone experience now "properly" assimilated. The new (if it is miraculous) is not a resuscitation of the old. On the contrary, it is a resuscitation of the new. This difficulty is the secret of miracle. The new resuscitates the new. The new resuscitates itself. This is precisely the hyperontological mechanism that allows Shakespeare to give intellectual life to a seemingly banal event like the animation of the statue of Hermione. What is resuscitated for the spectator is not an old Hermione, but a new one. The new, as new, breaks in. The new, as new, forces a theatrical entry. The new, lacking *any past at all* (what past has a statue? what previous lines has it spoken?), shatters all frames, all prior notion and preexisting category.

Miracle, I have suggested, presupposes some state of radical unimaginativeness. This unimaginativeness is on the empirical level related to despair, the abandoning not only of hope but of all hope. When we hope, we are in a state of imagining the object that hope is going to recover. But when hope is gone, the imaginative, future-oriented faculty too goes dead. This is Pericles' condition: his mind becomes dream without imaginative contour, awareness sluggishly recording the next meaningless move of fate.

Because of this extraordinary draining of imagination in the premiraculous waste, Shakespeare's hyperimaginative creativity looks at an aesthetic (and indeed imaginative) problem of the highest order when meeting the challenge of the theatrical miracle. Shakespeare has to conceive the hyperimaginative as something almost entirely shifted over into a horizon (that of vision) facing him. The hyperimaginativeness of miracle opposes Shakespeare as thing opposes mind. In this way, if you like, Shakespeare's own hyperimaginativeness becomes objectified (for him, for us, for the play). This objectification of imagination, this hyperobjectification of invention, is at once negative and positive. We witness the dual consequences in the last plays: on the one hand, imagination threatens to actually become a dead thing, what gives parts of the last plays a flavor of inventive mechanicalness; on the other hand, imagination flashes its objective reality (statue, glory, divinity) toward man as incoming icon, imaginative gift outside the pale of thinkable giving.

As we see in the iconography of religious miracle (a shameless and sometimes obscene overspending in gold, jewelry, and baroque magnificence), miracle hoards the imagination—depriving the viewer, as it were, of any independent right to his own imaginative powers. The miracle itself will imagine the miracle. You will not. To accept that fate is at once to surrender to miracle and to become the visionary spectator of the lost objects of one's own imagination.

Miracle, as we have been looking at it, is the most inorganic of things. It *is* miracle by not belonging to the order of things: being, existence, what is possible. That is why a culture based on an ideology of the organic cannot discuss miracle seriously; miracle does not fit a doctrine of belongingness, just as a Shakespearean miracle play does not fit an art supposedly devoted to the exclusive purposes of such belongingness.

This all-important loosening of miracle from context and organicist environment needs, as we have seen, to be appreciated in all possible directions: laterally, transcendentally, foundationally. Whether we look sideways, upward, or downward, the discovery is the same—there is empty "air" around miracle. Looking sideways, we see that miracle in the final analysis is plot-independent. Telling is a better soil for miracle than plot or tight discursive context. Looking upward, we see that the gods (Jupiter in *Cymbeline*) coexist rather awkwardly with miracles: the upward air too must be free for miracle; ideally, as in *Pericles*, upwardness is mere clearing and space—what tempestuousness (rather than tempest) makes available as the inorganicity of random weather. Looking downward, finally, we see that miracle needs no foundation; it has no origin that is not a liquefaction of origin, no bottom that is not itself without bottom. Pericles, like a ship, is made firm by infirmity.

Miracle is thus not a transcendental signified. It has no transcendental support. But this is not so because transcendentality is lacking in the world of miracles. On the contrary, the miracle eludes the transcendental signified by being *more* transcendental than a transcendental signified. In this way, miracle is larger than meaning: what happens at the end of *The Winter's Tale* is larger than the play itself—and therefore not strictly a part of it. What happens to Marina and Pericles is larger than the play they take part in, larger than the world their theater hastily sketches.

In her excellent work, *The Dramaturgy of Shakespeare's Romances*, Barbara Mowat calls attention to the various counterclassical features that remove the miracle plays from theatrical presence of an ordinary kind. I would like to quote Mowat in some detail, since her analysis provides a subtle and extensive platform of support for the various theatrical displacements that I have advanced in this book as the innovative conditions for the Shakespearean miracle play.

To begin with, Mowat recognizes what I have discussed as the *loss of the center* in these plays. This loss is not some sad misfortune that passively occurs in terms of authorial oversight; on the contrary, it is a mechanism deliberately implemented by the artist. Most of Shakespeare's plays have a midplay climax in which there is a sudden conflux of subsidiary actions, allowing actions to converge and collect themselves in the unifying and self-presencing realm of a central plateau; but in the last plays this centering middle of action is oddly missing.[40] There is no coming together of tributary actions at Milford-Haven in *Cymbeline*, but instead a slackening of tension in which Iachimo and Posthumus vanish from the story.[41] The same thing happens in *The Winter's Tale*: with the death of Mamillius, the crisis built up by the tension between Leontes and Hermione fails to carry further significant conflict into acts 4 and 5.[42] Together with Father Time, a new story line undercuts sustained dramatic intensity. Such deliberate Shakespearean undercutting of center and centered presence also operates through the behavior (not) given to the protagonist. The last plays "in large part, remove the hero from the play's center action, and avoid this intense midplay activity. The result is that the controlling dramatic frame is missing, and we are left with the narrative line alone."[43]

Critics, traditionally, have been reluctant to admit this sudden and radical refusal of Shakespeare to go on writing dramas of presence: they tend to want to persuade us (and themselves) that nothing really unorthodox is going on, and they refer to the reassuring generic rubric "romances" in order to argue that Shakespeare's final "turn" is a generic shift. But, as Mowat observes, the translation of Shakespeare's counterclassical plays into a classical rationale of critical analysis only blinds us to their otherness: "If we overlook the non-Aristotelian form of these plays and insist on seeing them as peculiar attempts to create 'normal' Shakespearean drama, we will tend . . . to misread these plays."[44]

What is at stake here, as Mowat indeed recognizes, is not only classicism as an aesthetic rationale (a world of aesthetic order in general, and of generic order in particular), but classicism as Reason—classicism as the quasi-theological ground and center of Western rationalism. It is possible to go on seeing Shakespeare's last plays as supplementary disquisitions on the fortunes and misfortunes of classical man; but it is also possible to see a final "turn" in Shakespeare (anticipated by *Macbeth* and *Timon*) in which he will have dismembered the very conditions (logical, aesthetic, and spiritual) that permit further inscriptions of the Logos of the metaphysical West.

> Pirandello, in describing his antirationalist theater, said that his task was to tear down the white columns which the Greeks had erected over the dark abyss. There is something of this in what Shakespeare has done in his last plays, where human reason and human cleverness (unless assisted by magic) are powerless in the face of the irrational; human goodness is a sometime thing, set upon by bestiality without and within; earthquake passions destroy the human constructs of tradition, rationality, and custom, unless an equally mysterious force—magic, the supernatural, a chance emotion—intervenes. Crucial to this 'tearing down' is the open form dramaturgy, which separates action from sequential action, action from acting character—and which allows Shakespeare to present isolated phenomena of human experience detached from the patterns which are normally imposed upon them by closed form drama.[45]

Meaning, then, is not something that can be extracted *from* action, character, structure, idea, plot, design, or whole—but is on the contrary what in arbitrary (sometimes whimsical) fashion gets *added* to the chaos of the life of the artifact as a pure exterior object. Only in retrospect, and by some act of absurdly tolerant aesthetic generosity, can we admit that such meaning inheres in the logic of the art that the dramatist has devised for our scrutiny. As meaning, miracle does not confirm (or deny) the "world" that it saves; miracle does not even save the world it saves. On the contrary, it is in the miracle itself that the spectator must put all his faith—indeed, finally, all his attention. The ultimate insult here—but also the ultimate emancipation—is that the spectator is denied the relevance of his own preexisting theatrical condition: spectatorship. What the spectator in the final analysis has to endure in the experience of the miracle play is the vanishing of his own significance and identity—the vanishing of his *importance*. The spectator is now important only insofar as he is a spectator of the miracle rather than of the play in which the miracle appears. In antirationalist theater of this kind, the miracle laughs at the action that leads up to it: just as a patient doomed by medical science but saved by miracle has to laugh at the therapeutic treatment that was to carry him through the terminal stages of decay. But this subtraction from the spectator is not only a subtraction. It is true that the spectator is being deprived of the right to his or her own performance, that of contributing to a play by being a witness to its logical unfurlings. But since the (absolutely inner) vanishing of the spectator is something that itself is staged (what Shakespeare *shows* the spectator, action devoid of action), the spectator is in the miracle play given access to supplementary transactions. The spectator becomes a witness to the theatralization of his own loss of proper rights.

If the miracle play, then, refuses to take the spectator quite seriously, this is so because (to follow Mowat again) the last plays present "a universe that refuses to take man seriously."[46] But that unseriousness, one would have to add, is itself a serious matter. Death, therefore, is not simply grotesque or unreal in the last plays, but a singular point where one seriousness disappears into another. The last plays do not focus a central conflict or seriously central idea, and they thus differ from the earlier tragicomedies by denying the all-powerfulness of intelligence and rational control. Insight itself is not enough. This means that Shakespeare no longer imposes a dominant mood or consistent perspective. Incidents do not serve the purpose of clearing a way for the logical order of further incidents, and the dramatist is "forgetting" to transform narrative (the mythic source) into drama (a closed aesthetic form). Shakespeare does not lead the spectator; he misleads him. The dramatist, in a new way, is telling a lie. The deceit of drama is no longer restricted to the fact that, as representation, it is an illusion. On the contrary, illusionism is itself sacrificed in order to engineer a more disturbing projection of "the real." In no previous play does Shakespeare do what he does in *The Winter's Tale:* lie to the audience about the fate of a central character. But as Mowat insists, this tactical move is typical of an entire policy of disinformation in the last plays:

> Shakespeare omits the usual preparatory speeches and scenes, he gives occasional bits of misleading information, he arranges circumstances so that one piece of action prepares us for no particular action as a consequence. Instead of [letting plot follow the arrows of desire created by dramatic expectations], he often leads us astray or springs on us some action for which we are totally unprepared. The effect created is that of wonder and surprise, rather than of fulfilled expectations.[47]

The jealousy of Leontes, the death of Mamillius, of "Hermione": these things are theatrical shocks. They do not, primarily, contribute to a dramatic design or significant expectation pattern, but serve on the contrary to break such a metaphysical mold. Thus we are not simply reminded that we are watching a play: *added* to this reminder there is given the sense that we are watching something other than a play. The dramatic tactics of the last plays, by mixing presentational and representational styles, do not simply distance the spectator from the reality of the theatrical illusion; instead audience engagement is controlled by a carefully oscillating distortion of tonal uniformity. The naive has to coexist with the sophisticated, the grotesque with the lyrical, the comic with the tragic, the possible with the impossible. We are not exposed to five acts of human suffering; but when suffering is presented, we find that the play has given us no shield of protection: neither the shield of "meaning" nor the shield of comic laughter. Evil has no true motivation, and suffering has no true context. Emotions soften the edges of such blunt items of action, yet these emotions are loosened from the characters and are no longer always the fixed properties of distinct individuals. Negativity, then, is massive and general in Shakespeare's miracle plays.

Mowat shows how the late plays become negations of rationalist drama as such. But the negativity that Shakespeare finally sets free in his imaginative theater can negate further limits. Throughout this book I have called attention to the ultimate object of such negation: language itself. Maire Jaanus Kurrik focuses this type of negation when she discusses the role played by negativity in *Timon of Athens*. Like Macbeth, Timon comes to a final phase of insight (or of blocked, negated, negative insight) where time, man, and linguistic reason are swamped by nothingness. The vanishing of man is thinkable only in the vicinity of the vanishing of language:

> *Timon.* Come not to me again; but say to Athens,
> Timon hath made his everlasting mansion
> Upon the beached verge of the salt flood,
> Who once a day with his embossed froth
> The turbulent surge shall cover. Thither come,
> And let my grave-stone be your oracle.
> Lips, let four words go by and language end
>
> (5.1.213–19)

Shakespeare's ability—demonstrated throughout the miracle plays—to make "language end" is a function of his unprecedented engagement with nothingness. Kurrik observes that "the

West has its first taste of willed, subjective nothingness in the tragic theater of Shakespeare."[48] And Timon is perhaps the "greatest figure of pure negation produced in the Renaissance."[49] Increasingly, in the cultural history of the West, there is a growing awareness that the self has powers and that negativity is one of these powers. Finally, the self discovers that one of its most indisputable forces is its capacity to negate itself.[50] This negation, power as the will not to be man, is what Timon ultimately personifies. He is a monument to human negation. Death, already loosened from its classical schema in the skewed negativities of *Antony and Cleopatra,* becomes the agent of counterclassical significance as soon as it starts to misfunction as a contrast to life. "Shakespearean tragedy, in that it gives birth to a sense of subjective nothingness, to lifelessness and feelinglessness, makes an end of classical tragedy which depended on the significance of life and death. Now tragedy is a struggle with absence."[51] Macbeth cannot feel Macbeth at the end of his tragedy, because he can feel neither death nor life. That dialectical distinction has ceased to be psychologically—and indeed dramatically—operative.

But if I extend this argument—if I trace this acceleration of the importance of negativity into the last plays, and if I understand its work there as negation more radical than tragic negation—then it will become clear that the self's "power to negate itself"[52] does not apply only to the heroes that Shakespeare depicts, but indeed to the dramatist himself, to his ownmost practice and dramatic outlook. This is really my main thesis in this book: that the final plays, and especially those identified here as miracle plays, signal the crowning ability of Shakespearean genius to "negate itself." Shakespeare could negate Shakespeare. And to fail to perceive that negation is to go on living in a quixotic realm of interpretation where one is chivalrously "saving" the very meanings that Shakespeare is shooting down with his own rifle. To call all of Shakespeare's last plays "romances" and to go on believing that they all solemnly celebrate the positive certitudes of "Shakespearean art" is to run enthusiastically in an opposite direction to the one that Shakespeare finally selected for his closing efforts. Even if we accept the sweeping term "romance," we need to recognize that the "romances" amount to more than just *another* batch of Shakespearean artifacts. In seeming "almost purposely to be avoiding design," Shakespeare is now practicing what Mark Rose calls "ostentatious artlessness."[53] Saying that much is not to hold the preposterous view that Shakespeare's last plays lack art or aesthetic power. It is to say that dramatic art is now incorporating into its positive structures all that appears to be the vanishing of the conditions for those structures. Shakespeare and his shadow (death, cessation, silence, negation, dissolution, dumbness) are now one—or *want* to be one. An empirical Shakespeare will be able to outlive this unification of artist and shadow; but an artistic Shakespeare will be incapable of outliving the contract between genius and its negation. *After* the "romances" Shakespeare has nothing left to write; and Shakespeare knows that. And he knows it, primarily, because the "romances" are not written at all.[54] They are completely nonexistent from the viewpoint of writing and only happen in a world where writing has chosen to identify itself with the contours of its pure opposite. It is difficult to imagine that Shakespeare took a "decision" to stop writing some time after *The Tempest;* his plays had themselves taken that decision several years earlier.

The consequences for language, in this phase of terminal countercreativity, are the consequences I have tried to map in this study. Once the Logos of the West had learned to negate itself, and once Shakespeare perceived himself as the sensitized medium of that negation, Shakespeare's negation of Shakespeare was also drama's negation of drama and language's negation of language. In the miracle plays, Shakespearean language does not primarily express meaning, character, thought, selfhood, presence, or truth. Shakespeare finally created a negative language and a negative drama that were "larger" than either language or drama. It is the language that gets spoken (and sometimes not spoken) in the miracle plays. It is the muteness, voiced or muted, that transforms truth into miracle.

As art and miracle meet in the zone where the fading of the one becomes the illumination of the other, negation cannot quite calculate its effects. Art and miracle, in order to touch, had to risk a dissolution of the one in the other. The outcome of such a collision was unforeseeable—and still is. What is certain, only, is that Shakespeare at one point aimed at the miraculous—and that in taking that aim he knew that he had not emptied his quiver.

Notes

Chapter 1. Miracle

1. Norman Sanders, "An Overview of Critical Approaches to the Romances," in *Shakespeare's Romances Reconsidered*, ed. Carol McGinnis Kay and Henry E. Jacobs (Lincoln and London: The University of Nebraska Press, 1978), p. 3.
2. Ruth Nevo, *Shakespeare's Other Language* (New York and London: Methuen, 1987), p. 7.
3. Ibid, p. 8.
4. Ibid.
5. Ibid.
6. Ibid.
7. Charles Frey, "Tragic Structure in *The Winter's Tale*: The Affective Dimension," in Kay and Jacobs, *Shakespeare's Romances Reconsidered*, p. 114.
8. Sanders, "An Overview of Critical Approaches to the Romances," p. 7.
9. Ibid., p. 6.
10. Nevo, *Shakespeare's Other Language*, p. 6.
11. Howard Felperin, "Romance and Romanticism: Some Reflections on *The Tempest* and *Heart of Darkness*, Or, When Is Romance No Longer Romance?" in Kay and Jacobs, *Shakespeare's Romances Reconsidered*, p. 75.
12. Ibid., p. 76; emphasis added.
13. Ibid., p. 60.
14. Ibid., p. 68.
15. Ibid., p. 67.
16. Ibid.
17. Ibid., p. 71.
18. Northrop Frye, "Romance as Masque," in Kay and Jacobs, *Shakespeare's Romances Reconsidered*, p. 11.
19. Ibid., p. 15.
20. Ibid., p. 16.
21. Ibid., p. 14.
22. Ibid., p. 13.
23. Nevo, *Shakespeare's Other Language*, p. 42.
24. Ibid., p. 43.
25. Ibid., p. 4.
26. Ibid., p. 105.
27. Frye, "Romance as Masque," p. 13.
28. See William Shakespeare, *The Complete Works*, ed. Stanley Wells, Gary Taylor, John Jowett, and William Montgomery (Oxford: Clarendon Press, 1986), p. 1167.

29. See David M. Bergeron, "The Restoration of Hermione in *The Winter's Tale*," in Kay and Jacobs, *Shakespeare's Romances Reconsidered*, pp. 126, 129. Greg once suggested that *The Winter's Tale* was revised for the wedding of Princess Elizabeth in February 1613.

30. Contemporary American deconstruction denies "belonging" (self-presence) in favor of irreducible differentialism ("*différance*"); thus, in much poststructuralist theory, it is fashionable to treat difference and belonging as opposites—difference going so far "back" that no ground ("origin") can be found without differential trace. "Belonging" is often used by traditionalists to counter such poststructuralist "salami" thinking (endless slicing of the object/text/foundation). Here I am thinking away this ideological opposition by ungrounding the ground *without* using an analytical procedure that privileges cognitive cutting. I am suggesting an absence or absencing of the ground/foundation that is not achieved by slicing it up or by differentiating it from itself.

31. Primitivity in plays like *Pericles* and *Cymbeline* is of course indirectly related to primitivity as archetypally figured in masques and antimasques: there was a ritualistic showing of a representation of social and cosmic lowness.

32. Nevo, *Shakespeare's Other Language*, p. 46.

33. Cyrus Hoy, "Fathers and Daughters in Shakespeare's Romances," in Kay and Jacobs, *Shakespeare's Romances Reconsidered*, p. 86.

34. Ibid., p. 84.

35. The Arden edition of *Pericles*, ed. F. D. Hoeniger (London and New York: Methuen, 1984), p. 145.

36. Stevie Davies, *The Idea of Woman in Renaissance Literature: The Feminine Reclaimed* (Brighton: Harvester Press, 1986), p. 150.

37. The Arden edition of *The Winter's Tale*, ed. J. H. P. Pafford (London and New York: Methuen, 1984), p. 126.

38. Davies, *The Idea of Woman*, p. 135.

39. Ibid., p. 137.

40. Ibid., p. 147.

41. Ibid., p. 146.

42. Ibid., p. 148.

43. Ibid., p. 149.

44. R. S. White, *"Let Wonder Seem Familiar": Endings in Shakespeare's Romance Vision* (Atlantic Highlands, N.J.: Humanities Press; London: Athlone Press, 1985), p. 156.

Chapter 2. Negative Miracle

1. G. Wilson Knight, *The Crown of Life: Essays in Interpretation of Shakespeare's Final Plays* (London: Methuen, 1948), pp. 15–17.

2. John F. Danby, *Poets on Fortune's Hill: Studies in Sidney, Shakespeare, Beaumont, and Fletcher* (London: Faber and Faber, 1952), p. 107.

3. Ibid., p. 91.

4. Ibid.

5. Donald A. Stauffer, *Shakespeare's World of Images: The Development of His Moral Ideas* (London and Bloomington: Indiana University Press, 1966), p. 268.

6. Wilbur Sanders, *The Winter's Tale* (Brighton: Harvester, 1987), p. xiv.

7. Ibid.
8. Ibid., p. 21.
9. Ibid., p. xiv.
10. Knight, *The Crown of Life*, p. 84.
11. E. M. W. Tillyard, *Shakespeare's Last Plays* (London: Chatto and Windus, 1938), p. 41.
12. F. W. Brownlow, *Two Shakespearean Sequences:* Henry VI *to* Richard II *and* Pericles *to* Timon of Athens (London: Macmillan, 1977), p. 120.
13. On the one hand, Time decides to "slide / O'er sixteen years" (4.1.5–6); on the other hand, Camillo says that "fifteen years" have passed since he saw his country (4.2.4).
14. Brownlow, *Two Shakespearean Sequences*, p. 123.
15. Quoted in Tillyard, *Shakespeare's Last Plays*, p. 5.
16. Knight, *The Crown of Life*, p. 96.
17. Ibid., p. 202.
18. Ibid., p. 142.
19. Wilbur Sanders, *The Winter's Tale*, p. 55.
20. Ibid., p. 37.
21. Ibid., p. 39. F. W. Brownlow tells us that "the decorum of criticism requires that critics should not play at theology" (*Two Shakespearean Sequences*, p. 166).
22. Frank Kermode, *William Shakespeare: The Final Plays* (London: Longmans, Green and Co., 1963), p. 22.
23. Kenneth Muir, *Last Periods of Shakespeare, Racine, and Ibsen* (Liverpool: Liverpool University Press, 1961), p. 6.
24. Danby, *Poets on Fortune's Hill*, p. 98.
25. Ibid.
26. Tillyard, *Shakespeare's Last Plays*, p. 41.
27. Danby, *Poets on Fortune's Hill*, p. 100.
28. Brownlow, *Two Shakespearean Sequences*, p. 161; emphasis added.
29. Knight, *The Crown of Life*, p. 82.
30. Ibid., p. 17.
31. Wilbur Sanders, *The Winter's Tale*, p. 32.
32. Arden, *The Winter's Tale*, p. 166.
33. Ibid., p. 94.
34. Knight, *The Crown of Life*, p. 16.
35. Wilbur Sanders, *The Winter's Tale*, p. 46.
36. Ibid., p. 36.
37. J. M. S. Tompkins, "Why Pericles?" *Review of English Studies* 3 (1952): 317.
38. Ibid., p. 318.
39. Ibid.
40. Ibid., p. 317.
41. See for instance Arden, *The Winter's Tale*, pp. 93–94.

Chapter 3. Miracle in Abyss

1. Danby, *Poets on Fortune's Hill*, p. 94.
2. Knight, *The Crown of Life*, p. 54.
3. Kermode, *Shakespeare: The Final Plays*, p. 14. Emphasis added.

4. The Arden edition of *Cymbeline*, ed. J. M. Nosworthy (London and New York: Methuen, 1980), p. 135.
5. Ibid., p. lxv.
6. Ibid.
7. Ibid., p. lxvi.
8. Ibid., p. lxv.
9. Ibid.
10. I am reintroducing the Folio question mark.
11. Inga-Stina Ewbank, "'My Name Is Marina': The Language of Recognition," in *Shakespeare's Styles: Essays in Honour of Kenneth Muir*, ed. Philip Edwards, Inga-Stina Ewbank, and G. K. Hunter (Cambridge: Cambridge University Press, 1980), p. 114.
12. Ibid., p. 115.
13. Anne Barton, "Leontes and the Spider: Language and Speaker in Shakespeare's Last Plays," in Edwards, Ewbank, and Hunter, *Shakespeare's Styles*, p. 138.
14. Ibid.
15. Ibid., p. 136.
16. Ibid.
17. Ibid., p. 137.
18. Ewbank, "My Name Is Marina," p. 128.
19. Ibid., p. 120.
20. Ibid.
21. Ibid., p. 115.
22. Ibid.
23. Ibid., p. 114.
24. Ibid., pp. 117, 125.
25. Ibid., p. 127.
26. Ibid.
27. Barton, "Language and Speaker in the Last Plays," pp. 144–45; emphasis added.
28. Ewbank, "My Name Is Marina," p. 127.
29. Arden, *Cymbeline*, p. 151.
30. Hazelton Spencer, *The Art and Life of William Shakespeare* (New York: Harcourt, Brace and Company, 1940), pp. 361–63.
31. Ibid., p. 363.
32. Danby, *Poets on Fortune's Hill*, p. 106.
33. Theodore Spencer, *Shakespeare and the Nature of Man* (New York: Macmillan; Cambridge: Cambridge University Press, 1945), p. 180.
34. Ibid., pp. 183–84.
35. Wilbur Sanders, *The Winter's Tale*, p. 70.
36. Ibid.
37. Ibid., p. 71.
38. Howard Felperin, *Shakespearean Romance* (Princeton: Princeton University Press, 1972), p. 5.
39. Ibid., p. 13.
40. Barbara A. Mowat, *The Dramaturgy of Shakespeare's Romances* (Athens: University of Georgia Press, 1976), p. 72.
41. Ibid.
42. Ibid., p. 73.
43. Ibid., p. 75.

44. Ibid., p. 109.
45. Ibid.
46. Ibid., p. 112.
47. Ibid., p. 77.
48. Maire Jaanus Kurrik, *Literature and Negation* (New York: Columbia University Press, 1979), p. 18.
49. Ibid., p. 15.
50. Ibid., p. 19.
51. Ibid.
52. Ibid.
53. Mark Rose, *Shakespearean Design* (Cambridge: Harvard University Press, 1972), p. 168.
54. "To write: to refuse to write—to write by way of this refusal." "Not to write—what a long way there is to go before arriving at that point . . . " "Not writing is among the effects of writing." "There is nothing negative in 'not to write.'" "The thought of the disaster . . . replaces ordinary silence—where speech lacks—with a separate silence." Maurice Blanchot, *The Writing of the Disaster*, trans. Ann Smock (Lincoln and London: University of Nebraska Press, 1986), pp. 10–13.

Bibliography

Alexander, Peter. *Shakespeare's Life and Art.* London: James Nisbet and Co., 1939.

Aquila, Richard E. *Matter in Mind: A Study of Kant's Transcendental Deduction.* Bloomington and Indianapolis: Indiana University Press, 1989.

Atkins, Douglas G., and Laura Morrow, eds. *Contemporary Literary Theory.* Amherst: University of Massachusetts Press, 1989.

Barton, Anne. "Leontes and the Spider: Language and Speaker in Shakespeare's Last Plays." In *Shakespeare's Styles: Essays In Honour of Kenneth Muir,* edited by Philip Edwards, Inga-Stina Ewbank, and G. K. Hunter, pp. 131–50. Cambridge and New York: Cambridge University Press, 1980.

Baudrillard, Jean. *The Mirror of Production.* Translated by Mark Poster. St. Louis, Mo.: Telos Press, 1975.

———. *Pour une critique de l'économie politique du signe.* Paris: Gallimard, 1972.

———. *Simulations.* Translated by Paul Foss, Paul Patton, and Philip Beitchman. New York: Foreign Agents; Semiotext(e), 1983.

Beilin, Elaine V. *Redeeming Eve: Women Writers of the English Renaissance.* Princeton: Princeton University Press, 1987.

Bergeron, David M. "The Restoration of Hermione in *The Winter's Tale.*" In *Shakespeare's Romances Reconsidered,* edited by Carol McGinnis Kay and Henry E. Jacobs, pp. 125–33. Lincoln and London: University of Nebraska Press, 1978.

Bevington, David, and Jay L. Halio, eds. *Shakespeare: Pattern of Excelling Nature.* Newark: University of Delaware Press; London: Associated University Presses, 1978.

Blanchot, Maurice. *The Writing of the Disaster.* Translated by Ann Smock. Lincoln and London: University of Nebraska Press, 1986.

Brockbank, J. P. "History and Histrionics in *Cymbeline.*" *Shakespeare Survey* 11 (1958): 42–49.

Brownlow, Frank W. *Two Shakespearean Sequences:* Henry VI *to* Richard II *and* Pericles *to* Timon of Athens. London: Macmillan, 1977.

Carr, Joan. "*Cymbeline* and the Validity of Myth." *Studies in Philology* 75 (1978): 316–30.

Cutts, John P. "Pericles' 'Downright Violence.'" *Shakespeare Studies* 4 (1968): 275–93.

———. *Rich and Strange: A Study of Shakespeare's Last Plays.* Pullman: Washington State University Press, 1968.

Danby, John F. *Poets on Fortune's Hill: Studies in Sidney, Shakespeare, Beaumont, and Fletcher.* London: Faber and Faber, 1952.

Dasenbrock, Reed Way, ed. *Redrawing the Lines: Analytic Philosophy, Deconstruction, and Literary Theory.* Minneapolis: University of Minnesota Press, 1989.

Davidson, Cathy N., and E. M. Broner eds. *The Lost Tradition: Mothers and Daughters in Literature.* New York: Frederick Ungar, 1980.

Davies, Stevie. *The Idea of Woman in Renaissance Literature.* Brighton: Harvester Press, 1986.

Dean, John. *Restless Wanderers: Shakespeare and the Pattern of Romance.* Salzburg: Salzburg Studies in English Literature, 1979.

Derrida, Jacques. "*Geschlecht* II: Heidegger's Hand." Translated by John P. Leavey, Jr. In *Deconstruction and Philosophy,* edited by John Sallis, pp. 161–96. Chicago and London: University of Chicago Press, 1987.

———. *Limited Inc.* Evanston, Ill.: Northwestern University Press, 1988.

Dufrenne, Mikel. *In the Presence of the Sensuous: Essays in Aesthetics.* Edited and translated by Mark S. Roberts and Dennis Gallagher. Atlantic Highlands, N.J.: Humanities Press, 1987.

Edwards, Philip. "Shakespeare's Romances: 1900–1957." *Shakespeare Survey* 11 (1958): 1–18.

Edwards, Philip, Inga-Stina Ewbank, and G. K. Hunter, eds. *Shakespeare's Styles: Essays in Honour of Kenneth Muir.* Cambridge: Cambridge University Press, 1980.

Ewbank, Inga-Stina. " 'My Name Is Marina': The Language of Recognition." In *Shakespeare's Styles: Essays in Honour of Kenneth Muir,* edited by Philip Edwards, Inga-Stina Ewbank, and G. K. Hunter, pp. 111–30. Cambridge: Cambridge University Press, 1980.

———. "The Triumph of Time in *The Winter's Tale.*" *Review of English Literature* 5 (April 1964): 83–100.

———. "The Word in the Theatre." In *Shakespeare: Man of the Theatre,* edited by Kenneth Muir, Jay L. Halio, and D. J. Palmer, pp. 55–75. Newark: University of Delaware Press; London and Toronto: Associated University Presses, 1983.

Farrell, Kirby. *Play, Death, and Heroism in Shakespeare.* Chapel Hill: University of North Carolina Press, 1989.

Felperin, Howard. "Romance and Romanticism: Some Reflections on *The Tempest* and *Heart of Darkness,* Or, When Is Romance No Longer Romance?" In *Shakespeare's Romances Reconsidered,* edited by Carol McGinnis Kay and Henry E. Jacobs, pp. 60–76. Lincoln and London: University of Nebraska Press, 1978.

———. *Shakespearean Romance.* Princeton: Princeton University Press, 1972.

———. "Shakespeare's Miracle Play." *Shakespeare Quarterly* 18 (1967): 363–74.

Flower, Anette C. "Disguise and Identity in *Pericles, Prince of Tyre.*" *Shakespeare Quarterly* 26 (1975): 30–41.

Frey, Charles. "Tragic Structure in *The Winter's Tale*: The Affective Dimension." In *Shakespeare's Romances Reconsidered,* edited by Carol McGinnis Kay and Henry E. Jacobs, pp. 113–24. Lincoln and London: University of Nebraska Press, 1978.

Frye, Northrop. *A Natural Perspective: The Development of Shakespearean Comedy and Romance*. New York: Columbia University Press, 1965.

———. "Romance as Masque." In *Shakespeare's Romances Reconsidered*, edited by Carol McGinnis Kay and Henry E. Jacobs, pp. 11–39. Lincoln and London: University of Nebraska Press, 1978.

———. *Spiritus Mundi: Essays on Literature, Myth, and Society*. Bloomington and London: Indiana University Press, 1976.

Gesner, Carol. *Shakespeare and the Greek Romance: A Study of Origins*. Lexington: University Press of Kentucky, 1970.

Gittings, Robert, ed. *The Living Shakespeare*. London: Heinemann, 1960.

Gorfain, Phyllis. "Puzzle and Artifice: The Riddle as Metapoetry in *Pericles*." *Shakespeare Survey* 29 (1976): 11–20.

Hall, Michael. *The Structure of Love: Representational Patterns and Shakespeare's Love Tragedies*. Charlottesville: University of Virginia Press, 1989.

Hart, Kevin. *The Trespass of the Sign: Deconstruction, Theology, and Philosophy*. Cambridge: Cambridge University Press, 1989.

Hartwig, Joan. *Shakespeare's Tragicomic Vision*. Baton Rouge: Louisiana State University Press, 1972.

Hastings, William T. "Shakespeare's Part in *Pericles*." *Shakespeare Association Bulletin* 14 (1939): 67–85.

Hegel, G. W. F., *Lectures on the Philosophy of Religion*. Translated by R. F. Brown, P. C. Hodgson, and J. M. Stewart. Berkeley, Los Angeles, London: University of California Press, 1988.

Heidegger, Martin. *Early Greek Thinking*. Translated by David Farrell Krell and Frank A. Capuzzi. San Francisco: Harper and Row, 1984.

———. *Introduction to Metaphysics*. Translated by Ralph Manheim. New Haven and London: Yale University Press, 1959.

———. *On the Way to Language*. Translated by Peter D. Hertz. New York: Harper and Row, 1982.

———. *Poetry, Language, Thought*. Translated by Albert Hofstadter. New York: Harper Colophon, 1975.

———. *The Question of Being*. London: Vision Press, 1974.

———. *What Is Called Thinking?* Translated by J. Glenn Gray. New York: Harper and Row, 1968.

———. *What Is Philosophy?* Translated by William Kluback and Jean T. Wilde. Plymouth: Vision Press, 1989.

Hoy, Cyrus. "Fathers and Daughters in Shakespeare's Romances." In *Shakespeare's Romances Reconsidered*, edited by Carol McGinnis Kay and Henry E. Jacobs, pp. 77–90. Lincoln and London: University of Nebraska Press, 1978.

Hunter, Robert Grams. *Shakespeare and the Comedy of Forgiveness*. New York and London: Columbia University Press, 1965.

Jacobs, Henry E. *Cymbeline*. New York and London: Garland, 1982.

Kermode, Frank. *William Shakespeare: The Final Plays*. London: Longmans, Green & Co., 1963.

Knapp, Robert S. *Shakespeare: The Theater and the Book*. Princeton: Princeton University Press, 1989.

Knight, G. Wilson. *The Crown of Life: Essays in Interpretation of Shakespeare's Final Plays*. London: Methuen, 1948.

———. *The Shakespearian Tempest*. London: Oxford University Press, Humfrey Milford, 1932.

Kurrik, Maire Jaanus. *Literature and Negation*. New York: Columbia University Press, 1979.

Levin, Carole, and Jeanie Watson, eds. *Ambiguous Realities: Women in the Middle Ages and Renaissance*. Detroit: Wayne State University Press, 1987.

Lewalski, Barbara Kiefer, ed. *Renaissance Genres: Essays on Theory, History, and Interpretation*. Cambridge, Mass., and London: Harvard University Press, 1986.

Logan, Robert A. "The Sexual Attitudes of Marlowe and Shakespeare." *Hartford Studies in Literature* 19 (1987): 1–23.

Long, John N. *Shakespeare's Use of Music: The Final Comedies*. Gainesville: University of Florida Press, 1961.

Marsh, Derek R. C. *Passion Lends Them Power: A Study of Shakespeare's Love Tragedies*. Manchester: Manchester University Press; New York: Barnes and Noble, 1976.

———. *The Recurring Miracle: A Study of* Cymbeline *and the Last Plays*. Pietermaritzburg: University of Natal Press, 1962.

McCormick, Peter J. *Fictions, Philosophies, and the Problems of Poetics*. Ithaca and London: Cornell University Press, 1988.

McFarland, Thomas. *Shakespeare's Pastoral Comedy*. Chapel Hill: University of North Carolina Press, 1972.

Mehl, Dieter. *The Elizabethan Dumb Show: The History of Dramatic Convention*. London: Methuen, 1964; Cambridge: Harvard University Press, 1966.

Milner, Marion. *Eternity's Sunrise: A Way of Keeping a Diary*. London: Virago, 1987.

Mowat, Barbara A. *The Dramaturgy of Shakespeare's Romances*. Athens: University of Georgia Press, 1976.

Muir, Kenneth. *Last Periods: Shakespeare, Racine, and Ibsen*. Liverpool: Liverpool University Press, 1961.

———. *Shakespeare as Collaborator*. London: Methuen, 1960.

———. *Shakespeare's Comic Sequence*. Liverpool: Liverpool University Press, 1979.

Neely, Thomas Carol. "*The Winter's Tale*: The Triumph of Speech." *Studies in English Literature* 15 (1975): 321–38.

———. "Women and Issue in *The Winter's Tale*." *Philological Quarterly* 57 (1978): 181–94.

Nevo, Ruth. *Shakespeare's Other Language*. New York and London: Methuen, 1987.

Nosworthy, J. M. "Music and Its Function in the Romances of Shakespeare." *Shakespeare Survey* 11 (1958): 60–69.

Olson, Charles. *Selected Writings*. Edited by Robert Creeley. New York: New Directions, 1966.

Palmer, D. J., ed. *Shakespeare's Later Comedies: An Anthology of Modern Criticism*. Harmondsworth: Penguin, 1971.

Parker, Patricia, and David Quint, eds. *Literary Theory/Renaissance Texts*. Baltimore and London: Johns Hopkins University Press, 1986.

Parrot, Thomas Marc. "*Pericles:* The Play and the Novel." *Shakespeare Association Bulletin* 23 (1948): 105–13.

Peterson, Douglas L. *Time, Tide, and Tempest: A Study of Shakespeare's Romances*. San Marino, Calif.: Huntington Library, 1973.

Pinkard, Terry. *Hegel's Dialectic: The Explanation of Possibility*. Philadelphia: Temple University Press, 1988.

Ranald, Margaret. *Women in Shakespeare's Last Plays*. Deland, Fl.: Everett/Edwards, 1976.

Reiss, Timothy J. *The Uncertainty of Analysis: Problems in Truth, Meaning, and Culture*. Ithaca and London: Cornell University Press, 1988.

Rose, Mark. *Shakespearean Design*. Cambridge: Harvard University Press, 1972.

Rudwin, Maximillian. *The Devil in Legend and Literature*. Chicago and London: Open Court Publishing Company, 1931.

Sallis, John, ed. *Deconstruction and Philosophy*. Chicago and London: Chicago University Press, 1987.

Sanders, Norman. "An Overview of Critical Approaches to the Romances." In *Shakespeare's Romances Reconsidered*, edited by Carol McGinnis Kay and Henry E. Jacobs, pp. 1–10. Lincoln and London: University of Nebraska Press, 1978.

Sanders, Wilbur. *The Winter's Tale*. Brighton: Harvester, 1987.

Schelling, Friedrich Joseph Wilhelm. *The Philosophy of Art*. Translated by Douglas W. Scott. Minneapolis: University of Minnesota Press, 1989.

Schleiermacher, Friedrich. *On Religion: Speeches to Its Cultured Despisers*. Translated by Richard Crouter. Cambridge and New York: Cambridge University Press, 1988.

Shepherd, Simon. *Amazons and Warriors: Varieties of Feminism in Seventeenth-Century Drama*. Brighton: Harvester, 1981.

Simpson, David, ed. *The Origins of Modern Critical Thought*. Cambridge and New York: Cambridge University Press, 1988.

Sitwell, Edith. *A Notebook on William Shakespeare*. London: Macmillan, 1965.

Smith, Hallett. *Shakespeare's Romances: A Study of Some Ways of the Imagination*. San Marino, Calif.: Huntington Library, 1972.

Spencer, Hazelton. *The Art and Life of William Shakespeare*. New York: Harcourt, Brace and Company, 1940.

Spencer, Theodore. *Shakespeare and the Nature of Man*. New York: Macmillan; Cambridge: Cambridge University Press, 1945.

Stauffer, Donald A. *Shakespeare's World of Images: The Development of His Moral Ideas*. London and Bloomington: Indiana University Press, 1966.

Szondi, Peter. *On Textual Understanding and Other Essays*. Translated by Harvey Mendelsohn. Minneapolis: University of Minnesota Press, 1986.

Tillyard, E. M. W. *Shakespeare's Last Plays*. London: Chatto and Windus, 1938.

Tobias, Richard C., and Paul G. Zolbrod, eds. *Shakespeare's Late Plays: Essays in Honor of Charles Crow.* Athens: Ohio University Press, 1974.

Tompkins, J. M. S. "Why Pericles?" *Review of English Studies* 3 (1952): 315–24.

Traister, Barbara Howard. *Heavenly Necromancers: The Magician in the English Renaissance.* Columbia: University of Missouri Press, 1984.

Traversi, Derek A. *Shakespeare: The Last Phase.* New York: Harcourt, Brace; London: Hollis and Carter, 1954.

Ulmer, Gregory L. *Applied Grammatology: Post(e)-Pedagogy from Jacques Derrida to Joseph Beuys.* Baltimore and London: Johns Hopkins University Press, 1985.

Uphaus, Robert W. *Beyond Tragedy: Structure and Experience in Shakespeare's Romances.* Lexington: University Press of Kentucky, 1981.

White, R. S. *"Let Wonder Seem Familiar": Endings in Shakespeare's Romance Vision.* Atlantic Highlands, N.J.: Humanities Press; London: Athlone Press, 1985.

Yates, Frances A. *Shakespeare's Last Phase: A New Approach.* London: Routledge and Kegan Paul, 1975.

Index

Index